DATE DUE

DEMCO 38-297

THE CONSCIENCE
OF WORDS

THE CONSCIENCE OF WORDS

by ELIAS CANETTI

Translated from the German by
JOACHIM NEUGROSCHEL

A *Continuum Book* · The Seabury Press · *New York*

FOR VEZA CANETTI

1979 · The Seabury Press
815 Second Avenue · New York, N.Y. 10017

Originally published in Germany under the title *Das Gewissen der Worte*
by Carl Hanser Verlag, copyright © 1976 by Carl Hanser Verlag Munchen.

English translation copyright © 1979 by The Seabury Press, Inc.

Printed in the United States of America

Library of Congress Cataloging in Publication Data

Canetti, Elias, 1905–
    The conscience of words.

    (A Continuum book)
    Translation of Das Gewissen der Worte.
    I. Title.
PT2605.A58G4513   1979   834'.9'12   78-15377
ISBN 0-8164-9334-0

CONTENTS

Prefatory Remark

This volume presents my essays from the years 1962 to 1974 in the order in which they were written. At first glance, it may seem odd to mingle figures like Kafka and Confucius, Büchner, Tolstoy, Karl Kraus, and Hitler, the most dreadful of catastrophes like Hiroshima, and literary reflections on keeping journals or on the genesis of a novel. But this adjacency was precisely what I was after, for these things are only seemingly disparate. The public and the private can no longer be separated, they overlap in ways that would never before have seemed possible. The enemies of mankind have rapidly gained power, coming very close to an ultimate goal of destroying the earth. It is impossible to ignore them and withdraw to the contemplation of only spiritual models that still have some meaning for us. These models have become rarer; many that may have sufficed for earlier times do not contain enough in themselves, comprise too little to still serve us today. Hence, it is all the more important to speak about those that have withstood our monstrous century.

But it would not be enough merely to grasp models and counter-models, even if one does succeed in grasping them. It is not, I think, superfluous to speak also about oneself—among countless other witnesses of this era—and to describe the efforts at keeping all those models at bay. Perhaps it is not purely private to show how a man of today has managed to produce a novel, so long as his aim was to truly confront the age; or how he arranges a diary to keep from being spiritually ground up in that age. I hope my readers will understand why I also included the short piece "Word Attacks." It refers to one aspect of being a refugee, but not at all because I wanted to lament about something that was the fate of millions, while many more people died as prisoners or soldiers. I wanted to depict what happens to a language that is resolved not to abandon itself; the real subject of that piece is language and not the person who uses it.

The essay "Power and Survival" recapitulates one of the main thoughts in *Crowds and Power,* though somewhat differently and more pointedly. It has repeatedly been shown that this essay, in this concentrated form, is an apt introduction for the larger book. "Hitler, According to Speer" applies the insights of *Crowds and Power* to a specific figure who is still close enough to allow everyone to check the usefulness of those insights.

The speech on Hermann Broch, which I have placed at the outset of this volume, stands out like a sore thumb from the designated framework. It was given in Vienna in 1936, for Broch's fiftieth birthday. Twenty-six years span the gap between that speech and the following essay, "Power and Survival." The reader may wonder what prompted me to include that lonesome early talk, and I do owe him an explanation. At the time, only a portion of Hermann Broch's oeuvre was completed; the most important part was the trilogy *The Sleepwalkers* and a few short prose pieces like "The Homecoming." I attempted, always thinking of Broch and acting out of personal knowledge of him, to define what we should ask of a writer so that he will be of some significance to our time. The three characteristics I arrived at then are such that I cannot alter anything about them even today. Years later, it struck me that, albeit very inadequately, I have since then striven to satisfy these demands myself. By thinking about Hermann Broch, I arrived at things that were to become demands on my own life. Since then, there has existed something by which I could measure any imminent failure. In times of weakening, not infrequent during the long years of work on *Crowds and Power,* I always held up the "three commandments," as I somewhat arrogantly called them, and I took heart from them, and a hope that was vehement and measureless, and yet indispensable. So I do not consider it senseless to begin the collection with that speech.

The chronological gap between that early speech and the subsequent essays is, incidentally, only a seeming one. For these essays often deal with early experiences and topics, and when I read through them in their present sequence, they struck me as a summing-up of the spiritual stations of my entire adult life.

Preface to the Second German Edition

The justification for this volume is, for me, its many different shapes, and ever since it was published I have been haunted by a feeling that something is missing: a conclusion that wraps it up from the inside. What can we expect today of a writer, a *Dichter,* when we know how little we have done ourselves? Would it be possible for a man beginning today to regain the sense of the German word *Dichter,* which has seemingly been destroyed? In the Munich speech "The Writer's Profession" (January 1976), I tried to say something about that. When I was writing it, it struck me as autonomous; when it was written, I realized that it belonged at the end of this volume. I very much wanted to add it to this second edition, as an expression of the hope for those who will succeed in more effectively satisfying its demand.

HERMANN BROCH

Speech for His Fiftieth Birthday
Vienna, November 1936

There is something fine and meaningful about using a man's fiftieth birthday to address him in public, to tear him almost violently from the dense network of his life and present him—heightened and visible on all sides and to all onlookers—as though he were all alone, condemned to a stony and unchangeable solitude, even though the actual, the secret solitude of his life, mellow and humble as it is, has certainly caused him sufficient pain. It is as though this address were saying to him: Don't be afraid, you have been afraid enough for us. We all have to die; but it is still not certain whether you too have to die. Perhaps your very words are what must represent us to posterity. You have served us with loyalty and honesty. The age will not release you.

To give these words their full effect, like a spell, the seal of fifty years is pressed upon them. For, in our thinking, the past is divided into centuries; there is room for nothing next to the centuries. To the extent that men may care about the vast context of their memory, they stuff everything they consider important and peculiar into the sack of the centuries. The very word designating those periods has gained a venerable overtone. As though using a mysterious sacerdotal language, people speak of the *secular*. The magical power that earlier, primitive nations gave to more modest numbers, three, four, five, seven, has now been transfered to the *saeculum*. Why, even the many people who romp and frolic in the past to rediscover their dissatisfaction with the present, these people who are filled with the bitterness of all known centuries—they like to demarcate the dreamt-of future in better centuries.

There can be no doubt: a century is exactly big enough for human desire. For if a man is very lucky, he will grow that old. It does happen now and then, but it is unlikely. The few who have really managed to achieve it are surrounded with amazement and many stories. Old chronicles will quite studiously list them by name and station. They receive even more attention than the rich. The fierce desire to conquer that much life may have raised the century to a high rank after the introduction of the decimal system.

Time, however, which celebrates its fifty-year-old, meets him half way. It hands him over to later people, as worth preserving. It makes him, perhaps against his will, distinctly visible in the scattered host of the few who existed more for them than for themselves. It enjoys the round height to which it has raised him, and links this to a quiet hope: perhaps he, who cannot lie, has seen a Promised Land, and perhaps he will speak about it, time would believe him.

Today, Hermann Broch is standing on that height, and so, to speak frankly, let us dare to maintain that we can honor him as one of the very few representative writers of our time. This statement would carry its full weight only if I could list the many who are not great writers even though they are regarded as such. But more important than this job of executioner is, I think, finding the characteristics that must lie close together in a great writer for us to consider him representative of his time. If we embark conscientiously on this enterprise, we will not come upon any convenient, much less harmonious picture.

The utter and dreadful tension in which we live, and from which none of the yearned-for thunderstorms can redeem us, has seized hold of all spheres, even the freer and purer sphere of astonishment. Indeed, if we had to sum up our time very briefly, we would have to describe it as one in which we can be *amazed* at the most contrasting things: For instance at a book that has been affecting us for thousands of years, and also at the fact that not all books can affect us any longer. At the faith in gods and also at the fact that we do not kneel down to new gods every hour. At the sexuality we are afflicted with and also at the fact that this split does not reach any deeper. At death, which we do not wish, and also at the fact that we do not already die in the womb, out of grief over coming things. Astonishment *used* to be the mirror people would talk about, the mirror that brought phenomena to a smoother and calmer surface. Today, this mirror is shattered, and the splinters of astonishment have become small. But no phenomenon is reflected by itself in even the tiniest splinter. Ruthlessly, each phenomenon pulls its opposite along. Whatever you see and how little you see, it cancels itself out when you see it.

Thus we will not expect the poet to be any different from the tortured gravel of everyday life when we try to capture him in that mirror. From the very start, we oppose the widespread erroneous idea that a great writer is above his time. No one is, in himself, above his time. Those who are above it all simply do not exist. They may live in ancient Greece or among some barbarians. Let them; many blindnesses are part of being so far away, and no one can be denied the right to close off all his senses. But such a man is not above us, merely above the sum of memory—the memory of ancient Greece, for example—that we carry inside us. He is, so to speak, an experimental cultural historian, ingeniously testing on himself what must be correct according to his reliable report. The man above it all is even more powerless than the experimental physicist, who merely busies himself in one part of his discipline but always retains the possibility of verification. The man above it all makes more than a scientific claim, he makes a downright cultic claim. Usually, he is not even the founder of a sect, he is a priest for himself alone; he celebrates himself for himself alone, *he* is the only believer.

However, the true writer, as we see him, is the thrall of his time, its serf and bondsman, its lowest slave. He is fettered to it on a short, unbreakable chain, shackled to it as tight as can be. His lack of freedom must be so great that he could not be transplanted anywhere else. In fact, if it did not sound a bit ludicrous, I would simply say: he is the dog of his time. He runs across its grounds, stops here and there; seemingly at random, yet tireless, receptive to whistles from above, but not always, easily roused to a fury, harder to call back, driven by some inexplicable viciousness. Indeed, he sticks his damp nose into everything, nothing is left out, he also returns, he starts all

3

over again, he is insatiable. Otherwise, he sleeps and eats, but that does not distinguish him from other creatures. What distinguishes him is the uncanny persistence in his vice, that heartfelt and thorough enjoyment, interrupted by running. He never gets enough, and likewise, he never gets it fast enough; why, it is as though he had learned to run especially for the vice of his nose.

I ask you to excuse me for an image that must seem highly unworthy of the topic at hand. But there are three attributes suitable for the representative writer of this age, and my aim is to top them with the one attribute that is never talked about, the one from which the others take their start, the very concrete and peculiar *vice,* which I demand for him, without which he would be like a dismal premature baby, very arduously nursed for something that he never really becomes.

This vice connects the writer as immediately to his environment as the nose connects the dog to his preserve. The vice is different in each writer, unique and new in the new situation of the age. It should not be confused with the normal cooperation of the senses, which all people have anyway. On the contrary, a disbalance in this cooperation, for instance the failure of any one sense or the overdevelopment of another can trigger the formation of the necessary vice. It is always recognizable, vehement, and primitive. It expresses itself clearly in the shape and the physiognomy. The writer who allows himself to be obsessed by it owes it the essentials of his experience.

Even the problem of originality, which has been more fought about than talked about, has a different light shed upon it. Originality, as we all know, must not be demanded. The man who wants to have it will never have it. And the conceited and well-contrived clowneries that some people have served up in order to count as original are certainly still in our embarrassed memories. However, there is a huge step from the rejection of straining for originality to the awkward claim that a writer does not have to be original. A writer *is* original, or he is not a writer. He is original in a very deep and simple way, through that which we have called his vice. He is so original that he does not even realize it. His vice drives him to exhaust the world, something that no one else could do for him. Immediacy and inexhaustibility, the two characteristics that people have always demanded of the genius and that he always has, are the offspring of this vice. We will have an opportunity to test a case and to see what kind of vice there is in Broch.

The second characteristic that one must demand of the representative writer today is an earnest desire to sum up his age, an urge for universality, unintimidated by any single task, ignoring nothing, forgetting nothing, omitting nothing, making nothing easy for himself.

Broch himself has dealt thoroughly and repeatedly with this universalness. Even more: one may say that his creative will was actually kindled by the demand for universality. At first, and for long years, a man of rigorous philosophy, he did not permit himself to truly take seriously what a writer accomplishes. Too many concrete and isolated things seemed to be there, piecework and subterfuge, the whole was never present. Philosophy, at the moment he began philosophizing, sometimes still indulged in its old demand for universality, timidly to be sure, for this demand was long out of date. But having a magnanimous mind, oriented towards all infinite things, Broch was willingly taken in by this demand. It was joined by the deep impression made on him by the universal intellectual and spiritual closure of the Middle Ages, an impression that he has never fully shaken off. He feels that a closed intellectual value-system existed in that period. And he has devoted much of his life to investigating the "decay of values," which, for him, began in the Renaissance, reaching its catastrophic end with the World War.

During this work, the creative writer gradually got the upper hand in him. On close inspection, his first comprehensive opus, the trilogy of novels entitled *The Sleepwalkers,* is the literary realization of his philosophy of history, though limited to his own period, 1888–1918. The "decay of values" materializes in distinct and highly literary figures. One cannot help feeling that their full validity, even occasional ambivalence arose against the author's will or at least with his embarrassed reluctance. It will always be strange to see that here a man tried to conceal what was his very own under a mountain of acquired thought.

With *The Sleepwalkers,* Broch found a possibility for universalness where he least expected it, in the piecework and subterfuge of the novel, and he talks about this in various places: "The novel has to be the mirror of all other images of the world," he once said. "The literary work must, in its unity, embrace the entire world." Or: "The modern novel has become polyhistorical." Or: "Creative writing is always an impatience of knowledge."

His new insight is probably formulated most clearly in his speech "James Joyce and the Present:"

> Philosophy itself terminated its age of universality, the age of the great compendiums; it had to remove its most urgent questions from its logical space or, as Wittgenstein says, expel them into mysticism.
>
> And this is the point at which the mission of literature begins, the mission of a knowledge that embraces totality, that remains beyond any empirical or social contingency, and that is indifferent to whether man lives in a feudal, a bourgeois, or a proletarian age—the duty of literature to the absoluteness of knowledge per se.

The third demand one has to make on a writer would be that he stand against his time. Against his entire time, not merely against this or that; against the comprehensive and unified image that he alone has of his time, against its specific smell, against its face, against its law. His opposition should be loud and take shape; he cannot simply freeze or silently resign himself. He has to kick and scream like an infant; but no milk of the world, not even from the kindest breast, may quench his opposition and lull him to sleep. He may wish for sleep, but he must never attain it. If he forgets his opposition, he has become an apostate, the way an entire nation abandoned its god in earlier, religious times.

This is a cruel and radical demand, cruel in its so powerful contrast to all that came earlier. For the writer is in no wise a hero who ought to overcome and subjugate his time. On the contrary, we saw that he is its thrall, its lowest slave, its dog. And this selfsame dog, running after his nose all his life, an epicure and meek victim, a sensualist and consumed prey at once, this same creature should, in the same breath, be against all that, oppose himself and his vice, never being freed of it, keeping on and waxing indignant and knowing about his own dichotomy to boot! It is a cruel demand, truly, and it is as cruel and radical as death itself.

For this demand evolves from the fact of death. Death is the first and oldest, one would even be tempted to say: the only fact. It is of a monstrous age and yet new every hour. Its degree of hardness is ten, and it also cuts like a diamond. It has the absolute cold of outer space, minus 273°. It has the wind speed of a hurricane, the highest. It is the very real superlative, of everything; but it is not infinite, for it is reached by every path. So long as death exists, any utterance is an utterance against it. So long as death exists, any light is a will-of-the-wisp, for it leads to it. So long as death exists, no beauty is beautiful, no goodness is good.

The attempts at coming to terms with death (and what else are the religions?) have all failed. The realization that there is nothing after death—a dreadful and fully inexhaustible realization—has shed a new and desperate holiness on life. The writer who, by virtue of what we, a bit summarily, have called his vice, is able to take part in many lives must also take part in all the deaths that threaten those lives. His own fear (and who is not afraid of death?) must become everybody's fear of death. His own hatred (and who does not hate death?) must become everybody's hatred of death. This and nothing else is his opposition to the time, which is filled with myriad deaths.

Thus, a legacy of religion has fallen to the writer's lot, and certainly the best part of the legacy. He has no small number of legacies to carry—Philosophy, as we have seen, has willed him its demand for a universalness of knowledge; religion has willed him the settled problems of death. Life itself, life as it was prior to all religion and philosophy, animal life unaware of itself or its end, gave him, in the concentrated and happily channeled form of passion, his insatiable greed.

It will now be our task to investigate the makeup of these legacies in a single man, in Hermann Broch. Only their togetherness gives them meaning, after all. Their harmony is what makes him representative. The very concrete passion with which he is possessed must offer him the material that he composes into a universal and binding picture of his time. His very concrete passion must, however, in each one of its vibrations, also reveal death, naturally and unambiguously. For that is how it nourishes the incessant and relentless opposition to the time, which mollycoddles death.

Permit me now to change the topic to something that will henceforth occupy us almost exclusively: *air*. It may astonish you to hear about something so very ordinary. You expect something about the peculiarity of our writer, about the vice he is addicted to, his terrible passion. You anticipate something embarrassing behind it, or, insofar as you are more trusting, at least something very mysterious. I have to disappoint you. Broch's vice is quite an ordinary thing, more ordinary than smoking, drinking, or cards, for it is older. Broch's vice is: breathing. He passionately loves to breathe, and he never breathes enough. He has an unmistakable way of sitting about, no matter where; seemingly absent, because he seldom and unwillingly responds with the normal means of language; actually present like no other man, for he is always concentrated on the wholeness of the space he finds himself in, on a kind of atmospheric unity.

Thus, it is not enough to know that there is a stove here and a closet there; to hear what one man says and what the other sensibly answers, as though the two of them had harmoniously discussed it beforehand. Nor is it enough to register the passage and the extent of time, when one man comes, when another stands up, when the third leaves; the clocks can take care of that for us. There is far more to sense wherever people are together in a room and are breathing. After all, the room can be full of good air and the windows open. It may have rained. The stove may be spreading warm air, and this warmth may reach the people unequally. The closet may have been shut for a good while; the different air, suddenly pouring from it now that it's opened, may change the people's behavior towards one another. They speak, certainly; and they have things to say; but they form their words out of air and, by speaking them, they suddenly fill the room with new and strange vibrations, catastrophic changes in the earlier status. And time, true mental time, is the last thing in the world to go by the clock; it is actually and to a very great extent a function of the atmosphere in which it passes. Hence, it is awfully difficult to even approximate when someone really entered, when someone else stood up, and when the third really left.

Of course, all this sounds very simple-minded, and an experienced master like Broch can smile at such examples. But I only mean to indicate how essential these things have become for him, all the things belonging to his breath metabolism. I mean to indicate how he made the atmospheric conditions all his own, so that, for him, they often stand directly for the relations between people. How he hears by breathing, how he touches by breathing, how he subordinates all his senses to his sense of breathing. And thus he occasionally seems like a big, beautiful bird whose wings have been clipped but whose freedom is otherwise intact. Instead of cruelly locking him in a single cage, his tormentors have opened all the cages in the world to him. He is still driven by the insatiable air-hunger of that fast, exalted time; to sate it, he dashes from cage to cage. From each he takes a sample of air, which fills him and he carries it away. Previously, he was a dangerous predator; in his hunger, he pounced upon any living thing; now, air is the only prey he lusts for. He stays nowhere long; as swiftly as he comes, he leaves. He eludes the actual masters and inmates of the cages. He knows that even after all the cages in the world, he will never gather all the air he had before. He always keeps his yearning for that great coherence, the freedom over all cages. Thus he remains the big, beautiful bird he once was, recognizable to others by the air fragments he gets from them, recognizable to himself by his restlessness.

But the matter isn't settled for Broch with the hunger for air and the frequent change of breathing-space. His abilities go further; he carefully retains what he has acquired by breathing; he retains it in the unique, precisely experienced form. And no matter how many new and perhaps more powerful things may come along, the danger of mixing atmospheric impressions—something quite natural for the rest of us—never exists with him. Nothing is blurred for him, nothing loses its clarity. His is a rich and well-ordered experience in breathing-spaces. It is his wish to make use of this experience.

One must therefore assume that Broch is gifted with something that I can only call a memory for breath. Next comes the question of what this breath-memory really is, how it works, and where it has its seat. I will be asked this question and I will have nothing precise to answer. And, at the risk of being scorned as a bungler by the appropriate science, I must point to certain otherwise inexplicable effects as demonstrating the existence of such a breath-memory. To make its scorn not so easy for that science, one would have to remind it how far Western civilization has drifted from all the more subtle problems of breathing and its experience. The oldest exact, nay, almost experimental psychology that we know of—which rightfully ought to be called a psychology of self-observation and inner experience—an achievement of India, had this very area as its subject. Science, that parvenu of mankind, has enriched itself shamelessly and at everyone's expense during the past few centuries. And one cannot be amazed enough that in the area of breathing, science has forgotten what was once, as we all know, the daily practice of countless adepts in India.

Of course, in Broch too, an unconscious technique is involved, facilitating his grasp, retention, and ultimate processing of atmospheric impressions. The naive observer can probably notice certain things in him that are connected to that technique. For instance, conversations with him have a very peculiar and unforgettable punctuation. He tends not to answer yes or no, that might be too violent a caesura. He arbitrarily divides the other person's speech into apparently meaningless sections. They are designated by a characteristic sound, which one would have to faithfully render with a phonograph, and which is taken as agreement by the other person, but actually only indicates the registration of what is said. One scarcely ever hears a negative. The other speaker is grasped not so much in the way he thinks and speaks; Broch is far more interested in finding out in what specific way the man makes the air shake. He himself yields little breath and, when reticent with words, he seems obstinate and absent.

But let us leave these personal matters, which would require a more thorough treatment to be of any real value. Let us, instead, ask ourselves what Broch undertakes in his art with his rich store of breathing experience. Does it give him the possibility of expressing something that could not otherwise be expressed? Does an art drawing upon it offer a new and different picture of the world? Indeed, can we actually conceive of a literature that stems from the experience of breathing? And what means does it employ in the medium of the word?

We would have to reply, above all, that the multiplicity in our world consists to a large extent in the multiplicity of our breathing-spaces. The room you are sitting in here, in a very definite arrangement, almost totally cut off from the world around us, the way each person's breath mixes into an air common to all of you and then collides with my words, the noises disturbing you, and the silence into which these noises relapse, your suppressed movements, rebuff or agreement—all those things, from the breather's standpoint, are a totally unique, unrepeatable, self-contained, and precisely delimited

10

situation. But then, go a few steps further and you will find the completely different situation of another breathing-space, in a kitchen perhaps or a bedroom, in a pub, in a tram, whereby we always have to think of a concrete and unrepeatable constellation of breathing beings in a kitchen, bedroom, pub, or tram. The big city is as full of such breathing-spaces as of individual people. Now none of these people is like the next, each is a kind of cul-de-sac; and just as their splintering makes up the chief attraction and chief distress of life, so too one could also lament the splintering of the atmosphere.

The diversity in the world, its individual splintering, the true material of artistic creation, is thus also a given for the breathing man. To what extent was earlier art aware of this?

One cannot say that the atmospheric was neglected in the older contemplation of human beings. The winds are among the most ancient figures in myth. Every nation paid heed to them; few spirits or gods are as popular as they. The oracles of the Chinese were very much oriented by the winds. Storms, tempests, tornadoes are basic plot elements in the earliest heroic epics. They are a recurrent prop later as well and even today; they of all things are popularly brought out from the lumber rooms of kitsch. A science coming on today with a very serious claim, for it makes forecasts, i.e. meteorology, deals to a great extent with the currents of the air. But all this is basically very rough, for the crux in all these things is always the dynamic quality of the atmosphere, the changes that nearly kill us, murder and manslaughter in the air, great cold, great heat, furious velocities, raging records.

Imagine if modern painting consisted merely in a gross and simple depiction of the sun or a rainbow! The feeling of an unparallelled barbarism would seize us in front of such pictures. We would want to punch holes in them. They would be altogether worthless. One would absolutely deny them the attribute "painting." For a long practice has taught people to draw on the diversity and changeability of colors as they experience them in order to abstract static, closed surface-works, endlessly refined in their repose—surface-works that they call pictures.

The literature of the atmospheric as a static thing is only just beginning its development. The static breathing-space has scarcely been treated. Let us call that which ought to be created here a

11

"breath-picture" in contrast to the painter's color-picture. And let us presume, given the deep relationship between breath and speech, that language is an appropriate medium for achieving the breath-picture. We also have to realize that Hermann Broch is the founder of this new art, its first conscious representative, who has likewise succeeded in making the classic model of his genre. One has to use the adjectives "classical" and "grand" for "The Homecoming," a tale of some thirty pages about a man arriving in a city, coming out to its railroad station square, and renting a room in the home of an old woman and her daughter. That is the content in terms of the old narrative art, the plot. But what is actually depicted are the square and the old lady's home. Broch's technique here is as new as it is perfect. Its study would require a whole treatise, and since it would have to be very detailed, it would certainly be out of place here.

His characters are not prisons for him. He floats away from them often. He has to float away from them; but he remains near them much of the time. They are bedded in air, he has breathed for them. His caution is timidity towards his own breathing, which affects the repose of others.

Yet his sensitivity also separates him from the people of his time, who, all in all, dwell in an illusion of security. Now, they too are not exactly insensitive. The sum total of sensitivity in culture has become very great. Yet this sensitivity too, odd as it may seem, has its orderly and unshakable tradition. It is determined by the things one already knows well. Tortures that have come down to us, which have been told about frequently, and told about in the same way as those of the martyrs for instance, arouse our deepest loathing. The effect of the stories and pictures is so powerful that whole ages have gotten the stamp of cruelty impressed on them. Thus, for the huge majority of readers and writers, the Middle Ages was the time of tortures, of witch burnings. Even the authentic information that the witch-hunts were actually the invention and practice of a later period can do little to change that notion. The average man thinks back to the Middle Ages with horror, he pictures the carefully preserved execution tower in a medieval town, which he has visited—perhaps on his honeymoon. The average man feels all in all, more horror for the remote Middle Ages than for the World War, which he has experienced personally. One can sum up this insight in a single shattering sentence:

Today it would be harder to condemn one man publicly to be burnt at the stake than to unleash a world war.

Thus, people are defenseless only when they have no experience or memory. New dangers may loom as vast as they like, but people will be only poorly and at most outwardly prepared. However, the greatest of all dangers ever to emerge in the history of mankind has chosen our generation as its victim.

It is the defenselessness of breathing, which I would like to talk about in conclusion. One can hardly form too great a notion of it. To nothing is man so open as to air. He moves in it as Adam did in Paradise, pure and innocent and unaware of any evil beasts. Air is the last common property. It belongs to all people collectively. It is not doled out in advance, even the poorest may partake of it. And if a man should starve to death, then at least he has breathed until the end—small as that comfort may be.

And this last thing, which has belonged to all of us collectively, shall poison all of us collectively. We know it, but we do not yet sense it, for breathing is not our art.

Hermann Broch's work stands between war and war, gas war and gas war. It could be that he still somewhere feels the poisonous particles of the last war. But that is unlikely. What is certain, however, is that he, who knows how to breathe better than we do, is already choking on the gas that shall claim our breath—who knows when!

POWER AND SURVIVAL

Among the most sinister phenomena in intellectual history is the avoidance of the concrete. People have had a conspicuous tendency to go first after the most remote things, ignoring everything that they stumble over close by. The elan of outgoing gestures, the boldness and adventure of expeditions to faraway places camouflage their motives. The not infrequent goal is to avoid what lies near because we are not up to it. We sense danger and prefer other and unknown perils. Even when these are found—and they are always found—they still have the glow of the sudden and the unique. One would have to be very narrow-minded to condemn this adventurousness of the mind, even though it sometimes comes from obvious weakness. It has led to an expansion of our horizon, of which we are proud. But the situation of mankind today, as we all know, is so serious that we have to turn to what is closest and most concrete. We don't even have an inkling of how much time is left for us to focus on the most painful things. And yet, it could very well be that our fate is contingent on certain hard knowledge that we do not yet have.

Today I wish to speak about *survival,* by which I naturally mean the survival of others. I also wish to try and show that this survival is at the core of everything that we—rather vaguely—call power. And I would like to begin with a very simple observation.

The *standing* man seems autonomous, as though standing for himself alone and as though still having the possibility of any decision. The *sitting* man exercises a pressure, his weight presents itself to the outside, arousing a sense of permanence. The way he sits, he cannot fall; he becomes larger when he stands up. The man, however, who has settled down to rest, the *lying* man, has disarmed himself. It is very easy to get at him in the defenselessness of his sleep. The lying man may have fallen, he may have been wounded. Before standing on his feet again, he will not be taken seriously.

14

However, the *dead* man, who never stands up again, makes an enormous impression. Incredulity is the first response when someone sees a dead man, especially if the dead man concerned him in some way, but not only then. Suspiciously if he was an enemy, with trembling expectation if he was a friend, one waits for any stirring of the body. He twitched, he's breathing. No. He's not breathing. He's not twitching. He is really dead. And now begins the terror at the fact of death, which one would like to call the only fact, and which is of such enormity that it takes in everything. The confrontation with the dead man is a confrontation with one's own death; less than this, since one does not really die of it, more than this since someone else is always there. Even the professional killer, who mistakes his insensitivity for courage and manliness, is not spared this confrontation; he too is frightened in some well-hidden part of his nature. Much could be said about this reception of the dead man in the observer, this deepest and most humane of all receptions; its precise description could fill hours and nights. The grandest testimony to it is the oldest: the grief of Gilgamesh the Sumerian over the death of his friend Enkidu.

Here too, we are not concerned with this open stage of an experience, for which we need not feel ashamed as victims and which therefore stands in the bright light of the religions. What we are concerned with is the next stage, which we do not like to admit, which was of greater consequence than the earlier one and not at all humane, which exists in the hearts of both power and greatness, and which we must focus on fearlessly and ruthlessly if we hope to understand what power is and what it does.

The terror at the dead man lying before one gives way to satisfaction: one is not dead oneself. One might have been. But it is the other who lies there. One stands upright oneself, unhurt, untouched. And whether he is an enemy whom one has killed, a friend who has died, it suddenly looks as though death, which one was threatened by, had been diverted from oneself to that person.

It is this feeling that very swiftly takes the upper hand; what was only just terror is now permeated with satisfaction. Never is the standing man, for whom everything is still possible, more aware of his standing. Never does he feel better upright. The moment holds him fast, the sense of superiority over the dead man binds him to the corpse. If the upright man had wings, he would not soar away now. He remains where he is, as close as possible to the lifeless man, facing him, and whoever that man may be, he has an effect on him, as though he had only just challenged him to a fight and threatened him, and now he turns into a sort of prey.

These facts are so dreadful and so naked that they are concealed in every way. Whether a person is ashamed of them or not is crucial for evaluating him. But it changes nothing in the facts themselves. The situation of survival is the central situation of power. Survival is not only ruthless, it is concrete, a precisely defined, unmistakable situation. Man never fully believes in death so long as he has not experienced it. But he experiences it in others. They die before his eyes, each as an individual, and every individual who dies convinces him of death. He nourishes his terror of it, and he has died in his place. The living man has used the other as a dummy, so to speak. The living man never considers himself greater than when confronted with the dead man, who is felled forever: at this moment, the living man feels as though he had grown.

Yet it is a growth that one normally does not flaunt. It may recede behind a genuine grief, which covers it entirely. But even if the deceased meant little to one and no special demonstration of grief is expected, it nevertheless would flout good taste to reveal any of the satisfaction at being confronted with the dead man. It is a triumph that remains concealed, that one admits to nobody else and perhaps not even to oneself. Convention has its value here: it tries to keep an emotion secret and small, since its heedless manifestation could have the most dangerous consequences.

This concealment is not all there is under all circumstances. The secret triumph in the face of death can become open and be admitted, it can bring honor and fame and be striven for. To understand this, it is indispensable to look squarely at the situation of *struggle*, and in its most original form.

The human body is soft and susceptible, and it is very vulnerable in its nakedness. Anything can penetrate it. Every injury makes it harder for the body to resist, and it is doomed in the twinkling of an eye. A man about to fight knows what he is risking. If he is not aware of any superiority, then he is risking the most. The man who has the good fortune to win feels a growth of strength and faces his

16

next opponent all the more eagerly. After a series of victories, he will win the thing most precious to a fighter, a sense of *invulnerability;* and once he has it, he will venture into more and more dangerous fights. Now he feels as though he had a different body, no longer naked, no longer assailable, armored by the instants of his triumphs. Ultimately, no one can do anything to him, he is a hero. One knows stories about constant victors from all over the world and from most nations. And even if the victors are vulnerable in some secret point of their body—which is not infrequent—this emphasizes their general invulnerability all the more. The hero's prestige, like his ego, is made up of all the moments in which he as the victor stood before his defeated enemy. He is admired for the superiority aroused by his invulnerability; that superiority is not considered an unfair advantage over his adversary. He unhesitatingly challenges anyone who does not give in to him. He fights, wins, kills; he gathers his victories.

"Gather" is meant quite literally. It is as though the victories were entering the victor's body and were now at his disposal. We have lost the grasp of this process as a concrete procedure, we do not really acknowledge it; but its subliminal effect is indisputable even in our century. It may be revealing to pursue it in a culture in which it is still open, one of those cultures that we somewhat inaccurately label primitive.

Mana, in the South Seas, refers to a kind of supernatural and impersonal force that can be transferred from one person to another. It is highly desired, it can be augmented in individuals. A courageous warrior can acquire it quite consciously. However, he owes it not so much to his experience in fighting or to his physical strength but to its transfer to him as the mana of his slain enemy. Let me quote from Handy's book on Polynesian religion:

> In the Marquesas, a member of a tribe could become a war chieftain through personal courage. It was assumed that the warrior's body contained the mana of all those he had killed. His own mana grew in proportion to his bravery. But in the native's mind, his bravery was the *result* and not the cause of his mana. With every successful killing, the mana of his spear also grew. The winner in a man-to-man fight took the name of the slain foe: that was the sign that the other man's power now belonged to him. In order to incorporate the mana immediately, he ate of

17

the man's flesh. And in order to rivet this growth of power in a battle, to ensure the intimate rapport with the captured mana, his war gear would include some physical remnant of the conquered enemy: a bone, a dried hand, sometimes even an entire skull.

The effect of victory on the survivor cannot be put more clearly. By killing the other, he has become stronger, and the increase of mana makes him capable of more victories. It is a kind of blessing that he wrests from the foe, but he can achieve it only if the other is dead. The physical presence of the enemy, alive and then dead, is indispensable. There has to have been fighting and killing; the personal act of killing is crucial. The handy parts of the body, which the victor makes sure to keep, incorporate, and hang upon himself, always remind him of his increase in power. They make him feel stronger and inspire terror in others: every new foe he challenges trembles before him and sees his own fate dreadfully before him.

Other peoples have other sorts of concepts with the very same goals. The emphasis is not always on the openness of the fight. Among the Murngins in the Australian Arnhem Land, each young man seeks out an enemy to gain control of his strength. However, he has to kill him secretly, at night. And this alone makes the spirit of the victim pass into him and give him double strength. It is explicitly said that the victor *grows* through this process, he actually gets *bigger*. In lieu of the impersonal strength of the mana that we have found in the previous case, we now have a personal spirit that a man tries to capture. And this spirit must not see the murderer during his deed, otherwise it will get angry and refuse to pass into him. For this very reason, it is indispensable that the assault take place in the darkness of night. The way the dead man's soul then enters the murderer's body is described in detail. Once mastered and incorporated, this soul becomes useful to him in every way. Not only does the murderer become physically larger, but even the prey it helps him get, whether a kangaroo or a turtle, grows after being hit, even when dying, and it puts on fat for the happy man in its final moments.

Heroes more in line with our well-known tradition can be found in the Fiji Islands. We are told about a boy who has lived far away from his father and is not yet fully grown; he finds his way to him and, in

18

order to impress him, he challenges all his father's enemies by him-self:

"Very early the next morning, the enemies came up to the town with warwhoops. . . . The boy arose and said: 'No one is to follow me. All of you, remain in town!' He took hold of the club, which he had made himself, plunged out into the midst of the foes and slashed about furiously, right and left. With each blow, he killed one, until they finally fled from him. Sitting down upon a heap of corpses, he called to his people in town: 'Come out and drag away the slain!' They came out, they chanted the death chant, they dragged off the forty-two corpses of the slain, while the drums boomed in the town."

The boy not only fought a whole pack of enemies, but he also killed one with each swoop of his club, and no blow was in vain. In the end, he sits as victor on a pile of the dead, having personally killed each one. The prestige of such warlike ability in Fiji was so great that there were four different names for heroes, according to the number of slain foes. The lowest on the scale was Koroi, the killer of *one* man; Koli meant having killed ten, Visa twenty, and Wangka thirty. The man who achieved more received a compound name. One famous chieftain was called Koli-Visa-Wangka, he was the killer of $10 + 20 + 30$, i.e. 60 men.

It is never quite without danger to go among the so-called primi-tives. One seeks them out in order to shed, from them, an unsparing light on oneself. Yet the effect they have is often the opposite. We feel terribly superior to them because they use clubs instead of atomic bombs. In reality, all we can pity Chief Koli-Visa-Wangka for is the fact that his language causes him such difficulties in counting. We have an easier time of it—far too easy.

I have cited this last example merely to show how far the open habituation to survival can lead. It does not end with the, as it were, "clean" case of the hero who gradually gains his feeling of invulnera-bility in sought-out duels in order to put it forward when his people are threatened by monsters or enemies. Perhaps such restrained heroes truly existed. I tend to regard them as ideal cases. For the sense of happiness in concrete survival is an intense pleasure. Once it is admit-ted and approved of, it will demand repetition and quickly mount into an insatiable passion. The man possessed with it will appropriate

19

the forms of social life around him in such a way as to make them serve this passion.

The passion is that of *power*. It is so closely attached to the fact of death that it strikes us as natural; we take it for granted, like death, never questioning it, never even seriously investigating its ramifications and repercussions.

The man who has acquired a taste for survival wants to *accumulate* it. He will try to cause situations in which he survives many people at once. The scattered moments of survival in daily existence will not suffice. Everything takes too long, he cannot speed it up. Nor does he want to among people really close to him. Peaceful existence in most human societies has its deceptive course, it tries to camouflage dangers and ruptures. The incessant disappearance of people, who are occasionally and suddenly no longer alive, is grasped and presented in such a way as though they weren't really fully gone. In propitiating acts of a special nature, one addresses them as though they could still take part. Usually, people have really believed in their existence somewhere and feared their envy of the living, it might have some dangerous effect on them.

This is a dense network of relationships, so dense that no one, not even a dead man, can fully drop from the world. And this network has always been opposed by the activity of those who were after physical survival. If they were otherwise relatively simple people, they felt fine in wars and battles. In such instances, people always speak of the attraction of danger, as though danger were the actual meaning of military situations. And yet the real goal of war is obvious: killing, mass killing. The goal is a heap of enemy corpses, and the man who wants to win imagines quite clearly that he will survive that heap of enemy corpses. But these are not the only dead, many of his people also die, and they too are survived. The man who willingly goes to war feels he shall return, he shall not be hit. It is a kind of reverse lottery, won only by the numbers that do *not* come out. The man who willingly goes to war goes with *confidence*, and this is the expectation that the fallen men on both sides, including his, are only *others,* and that he is the survivor. Thus, in war, the simple man, who does not see himself as anything special in peacetime, is offered the chance of a feeling of power, in the very place where this feeling has its root, in repeated survival. The presence of dead men here cannot be sidestepped, everything is geared to that. And even the man who has not personally done a great deal in that direction is exalted at the sight of all the fallen soldiers, who do *not* include him.

In peacetime, the heaviest sanctions are aimed at the one thing that is not only demanded in war, but massively achieved. The survivor returns with an increased sense of himself, even if the war did *not* turn out well for his side. One could not otherwise explain why people, having so well grasped the horrifying aspects of war, quickly forget or transfigure them. Something of the radiance of invulnerability surrounds every man who comes back alive.

But not all people are simple, not all are content with that. There is a more active form of this experience, and it is this form that interests us here. An individual cannot possibly kill as many people as his passion for survival may wish. Still, he can induce or direct others for that. As a general, he determines the shape of the battle. He plans it in advance and issues the order for it to start. He gets reports on it. In earlier days, he used to observe its course from an elevated point. He is thus removed from the immediate fight; he may not even manage to kill a single foe. But the others, who are under his command, take care of that for him. Their successes are attributed to him. He is regarded as the real victor. His fame and his power grow with the number of dead. He will not be particularly respected for a battle in which there is no serious fighting, which is won too easily and quickly with almost no victims. No true power can be built up on easy victories alone. The terror that power wants to arouse, that power is actually after is contingent on the mass number of victims.

The famous conquerors in history all went this way. All kinds of virtues were later attributed to them. Even after centuries, historians are still conscientiously balancing their character traits in order to reach what they believe is a fair judgment of them. The fundamental naïveté of this activity is virtually palpable. These historians are in fact giving in to the fascination of a power that is long past. By thinking themselves into an age, they become contemporaries, and they absorb something of the fear that the real contemporaries had for the ruthlessness of the power-wielders. They fail to realize that they are *yielding* to it while honestly sifting facts. There is also a more noble motive, of which even great thinkers were not free: they cannot get themselves to admit that a huge number of persons, each containing all possibilities of mankind, were slaughtered for nothing, absolutely nothing. And so, afterwards, they hunt for a meaning. Since history has always gone on, an apparent meaning in its continuity can always easily be found. And historians make sure that this meaning is given a kind of dignity. For truth has no dignity whatsoever here. It is as shameful as it was destructive. The crux is a private passion of the power-wielder: his lust for survival grows with his power; his power allows him to give in to that passion. The actual substance of this power is the desire to massively survive other people.

It is more useful for him if his victims are enemies; but friends can do the trick too. In the name of manly virtues, he will demand the most difficult, the most impossible things from his subjects. It makes no difference to him if they perish. He is able to convince them that it is an honor since it is happening for him. He binds them to him through booty, which he gets for them at the start. He uses orders, which are practically made for his purposes (for the moment, we cannot undertake a vastly important investigation of the phenomenon of orders). If he knows what he's doing, he will try to arouse them into warlike crowds and create so many dangerous enemies for them that it will ultimately be impossible for them to leave their own war crowd. He does not reveal his deeper aim to them; he can readily hide his aims and find a hundred convincing pretexts for anything he orders. He may, of course, give himself away in his exuberance, only among closest friends, but very thoroughly, like Mussolini with Ciano, when he scornfully called his subjects sheep, whose lives naturally were unimportant.

For the true goal of the real power-wielder is as grotesque as it is incredible: he wants to be the *only* one. He wants to survive them all so that no one will survive *him*. He wants to elude death at any price, and thus there must be no one, absolutely no one who could cause his death. So long as people exist, no matter who, he will not feel safe. Even his guards, protecting him from his enemies, might turn against him. It is not hard to prove that he always secretly fears the people he commands; and he is always overcome with fear of the people immediately surrounding him.

There were power-wielders who, for that very reason, did not want any son. Shaka, the founder of the Zulu kingdom in South Africa, a very courageous man, never could quell his fear of a son. He had

22

twelve hundred wives, with the official title of "sisters." They were not allowed to be pregnant, the penalty was death. His mother, the only person he cared for, and whose advice he could not do without, yearned for a grandson. When one of his wives did become pregnant, his mother concealed her in her own residence and helped her bear a son. For several years, the boy grew up with her secretly. One day, during a visit, Shaka caught his mother playing with a boy. He instantly recognized him as his own son and killed him on the spot with his own hands. But he did not escape the fate he so feared. Instead of being killed by a son, he was murdered at the age of forty-one by two of his brothers.

This fear of a son appears strange to us. Shaka was unusual in not even permitting a son. Otherwise, fights between rulers and their sons are quite normal. Oriental history is so full of them that they must be seen as a rule rather than an exception. But what is the meaning of the statement that the power-wielder wants to be the *only one?* It seems natural, and we have experienced, that he wants to be the *strongest,* that he fights against other power-wielders in order to subjugate them, that he hopes to conquer them all and become lord of the greatest and—in his ultimate goal—perhaps only kingdom. One will agree with me that he would like to be the only *ruler;* too many conquerors have played this part, and a few have even made it come true within their horizon. But the only person? What can it mean that the power-wielder wants to be the only person? It is essential to power that there are others to be ruled; without them, no act of power is thinkable. However, with this objection, one overlooks the fact that the act of power can consist in *removing* others; and the more radical and comprehensive it is, the greater the act.

An event of such proportions has come down to us from fourteenth-century India. Its exotic coloring withal, it sounds so modern that I would like to tell it briefly. The most active and ambitious king of his time, Muhammad Tughlak, the Sultan of Delhi, kept finding letters that were thrown over the walls of his audience hall. Their exact contents are not known, but supposedly they were insulting and injurious. He decided to reduce Delhi, one of the biggest cities in the world back then, to ruins. Since, as a strict Mohammedan, he cared greatly for justice, he *bought* up all the houses and homes, paying the full prices. Then he ordered the inhabitants to move to a new, very distant city, Daulatabad, which he wanted to make his capital. They refused. Whereupon he had his herald announce that no one was to be found in the city after three days. The majority gave in to the order, but some people hid in their houses. The sultan had the city combed for any remaining inhabitants. His slaves found two men in the streets, one crippled, one blind, and brought them before the sultan. He ordered that the cripple be shot from a catapult and the blind man be dragged from Delhi to Daulatabad, a voyage of forty days. En route, he fell to pieces, and all that arrived in Daulatabad was a leg. Now everyone else fled from Delhi, leaving furniture and property behind; the city was utterly deserted. The destruction was so total that not a cat, not a dog remained in the buildings of the city, in the palaces or suburbs. One night, the sultan climbed to the roof of his palace and gazed across Delhi, where no fire, no smoke, no light was to be seen, and he said, "Now my heart is tranquil and my wrath appeased."

It is true that he later wrote to the inhabitants of other cities, ordering them to move to Delhi and repopulate it. It is equally true that very few came, and Delhi, in its immeasurable hugeness, remained almost empty for a long time. But the crucial moment is the moment of the sultan's *onliness,* when he gazed from the palace roof across the empty city at night: all its inhabitants, even dogs and cats, removed from it, forty days away; no fire, no smoke, no light; and he all alone: "Now my heart is tranquil."

It must be added that this utterance of the sultan's "Now my heart is tranquil," is not a later invention or embroidery. We have it from a good source, the famous Arab traveler Ibn Batuta, who spent seven years at the sultan's court and knew him very thoroughly. His heart is at peace because there is no man far or wide who could turn against him. He also feels as though he had outlived all men, the population of his capital stands for the whole of mankind. This moment of *onlyness* was certainly just temporary. But the resolute way it was brought about, the huge expenditure, the consequences (a rich and brilliant capital depopulated for years), the fact that a circumspect, active, and practical ruler, lauded for his wisdom and justice, could find it in his heart to treat his capital city like that of his worst enemy—all these things would tend to show that the urge for this

24

onlyness is something very real, a prime force to be taken seriously and fathomed wherever an opportunity presents itself.

Like so many other things, it can best be grasped from within, namely by observing certain mental diseases, especially paranoia. By far the most important document on the "only" man in this sense is, to my knowledge, *Denkwürdigkeiten* by Schreber, the former president of the Senate of Dresden. A paranoiac, institutionalized for nine years, he presents his system here, completely and coherently. This book, incidentally, is interesting not just for our purpose; it touches on such diverse and frequent phenomena that I would not hesitate to call it the most important document in psychiatric literature. As a manuscript, it led to the legal termination of Schreber's being declared incompetent. As a book, it was published by the author himself in 1903. His family, embarrassed by the book, bought up most of the edition, and any copies of it must be quite rare by now.

One should, apropos, ignore an essay on Schreber—"Psychoanalytical Remarks on an Autobiographically Described Case of Paranoia (Dementia paranoides)"—that Freud brought out in 1911. It is not one of his most felicitous works. It reads like a first, groping attempt, and one senses that Freud himself was aware of the defects. He took only a tiny portion of the material into account, and rarely has he come up with such an utter misinterpretation. One can see this only if one really knows *Denkwürdigkeiten.* Subsequent discussion of Schreber's book referred purely to those passages that Freud quoted. Only in the past few years have one or two authors taken the trouble to go back to the original. No one has exhausted it, and it will not so readily be exhausted. To be fair, however, one has to stress that Freud was writing in 1911—i.e., before our century really commenced, with the outbreak of World War I. What man who has experienced the nearly sixty years since then as a thinking person has remained the same? For whom have not all problems been cast anew? It is only the people in our generation who can possibly understand Schreber and interpret him in such a way as not to leave out the greater part of what he presents.

Below, I am underscoring two of the most essential ideas that ruled Schreber. One has a right to emphasize them, for there can be no doubt that they were at the center of his madness.

All mankind has perished. The only man to remain, the only man still alive is *he*. He has thought about the catastrophe leading to the end of mankind, and he has more than *one* conjecture about it. Perhaps the sun moved from the earth, causing it to freeze over. Perhaps it was an earthquake, like the one in Lisbon. But he dwells longest on the notion of devastating epidemics, leprosy and plague. To make sure of it, he thinks of new and unknown forms of the plague. While other people all perished, he alone was healed by "beneficial" rays.

During the turbulent early period of his disease, he had grand visions. One of these visions led him in a kind of elevator deep into the earth. He thereby experienced all geological ages and suddenly found himself in a hard-coal forest. Once he left the elevator for a while and walked through a cemetery, where the entire population of Leipzig was buried. There he visited his wife's grave.

In reality, his wife was still alive, visiting him regularly in the Sonnenstein Asylum near Dresden, where he was a patient for eight or nine years. He was quite aware of these visits. He also saw and heard his doctor and the other physicians and attendants in the institution. When his states of excitement mounted, there were bad clashes with them. He also saw other patients. How did these circumstances chime with his solid conviction of onlyness? He did not dispute what his eyes saw, but he explained it away. The people he saw were not *real,* they were "fleetingly sketched men." That is what he calls them; and these mirages, coming and vanishing and not taken earnestly by him, were merely intended to deceive and confuse him.

One should not assume, however, that he, as an only man, led a lonesome life. He was in contact with the stars, and this contact was a very special one. For, you see, the souls of the dead continued living on the stars, enormous hosts of them hung from familiar constellations like Cassiopeia or the Pleiades. Indeed, he even felt that these heavenly bodies actually consisted of the souls of the dead. And he now exerted a powerful attraction on these souls. They gathered about him in large groups, evaporating into his head or his body. At night, thousands of them dripped down on him from the stars as "small men," tiny human-shaped figures, a few millimeters tall, and they existed briefly on his head. But they were quickly doomed, his body sucked them up, and they vanished within him. At times he would hear something like a terse and final death-rattle before they were absorbed. He warned them of his power of attraction, but they kept coming all the same. Whole constellations dissolved, one ill tiding after another arrived. By pulling stars together, they tried to save one or the other constellation. But basically, it was all futile, his catastrophic effect on the universe could not be halted.

Because of this contact with souls, he calls himself the greatest "seer of spirits" of all millennia. But according to his own descriptions of his effect, this term is inaccurate, or even—one would be tempted to say—too modest. The actual image he offers is quite different. He presents two distinct stages of *power* in one. By appearing simultaneously and together, they may, at first glance, be confusing. But they can easily be taken apart and comprehended in their precise meaning. As far as his fellow men are concerned, they have all perished, and he is, as he wishes to be, the *only one.* This is the final and most extreme phase of power. One can work towards it, but it can be realized only in madness. In regard to the *souls,* however (which he sees in human guise, i.e., somehow as human beings), he is still the great man. He is their leader, and they cluster around him in thousands and thousands. But they do not merely remain gathered about him like a people about its leader. What happens to them immediately is what happens gradually, through the years, to any people collected around its leader: they are *reduced* by him. The moment they reach him, they swiftly shrink down to a size of a few millimeters, and the true relationship between them thereby comes out convincingly. He, compared with them, is a giant, while they are tiny creatures striving around him. But that's not all: the great man swallows them. They literally enter him and vanish. His effect on them is annihilatory. He attracts and collects them, he reduces and devours them. Everything they once were now benefits his own body.

Though he may not be fully the only one, he is nevertheless the only one of any significance whatsoever. For this stage of power, which we are all familiar with, he offers a picture that could not be clearer and more penetrating. We should not be put off by the fact that this picture is part of a madness. We have to learn things wherever they offer themselves, and real power, in the extreme forms that we know, is no less a madness. Schreber certainly cannot tell us how to *achieve* power; that would require an observation of its practice.

But it strikes me as quite valid to find out from him what the *goal* of power is.

I hope I am not disappointing my readers if I conclude with Schreber. One would have to be as blinded as he, or as a real power-wielder of the kind described, to be satisfied with that. After all, people like us are involved too, and a far more significant portion of any investigation of such power ought to deal with the question of why we obey it. My aim was to limit myself to that inner aspect of the power-wielder that seems incomprehensible, that goes thoroughly against our grain, and that we therefore have to focus on very sharply.

1962

KARL KRAUS
The School of Resistance

It is intrinsic to both the insatiability and the vehemence of youth that *one* phenomenon, *one* experience, *one* model drives out the other. One is heated and expansive, one grabs at this or that, makes an idol of it, kowtows to it, and is devoted to it with a passion that excludes everything else. The moment it disappoints us, we pull it down from its height and unhesitatingly smash it; we don't *want* to be fair, it meant too much to us. The new idol is placed among the ruins of the old. One hardly cares that the new one feels uneasy here. One is moody and arbitrary with one's idol, one doesn't ask about its feelings, its only purpose is to be elevated and toppled, and the idols follow one another at an amazing speed, and in a variety and mutual opposition that would be terrifying if one ever thought of focusing on all of them together. One or the other idol manages to become a god, he remains and is spared, one does not lay hands on him. Only time is hard on him, not one's own ill will. Such a god may decay or gradually sink into the ground, which is yielding. But nevertheless: by and large, he remains intact, he never loses his shape.

Imagine the devastation of this temple precinct inside a man when he has lived a while. No archeologist could attain a reasonable grasp of the layout. Even the intact, the recognizable effigies form a pantheon that is enigmatic. Yet he would find ruins upon ruins, more and more peculiar, more and more fantastic. How is he to understand why precisely these ruins come to those? All they have in common is the way they were destroyed, and thus he could conclude only one thing: that it was always the same barbarian who raged here.

The wisest thing would probably be to avoid touching this whole temple precinct of ruins. However, I am now planning to be unwise and to speak about one of my idols, who was a god, but nevertheless, after perhaps five years of autocracy, was replaced and, after a few more years, completely toppled. That was a long time ago, and so I have some perspective on it. Today I know why Karl Kraus was just the right man for me, why I became addicted to him, and why I ultimately had to liberate myself from him.

In spring 1924—I had only just returned to Vienna a few weeks earlier—friends took me to my first lecture by Karl Kraus.

The huge concert-house auditorium was jammed. I sat far in back, able to see very little at that distance: a small, rather frail man, slightly hunched, with a face that came to a point below, of an incredible agility, the movements of whom I did not understand, they had something of an unknown creature to them, a newly discovered animal, I could not have said which. His voice was sharp and agitated and easily dominated the auditorium in sudden and frequent intensifications.

I could, however, very carefully observe the people around me. The auditorium had a mood that I knew from large political meetings: as though everything the speaker had to say was familiar and expected. The newcomer had been away from Vienna for eight years, perhaps the most important, those from eleven through nineteen. And for him, everything, down to the last detail, was new and astonishing because all the things that were said and passionately spoken with great emphasis as very important, referred to countless particulars of public and also private life. First of all, it was overpowering to feel that so much was happening in a city, so much that was worth being underscored, that concerned everybody. War and its aftermath, vice, murder, profiteering, hypocrisy, even typographical errors were pulled from some kind of context with the same vehemence, named, pilloried and then hurled in some sort of fury over a thousand people, who understood every word, disapproving, acclaiming, laughing, cheering.

Shall I confess that the abruptness of the mass effect was what at first astonished me the most? How could it be that all the people knew exactly what it was about, being familiar with it and disapproving of it beforehand, and now thirsting for its condemnation? All charges were presented in a strangely cemented diction that had something of legal paragraphs, never stopped, never ran out, sounding as if it had begun years ago and could be prolonged in the exact same way for many years more. The proximity to the legal sphere was also palpable in the presumption of an established and absolutely certain and inviolable law. It was clear what was good and it was clear what was bad. It was as hard and natural as granite, which no one could have scratched or notched.

Yet it was a very special kind of law, and thus, despite my unfamiliarity with the punishable offenders, I could already feel myself surrendering to him that first time. For the incomprehensible and unforgettable thing (unforgettable to anyone who experienced it, even if he lived to be three hundred) was that this law *glowed:* it radiated, it scorched and destroyed. These sentences, built like cyclopean fortresses and always carefully dovetailing, shot out sudden flashes of lightning, not harmless, not illuminating, not even theatrical flashes, but deadly lightning. And this process of annihilatory punishment, occurring in public and in all ears at once, was so fearful and dreadful that no one could resist it.

Every verdict was carried out on the spot. Once pronounced, it was irrevocable. We all witnessed the execution. The raging expectation among the auditors was not so much the pronouncement itself as its immediate fulfillment. Some of the usually unworthy victims put up a fight, refusing to accept execution. Many avoided a public struggle, but some did face up to him; and the ruthless persecution that ensued was the spectacle most relished by the audience. It took me decades to realize that Karl Kraus had succeeded in forming a hunting pack of intelligentsia—gathering at every lecture and existing acutely until the victim was brought down. Once he fell silent, the hunt was exhausted. Then another could begin.

The world of laws, which Karl Kraus protected with a "crystal voice" as a "wrathful magician" (those are Trakl's words) united two spheres that were not always in such close contact: morality and literature. Perhaps, in the intellectual chaos following World War I, nothing was more crucial than this blend.

What means did Kraus have at his disposal for achieving his effect? Today, I will name only two main devices: *literalness* and *horror.*

Literalness, to begin with the former, was shown in his sovereign use of quotations. The quotation, as he employed it, testified against the quoted man; it was often the high point, the perfection of what the commentator was accusing the man of. Karl Kraus had a gift for condemning people out of their own mouths, as it were. However the origin of this mastery—and I don't know if the context has already been seen clearly—lay in something that I should like to call the "acoustic quotation."

Kraus was haunted by voices, something that is not as rare as one might think—but with one distinction: The voices pursuing him *did exist,* in the Viennese reality. He could hear them everywhere, on streets, squares, in restaurants. Most writers knew how *not* to listen. They were willing to deal with their peers, sometimes listening to them, more often countering them. It is the hereditary vice of the intellectual that for him the world consists of intellectuals. Kraus, too, was an intellectual, otherwise he couldn't have spent his days reading newspapers, and the most diverse ones at that, all of them apparently running the same things. But since *his* ear was constantly open (it never closed, it was always in action, it was always listening), he also had to read these newpapers as though he were *hearing* them. The black, printed, dead words were audible to him. When he quoted them, he seemed to be letting voices speak: acoustic quotations.

But since he promiscuously quoted everything, hearing every voice, suppressing none, since they all existed in a kind of curious equality next to one another, aside from rank, weight, and value, Karl Kraus was by far the liveliest attraction that Vienna had to offer back then.

He was the oddest of all paradoxes: this man who loathed so much, the most steadfast scorner in world literature since the Spaniard Quevedo and since Swift, a kind of scourge of God for guilt-ridden mankind—this man let *everybody* speak. He was incapable of sacrificing even the least, the lowliest, the emptiest voice. His greatness consisted in the way he, all alone, literally alone, confronted, heard, eavesdropped on, attacked, and whiplashed the world, to the extent that he knew it, his entire world, in all its representatives (and it had countless representatives). He was thus the opposite of the writers, the huge majority of writers, who butter people up in order to be loved and lauded by them. We certainly need not waste any time discussing the necessity of such figures as he, precisely because there is such a lack of them.

In this essay, I am putting the main accent on the *living* Kraus, that is to say, Kraus as he was when speaking to many people at once.

It cannot be repeated often enough: The real, the rousing, the tormenting, the shattering Karl Kraus, the Kraus who became part of our very being, who moved and shook us, so that we needed years to gather enough strength and stand up against him—the real Karl Kraus was the *speaker*. There has never existed such a speaker in my lifetime—not in any European language that I know.

When he spoke, all his affects—and they were richly developed —imparted themselves to his listeners and were suddenly theirs. It would require a whole book to deal seriously with these affects, to depict his wrath, his scorn, his bitterness, his loathing, his worship, in regard to love and women (for whom he always had something of a chivalrous gratitude), his compassion and tenderness for the fully powerless, his murderous courage in pursuing the powerful, his marked relish at seeing through them when he tore the mask of feeblemindedness from their Austrian version, his arrogance, with which he created a distance around him, his ever-active veneration for his gods, which included such diverse beings as Shakespeare, Claudius, Goethe, Nestroy, Offenbach.

I can only list these affects now, though I am itching to add all sorts of concrete details, indeed, even imitate him as accurately as if I had just left his lecture. However, there is one affect, mentioned earlier, which I do have to emphasize. It was something that I would call his truly Biblical quality: his *horror*. If we had to limit ourselves to a single feature distinguishing him from all other public figures of his time, it would be this one: Karl Kraus was the master of horror.

It is easy even today for anyone to convince himself of that if he just opens *The Last Days of Mankind*. It is obvious in his continuous juxtaposition of the people whom war has degraded or puffed up: war cripples next to war profiteers, the blind soldier next to the officer who demands to be saluted, the noble face of the hanged man under the fat mug of the executioner—these are not things that the cinema with its cheap contrasts has accustomed us to, they are still charged with their full and unquellable horror.

When he uttered them, a thousand people sat paralyzed before him. No matter how often he recited from this play, his horror, always regenerating the force of the original vision, imbued everyone. Thus he suceeded in creating at least one uniform and unchangeable attitude among his listeners: an absolute hatred of war. It took another world war, the destruction of entire breathing cities, and the war's most specific product, the atomic bomb, to make this attitude universal and almost self-evident. In this way, Karl Kraus was something like a forerunner of the atomic bomb, its terrors already existed in his words. His attitude has today become a realization, to which even the power-wielders have to open themselves more and more: namely that wars are now absurd for both winners and losers and hence impossible, and that their irrevocable prohibition is only a matter of time.

Aside from that, what have I learned from Karl Kraus? What of his have I so thoroughly absorbed that I could no longer separate it from my own person?

First of all, there is the feeling of absolute responsibility. I had it before me in a form bordering on obsession, and nothing less seemed worthy of life. That model is before me even today, so powerful that all later formulations of the same demand would have to appear inadequate. There is that wretched word "commitment," which was born to be banal and is now rampant everywhere like weeds. It sounds as if one were an employee of the most important things. True responsibility is a hundred degrees harder, for it is sovereign and self-determining.

Second of all, Karl Kraus opened my ear, and no one could have done it like him. Since hearing him, it has not been possible for me not to do my own hearing. He began with the sounds of the city about us, the calls, yells, randomly caught distortions of language, and especially things that were wrong and out of place. It was all funny and terrible at once, and the connection of these two spheres is something I have taken for granted ever since. Thanks to him, I started realizing that each individual has a linguistic shape distinguishing him from all others. I understood that people talk to but fail to comprehend one another; that their words are thrusts ricocheting off the words of others; that there is no greater illusion than thinking that language is a means of communication between people. One speaks to another person but in such a way that he does not understand. One keeps talking and he understands even less. One screams, he screams back; ejaculation, eking out a miserable existence in grammar, takes control of language. The exclamations bounce to and fro like balls, deliver their blows, and drop to the ground. Seldom does anything penetrate the other person, and if it does, it is usually twisted awry.

But the same words that cannot be understood, that have an isolating effect, that create a kind of acoustic shape, are not rare or new, are not invented by these creatures who aim at isolation. They are the words that are used most often, phrases, the most general things, things said a hundred thousand times, and that is exactly what they use to manifest their self-will. Lovely, ugly, noble, common, sacred, profane words, they all wind up in this tumultuous reservoir, and each individual fishes out whatever suits his indolence; and he keeps repeating it until it is unrecognizable, until it is totally different, until it says the very opposite of what it once meant.

The warping of language leads to a primal chaos of the separated figures. Karl Kraus, whose sense for the abuse of language was honed as sharp as could be, had a knack for catching the products of this abuse *in statu nascendi* and never losing them again. For anyone who heard him, a new dimension of language was thereby opened, an inexhaustible dimension, which was used in earlier days just sporadically and inconsequentially. The great exception was Nestroy, from whom Karl Kraus learned as much as I did from him, and whom I can mention today only in passing.

For I would now like to speak about something else, which contrasted blatantly with the spontaneity of his ear: I would like to speak about the form of his prose. One can cut up every long prose piece of Kraus's into two, four, eight, sixteen parts, without really depriving it of anything. Pages are strung evenly on pages. They may have turned out better or worse—but in a peculiar concatenation, which is purely outward, they keep on going with no necessary end in sight. Every piece, designated as such by a title, could be twice or half as long. No unbiased reader could tell why it doesn't stop much earlier, why it won't stop for a long time. There is something arbitrary in the continuation, which has no recognizable rule. So long as ideas occur to him, he keeps going; usually, ideas keep occurring for a very long time. An overall structural principle is never present.

For the structure, lacking as a whole, is present in every sentence and is instantly conspicuous. All structural yearnings, in which writers ought to be rich, are exhausted for Karl Kraus in any one sentence. That's all he cares about: the sentence must be untouchable, no gap, no crack, no false comma. Sentence joins sentence, piece joins piece into a Great Wall of China. It is joined equally well everywhere, its character is unmistakable everywhere; but no one knows what it actually encloses. There is no empire beyond this wall, the wall itself is the empire; all the juices of the empire that may have existed went into this wall, into its construction. No one can tell what was inside or what was outside; the empire lay on both sides, the wall stands towards both the inside and the outside. The wall is everything, a cyclopean end in itself, wandering through the world, uphill, downhill, through dales and plains and very many deserts. Since the wall is alive, it may think that everything else is destroyed. Of its armies, which populated it, which had to guard it, only a single, lonesome sentry is left. This lonesome sentry is also its lonesome expander. Wherever he looks into the countryside, he feels the need to erect a further section. The most diverse materials offer themselves, he is able to form them all into new ashlars. One can promenade on this wall for years, and it will never come to an end.

I believe it was an uneasy feeling about the nature of this wall and the bleak view of the desert on either side that gradually made me rebel against Kraus. For the ashlars he built with were *judgments,* and everything that had lived in the surrounding landscape went into them. The sentry had become addicted to judgments. The production of his ashlars and the construction of his wall, which never stopped, required more and more judgments, and he procured them at the expense of his own empire. He sucked out what he was supposed to guard: for his high goals, to be sure, but everything around him became emptier and emptier; and eventually, one could readily fear that the erection of this indestructible wall of judgments had become the true purpose of life.

The heart of the matter was that he had appropriated all judging and did not permit anyone whose model he was to do any judging of his own. Anyone attached to him very quickly noticed in himself the result of this prohibition.

After you heard ten or twelve lectures by Karl Kraus, after you read his journal *Die Fackel* for a year or two, the first thing to happen was a general shrinkage of the desire to do your own judging. There was an invasion of powerful and relentless decisions that did not brook the slightest doubt. Once something was decided by this supreme authority, it was considered settled; people would have regarded it as impudent to even test it for themselves, and so they never so much as looked at any author condemned by Kraus. And even small, scornful marginalia, growing like grass between the ashlars of his sentence fortresses, were enough to make you avoid their subjects forever. A kind of reduction occurred; previously, during my eight years' absence from Vienna, which I spent in Zurich and Frankfurt, I had gone through all kinds of literature, a raging wolf of reading; but now came a period of limitation, of ascetic reserve. It had the advantage that one concentrated all the harder on the authors Kraus approved of: Shakespeare and Goethe, of course; Claudius; Nestroy, whom he was the first to revive and make accessible, his most personal and most consequential achievement; early Hauptmann, say, up to *Pippa,* whose first act he used to read aloud to his audiences; Strindberg and Wedekind, who had the honor of appearing in *Die Fackel* during their early years; and, as for other moderns, Trakl and Lasker-Schüler. We see it was by no means the worst that he reduced one to. I did not need him for Aristophanes, whom he adapted into German; nor could he have driven him out of me either, anymore than *Gilgamesh* or the *Odyssey;* all three had long since become part of the innermost marrow of my intellect. Novels, fiction in general, were left out of the game altogether; I think he wasn't much interested in them, and that was a boon. Thus under his most ruthless dictatorship, but untouched by it, I could read Dostoievsky, Poe, Gogol, and Stendhal, and absorb them as if Karl Kraus had never existed. I would like to call that my secret underground existence during that period. It was from them as from the painters Grünewald and Breughel, whom his words never reached, that I unwittingly took the strength for a later rebellion.

For at that time, I truly experienced what it means to live in a dictatorship. I was its voluntary, its devoted, its passionate and enthusiastic follower. Any foe of Karl Kraus's was a corrupt, an immoral creature. And even though it never reached the point, as was customary in subsequent dictatorships, of exterminating the alleged vermin, I nevertheless had what I must confess, to my shame, I had what I cannot term any differently, I had my "Jews"—people whom I snubbed when passing them in restaurants or on the street, whom I did not deign to look at, whose lives did not concern me, who were outlawed and banished for me, whose touch would have sullied me, whom I quite earnestly did not count as part of humanity: the victims and enemies of Karl Kraus.

Still and all, it was not a totally fruitless dictatorship, and since I had surrendered to it myself and ultimately also managed to liberate myself, I have no right to accuse it. Besides, my experience with that dictatorship has forever ruined for me the deplorable custom of accusing others.

It is important to look up to a model who has a rich, turbulent, unmistakable world, a world that he has smelled for himself, seen for himself, heard for himself, felt for himself, devised for himself. The authenticity of the model's world is what the model gives one, is what most deeply impresses one. One lets oneself be overridden and overpowered by this world, and I cannot imagine a writer who was not controlled and paralyzed by someone else's authenticity at an early time. In the humiliation of his rape, when he feels that he has nothing of his own, that he is not himself, does not know what he himself is, his concealed powers begin to stir. His personality articulates itself, arising from the resistance; wherever he liberated himself, there was something that liberated him.

But the richer the world of the man who kept him subjugated, the richer his own world when it shakes off the other. Thus, it is good to wish for strong models. It is good to be at their mercy, insofar as one secretly, in a kind of slavish darkness, goes after one's own world, which one rightfully is ashamed of still because one does not yet see it.

There is something fateful about models who reach down into this darkness, cutting off one's breath even in the last, wretched cellar. But equally dangerous are those very different models who practice bribery and far too quickly become useful to one in details, who make one think that one's own world already exists merely because one bows to them in humility. One ultimately lives by their grace as a well-trained animal and is content with delicacies from their hand.

For no one who begins can know what he will find in himself. And how could he have any inkling of it since it does not yet exist. With borrowed tools, he pierces the ground, which is itself borrowed from others. When he suddenly and for the first time stands in front of something that he does not recognize, that came to him from no-where, he is frightened and reels: for that is his own.

It can be little, a peanut, a root, a tiny rock, a poisonous bite, a new smell, an inexplicable sound, or even a somber, far-reaching artery. If he is courageous and circumspect enough to wake up from the first terrified reeling, to recognize and name it, then his own actual life will commence.

1965

DIALOGUE WITH
THE CRUEL PARTNER

It would be hard for me to get any further with the things I like to do best if I didn't sometimes keep a diary. Not that I use these jottings; they are never the raw material for what I am working on. But if a man knows the vehemence of his impressions, feels every detail of every day as though it were his only day, if—one cannot put it otherwise—he actually consists of exaggeration, but does not fight this faculty because his goal is to emphasize, to experience the sharpness and concreteness of all things that make up a life—that man would have to either explode or otherwise burst into bits unless he could *calm down* in a diary.

This calming down is perhaps the main reason why I keep a diary. It is incredible how the written sentence can calm and tame a man. The sentence is always something different from the man writing it. It stands before him as something alien, a sudden solid wall which cannot be leaped over. One might walk around it, but before one even arrives on the other side, there is a new wall at a sharp angle to the first, a new sentence, no less alien, no less solid or high, and likewise beckoning one to walk around it. Gradually, a labyrinth arises, in which the builder just barely knows his way. He is calmed by its tangled paths.

The people closest to a writer could not stand hearing everything that has excited him. Excitement is catching, and others hopefully have their own lives, which cannot consist only of someone else's excitement, otherwise they would suffocate. Then there are the things one cannot tell anybody, even the closest people, because one is too ashamed. It is not good if they are not articulated at all; it is not good if they pass into oblivion. The mechanisms one uses to make life easy are far too well-developed. First a man says, somewhat timidly:

"I really couldn't help it." And then, in the twinkling of an eye, the matter is forgotten. To escape this unworthiness, one ought to write the thing down, and then much later, perhaps years later, when self-complacence is dripping out of all one's pores, when one least expects it, one is suddenly, and to one's horror, confronted with it. "I was capable of *that*, I did *that*." Religion, absolving a man once and for all from such terrors, may be good for those people whose job is not to reach a full and waking consciousness of inner processes.

The man who truly wants to know everything will learn best from his own example. But he must not spare himself, he must treat himself as though he were someone else, not less but more harshly.

The bleakness of many diaries is due to the total lack of anything to be calmed down. One can hardly believe it, but some people are satisfied with everything around them, even with a world about to collapse. Others, despite all vicissitudes, are satisfied with themselves.

Thus, as we can see, calm as a function of a diary is no great shakes. It is a calming of the moment, of momentary weakness, which clears the day for work, and nothing more. In the long run, a diary has the reverse effect, it does not permit one to go to sleep, it interferes with the natural process of transfiguring a past which is left to itself, it keeps one awake and mordant.

But before going into detail about that and about some of the functions of diaries or journals, I would like to separate the things that I do not count among them. I distinguish between notes (or jottings) memo books, and real diaries.

Notes

I spoke about notes in the foreword to my selection of *Notes 1942–1948*. But in order to make myself clear, I would have to repeat at least the gist of what I said. "Notes" are spontaneous and contradictory. They contain sudden ideas, sometimes from unbearable tension, but often from great ease. One cannot avoid the fact that a work being continued daily through the years may occasionally strike one as clumsy, hopeless, or belated. One loathes it, one feels besieged by it, it cuts off one's breath. Suddenly, everything in the world seems more important, and one feels like a bungler in that constriction. How can anything deliberately leaving out so much be good? Every outside sound seems to come from a forbidden paradise; whereas every word one joins to the labor that one has been continuing for so long, every such word, in its pliant adjustment, its servility, has the color of a banal and permitted hell. The unbearableness of the task can be very dangerous to it. A man, and this is his greatest fortune, is versatile, in myriad ways, and he can live only for a certain time as if he weren't. In such moments, when he views himself as the slave of his goal, only one thing can help: he has to yield to the diversity of his faculties and promiscuously record whatever passes through his mind. It has to emerge as though coming from nowhere and leading nowhere; it will usually be brief, quick, often lightning-fast, untested, unmastered, unconceived, and aimless. The same writer, normally keeping a strict discipline, briefly becomes the voluntary plaything of his chance ideas. He writes down things that he would never have expected in himself, that go against his background, his convictions, even his form, against his modesty, his pride, and even his otherwise stubbornly defended truth. Eventually, the pressure that triggered everything vanishes; and all at once, he may actually feel light and jot down the freest things in a kind of bliss. The results, and there are many, had best be put aside unheeded. If he can truly manage this for many years, he will maintain his faith in spontaneity, which is the life-giving air of such jottings; once he has lost this faith, they become totally useless, and he might as well stick to his real work. Much, much later, when everything seems to be by someone else, certain things in the jottings, no matter how senseless they once may have seemed to him, suddenly acquire meaning for others. Since he is now one of these others, he can pick out the serviceable parts without much effort.

Memo Books

Each person, going by the model of all humanity, would like to create his own calendar. The chief attraction of the calendar is that it keeps going forever. So many days have been, and others will follow. The names of the months recur, those of the days more often. But the number marking each year is always different. It grows, it can never wane, it is always one year more. It grows steadily, no year is ever omitted, it is just like counting, you always add only *one*. Chronology expresses precisely what people wish for most. The recurrence of the days, whose names they are conscious of, gives them *security*. A man wakes up: "What's today?" Wednesday, it's Wednesday again, there have been many Wednesdays. But he has passed more than Wednesday. For it is October 30, that is something bigger, and he has known a whole bunch of them too. But in regard to the number of the year, with its linear increase, he hopes it will pull him along to higher and higher numbers. Security and the wish for a long life come together in our reckoning of time, which seems almost made for them.

However, the *empty* calendar is everyman's calendar, he wants to make it his own, and to do so he has to fill it. There are good days and bad, open and afflicted ones. If he records them, in just a few words or letters, the calendar will be unmistakably his own. The most important events establish commemoration days. In his youth, they are rare, the year maintains a sort of innocence, most days are still free and unused for the future. But gradually, the years fill in, more and more crucial things recur, and eventually there is hardly an unused day in his calendar: he has his own history.

I know people who make fun of other people's calendars, "because there's so little in them." But only the man who has made one for himself can truly know what's in it. The leanness of these signs makes up their value. They exist by dint of their concentration, the experiences preserved in them are well-nigh magically sealed, they are unused and can suddenly grow into something enormous through other proximities in some other year.

Now there is no living person who would not have the right to such memo books. *Everyone* is the midpoint of the world, absolutely everyone; and the world is precious only because it is full of such midpoints. That is the *meaning* of the word "human:" each person a midpoint next to countless others, who are midpoints as much as he.

Memo books were and are the seed of actual diaries. Many writers, distrusting a diary because too much of their substance could be squandered in it, do keep their memo books. Normally, the two are mixed. But I keep them strictly apart. In the memo books, which are nearly always small calendars, I briefly jot down the things that especially concern or content me. They hold the names of the few people through whom one has breathed and without whom one could never endure all the other days. The encounter with them, the first proximity, their departure, their return, their serious illnesses, their recovery, and the most horrible thing of all, their deaths. Then there are the days of sudden ideas that plunge upon one first like swords, that submerge, then surface, and finally, transformed, carry a good portion of life. At times, one records the days when something of these ideas has acquired shape and satisfies one. These days of expansive overcoming are the opposite of those days in which one was overcome instead: one has read something which one feels will never abandon one again, *Woyzeck, The Possessed,* the *Ajax* of Sophocles. Then there are the moments in which one has heard of unparallelled customs, an unknown religion, a new science, an expansion of the world, a further threat to mankind, or, very seldom, a hope for mankind. Then the places one finally reaches after yearning one's heart out for them. All these things are mentioned in only three or four words. Names are the main things, the crux is the day on which the new thing, the new people enter one's life or on which some vanished thing crops up again as though new.

We can say one thing with certainty about these memo books: they are no one else's business. For outsiders, they are incomprehensible; or if not, then the monotonous language of the registration makes them utterly boring.

As soon as it becomes more, as soon as one deals with the things themselves, they leave the framework of the memo calendar and enter the diary.

Diaries

In a diary, one talks to oneself. The man who cannot do this, who sees an audience before him, even a later one, even after his death, is a forger. Such forged diaries are not the issue here. They too can have their value. Some of them are incredibly fascinating; their interest lies in the extent of the forgery: their attraction depends on the forger's talent. But what I want to focus on now is the genuine diary, which is much rarer and much more important. What meaning does it have for the writer, that is, for a man who writes a lot anyway because writing is his profession?

Conspicuously, a diary cannot *always* be kept, there are long periods in which one avoids it, like something dangerous, almost a vice. One is not always dissatisfied with oneself and with others. There are times of exaltation and undoubted personal happiness. In the life of a man for whom a penchant for knowledge has become second nature, such times cannot be very frequent. Hence, they will seem all the more precious to him. He will hesitate to touch them. Since they carry him, like anyone else, through the much bigger remainder of his existence, he *needs* them and therefore doesn't touch them, he leaves them with their aura of uncomprehended miracles. Only their collapse will bring him to his senses. How did he lose them? What destroyed them for him? In this moment, his soliloquy resumes.

At other times, it may be that the entire day is absorbed in one's own work. This work is going forward well and soundly, it has reached a level beyond any goal or doubt, it coincides so accurately with what one is that nothing happens outside it, nothing remains outside it. There are good, even important writers who, in this frame of mind, can write one book after another. They have nothing to say to *themselves,* their book says it all for them. They succeed in dividing themselves totally over their characters. They have often worked out a surface, a texture so rich and peculiar as to incessantly occupy their attention and sensual memory. They are the true work masters of literature, the happy writers. They find it natural to reduce to a minimum the periods between books. The peculiarity of their surface lures them back to work. The changes and iridescence of the world, the peculiar motion of outer life have been bound by them to this surface, and they are now frolicking in it like others in the world.

I would be the last to feel irony or even scorn for such writers. They have to be evaluated according to the necessity of their peculiarity; they include a good number of the best men in world literature. At moments, one yearns for a world in which any other kind of writer would be impossible. However, no genuine diaries can be expected from them. They probably doubt that such diaries are at all possible. Their self-assurance and their success have to make them scornful of other, less even-keeled natures. Yet one need simply mention the name Kafka, against whose substance and originality even the best of the self-assured would not dare measure themselves; and his name is all it takes to prove how inadmissible their intolerance is. Perhaps it should even give them pause to think that our most important possession by far from a man like Pavese is his diaries; his permanent creation is here and not in his works.

Thus, in a diary, one speaks to oneself. But what does that mean? Does one, de facto, become two figures properly conversing with one another? And who are the two? Why are there only two? Couldn't there, shouldn't there be many of them? Why would a diary be worthless if one spoke to many instead of to oneself?

The first advantage of the fictional "I" that one addresses is that it really listens. It is always at hand, it never turns away. It never feigns interest, it is not polite. It does not interrupt, it lets one finish speaking. It is not only curious, it is also patient. I can speak here only out of my own experience: yet I am always amazed that there is someone listening to me as patiently as I listen to others. Still, one should not imagine that this listener makes things easy for one. Since he has the advantage of understanding one, one cannot put anything over on him. He is not only patient, he is also malicious. He won't let anything pass, he sees through everything. He notices the tiniest detail, and the instant one begins falsifying, he goes back vehemently to that detail. Never in my entire life—and sixty years count for something—have I met such a dangerous interlocutor, and I have had a few whom no one need be ashamed of. Perhaps there's a special advantage to his not representing his own interests. He has all the reactions of a person in his own right, but without the motives. He defends no theory, he does not preen himself on any discoveries. His instinct for stirrings of power or vanity is unbelievable. Naturally, his knowing someone thoroughly stands him in good stead.

When challenging me for some inaccuracy, some lack of knowledge, some foible, some indolence, he pounces on me like a thunderbolt. When I say, "That's not important, I'm interested in more than myself, the condition of the world, I have to warn, that's all," he laughs in my face. "Nevertheless," he says, "nevertheless." Let me quote him verbatim: "It is a mistake of the do-gooders" (how that vile expression stings) "that the responsibility they feel and the good they perhaps truly want to do make them forget to develop the instrument enabling them to know people and grasp them in a thousand rough and fine details. For these same people bring forth the worst and most general, the most dangerous things that occur. There is no other hope for the survival of mankind than knowing enough about the people it is made up of. How can you dare to come out with something so wrong about yourself merely because it's convenient for you?"

Sometimes, I have foreseen something terrible—in the world, I mean—which then came true precisely. I had nothing better to do than write it down. I could prove it to myself, it was written down long before it came about. I probably wanted to arrogate the right to further forecasts. Let me quote my partner's demolishing retort, it is more important than the woeful vanity of the prediction that materialized:

"The warner, the prophet, whose forecasts come true is an unfairly respected figure. He has made things too easy for himself and permitted the terrible things he loathes to overpower him before they even happen. He thinks he is warning; but measured by the passion of his foresight, his warning is worthless. He is admired for his foresight; but nothing is easier. The more terrible his foresight, the more likely its materialization. We ought to admire the prophet who foretells something *good*. For this, and only this, is improbable."

The conscience, the good old conscience, I hear a reader say triumphantly, he's conversing with his conscience! He's boasting about keeping a diary to converse with his conscience! But that's not quite so. The other, to whom one speaks, *changes* his roles. It is true, he can appear as a conscience, and I am very beholden to him for that since the others make things much too easy for one, it seems to be a human pleasure to let oneself be *persuaded*. But it is not always a conscience. Sometimes it is *I,* speaking to him in despair and self-accusal, with a vehemence such as I would wish on nobody. He then suddenly turns into the keen-eyed comforter, who knows precisely in which way I am going too far. He sees that as a writer I often help myself to some malice or bad attitude that isn't mine at all. He reminds me that ultimately the important thing is what one *does,* for anyone can think anything. Sarcastic and cheerful, he pulls off the masks of evil in which one struts about, and he shows that one is really not so "interesting." I am even more thankful to him for this role.

He has many other roles, it would be tiresome to go into all of them. But one thing is obvious: a diary that doesn't have this consistent dialogue-character strikes me as worthless; I could not keep my diary except in the form of such a monologue.

I cannot think that the alertness of these two figures, who often go hunting after each other, is an empty game. One must bear in mind that a man who does not recognize the external authority of faith has to put up some corresponding thing inside himself; otherwise he will turn into a helpless chaos. His permitting them to change roles, his letting them play them does not mean that he does not take them seriously. In this game, if he can just succeed, he will ultimately achieve a finer moral sensibility than is offered him by the usual rules of the world. For these prescriptions are dead for most people because they can never play, their rigidity deprives them of their life.

That might be the most important function of a diary. It would be wrong to call it the only one. For in a diary, one speaks not only to oneself, but also to others. All the conversations that one can never finish in real life because they would end in violence, all the absolute, unsparing, demolishing words that one would often have to say to others—all those things wind up here. And here they remain secret; for a diary that is not secret is no diary, and the people who read their diaries to others ought really to write letters or, even better, put on recitation evenings about themselves. In my early Berlin period, I knew a man who never made a journal entry without reading it to me that same evening. By inviting enough guests, I managed to reduce the readings to one a week, and he was very happy, they lasted longer, and he also preferred spreading his tail in front of more than two eyes.

There cannot be enough ruses and cautionary measures for keeping a genuine diary a secret. Locks cannot be trusted. Codes are better. I myself employ an altered stenography that would take weeks of drudgery to decipher. Thus I can write down whatever I like, never hurting or damaging another person, and when I am finally old and wise, I can decide whether to make it disappear entirely or confide it to some secret place, where it would be found only by chance, in some harmless future.

I have never managed to keep a diary while traveling in a new country. I cannot possibly pick up a pencil because I am much too full of the many unknown people one talks to in either signs or supposed words without mutual understanding. Language, otherwise an

48

instrument that one thought one could manipulate, suddenly becomes wild and dangerous. One yields to its seduction and one is manipulated by language instead. Disbelief, confidence, ambivalence, boasting, strength, threat, rejection, annoyance, deception, tenderness, hospitality, amazement—everything is there, and so immediate, as though one had never noticed it before. A written word about these things will rest on the paper like its own corpse. Amid such splendors, I would rather not become a killer. But no sooner am I at home than I make up for every lost day. From memory, sometimes with great effort, I distribute to the days what is theirs. There have been journeys whose belated diary entries are three times as long as they were.

I believe that with such travel memories one is most apt to think of readers. One feels they are possible without falsifications. Onc recalls other people's accounts, which lured one into the voyage. It is nice to show gratitude with one's own things.

Altogether, the diaries of others mean a great deal to one. What writer has not read diaries that have never let him loose again? This might be a good place to say something about that.

One can begin with those one read as a child: the diaries of great travelers and discoverers. First, one is enticed by adventure per se, independent of the customs and cultures of exotic people. The eeriest thing for a child is emptiness, which he never knows, he is never left all alone, he is always surrounded by people. So he plunges into journeys to the North or South Pole or long sea voyages in small vessels. The exciting thing is the emptiness all around, most dangerous at night, which he himself fears. In this remoteness and emptiness, he indelibly registers the sequence of day and night, for the journey, always continuing, has a goal, it never ceases before reaching it or before some final catastrophe. I truly believe that the child thereby has the terrifying experience of the calendar.

Then there are the travels to secretly populated areas: Africa and the jungle, and the first alien customs to cut into his flesh are those of cannibals. His curiosity is egged on by these terrors, he now wants to know something about other alien people. The path through the jungle goes step by step, the number of daily miles is carefully recorded. All the forms in which one later discovers new things are already prefigured in these. Danger upon danger, but day by day, and then the dreadful waiting of the vanished travelers, attempts at saving them, or else their tormented ends. I do not think that there are any subsequent diaries that mean so much to an adult.

However, the feeling for distant places remains, and the interest in them is never sated. So one frolics insatiably in past times and foreign cultures. The rigidity of one's own existence increases, and those are the most inexhaustible means of transformation. There are experiences that one longs for and that are taboo at home; and suddenly, somewhere else, in a place one has read one's way to, they are a universal custom. The situation one lives in at home is overdetermined: one's activities go by hours that are the same every day; the people one knows all know one another; one is talked about and watched; ears on all sides and familiar eyes. Since everything is bound and always more and more bound, there is a gigantic reservoir of unsated desire for transformation, and only news from genuinely foreign places can get that desire going.

It is a special and much too unused fortune that there are travelogues from foreign cultures, written by their own people and not by Europeans. Let me mention just two of the most detailed ones, which I keep rereading: the book by the Chinese Pilgrim Huan Tsang, who visited India during the seventh century; and the book by the Tangiers Arab Ibn Battuta, who spent twenty-five years traveling through the entire Islamic world of the fourteenth century, as well as India and probably China. But they do not exhaust the hoard of exotic diaries, Japan has literary diaries as subtle and precise as anything by Proust: *The Pillow Book* by Sei Shonagon, a lady-in-waiting—hers are the most perfect "jottings" that I know—and the diary of Lady Murasaki Shikibu, who also wrote the novel *Genji;* both lived at the same court around the year 1000, knowing but not liking one another very much.

The exact opposite of these accounts from far away are diaries from nearby. They are by closely related people in whom one recognizes *oneself.* The finest example in German literature is the diaries of Hebbel. One loves them because they scarcely have a page without something concerning one personally. One may feel that one has already written down this or that at some moment. Perhaps one really has. If not, one could certainly have done so. This process of an intimate encounter is exciting if for no other reason than because, next to things that are "one's own," one finds something else that one could never have thought or written down in that way. It is the spectacle of two minds interpenetrating: they touch at certain points; at others, empty spaces form between them not to be filled out in any way. The similar and the dissimilar are so close together as to force one to think; nothing is more fruitful than such diaries from nearby, as one might call them. However, an inherent feature is that they are "complete," i.e. very rich, and not written in terms of a specific purpose.

Religious diaries depicting the struggle for a faith, are excluded here; they offer strength only to those people caught in a similar fight. They will tend to depress the man with a truly free, a real mind, who takes it so seriously that he could not yet pledge himself. The traces of freedom still remaining in them, the reluctance, which is regarded as weakness, will touch the reader more quickly than what the writer considers his strength: the gradual surrender. The most astonishing examples, going beyond the form of a diary—Pascal and Kierkegaard—would be excluded from this restriction: they are greater than their purpose, and thus they have everything.

One often hears that other people's diaries encourage truth in one's own. Confessions of important men, once brought to paper, have lasting effect on others. *"This* man says he has done this and that. I need not despair if I have done the same." The value of a *model* is expanded here in a strange way. Its negative aspect gives one the courage to fight against one's own negative features.

It is certain that nothing comes about without great paragons. But their works are also paralyzing: the deeper one grasps them, i.e. the more gifted one is, the more convinced one becomes that they are not to be reached. Experience, however, proves the opposite. Modern literature came into being *despite* the overwhelming model of Antiquity. *After* writing *Don Quixote,* that is to say, outdoing anything like a novel that Antiquity had to offer, Cervantes would have been proud to equal Heliodorus. The exact functioning of the model has not yet been researched, and this is not the place to tackle this enormous theme seriously. Yet it is amusing to see the part that Walter Scott, one of the most unenjoyable writers of all time, played for Balzac, with whom he has nothing in common. The addiction to originality, so characteristic of the modern age, is revealed in its quest for models, that are only seeming, that it destroys in order to hold out conspicuously *against* them; the real models it is dependent on remain all the better concealed. This process can be unconscious; often, it is conscious and dishonest.

For those, however, whose originality is not due to trickery or force, for whom the impetus of the great minds that have virtually pushed them into the world is never fully exhausted, who can always return to them without compromising themselves—for those men, it is an inestimable good fortune to find diaries by their forebears that expose the weaknesses they themselves are laboring under. The finished work has an oppressive supremacy. The man still caught in his own work, not knowing where it will lead, not knowing whether he can ever end it, can despair a thousand times. It will give him strength to see the doubts of those who succeeded in their work.

Along with this practical value of diaries, there is an effect of a more general nature, *obstinacy,* which they manifest. Every diary deserving of the name has certain recurrent obsessions, worries, private problems. They continue throughout a lifetime, they constitute the peculiarity of that life. The man who has gotten rid of them seems virtually snuffed out. The struggle against them is as necessary as their doggedness. They are by no means always interesting per se, and yet they make up the most definite feature of this man, he can no more do without them than he can do without his bones. It is infinitely important to see this hardest, most indissoluble aspect in others so as to focus more calmly on, and not despair in, the corresponding aspect in oneself. The characters in a literary work cannot have this impact, for they exist by dint of a successful detachment from their creator, they are removed as far as possible from his own inner processes.

It seems to me that there are certain contents in a life that can be best captured in diary form. I do not know whether they should be the same for everyone. One could imagine that a *slow* person, to whom everything unfolds very gradually anyway, would have to acquire the very opposite. The lightning speed of jottings would be his most crucial exercise, he could thereby learn how to fly at times and to gain those aspects of the world that are part of rapidity; he would thus complement his natural talent for gradual development.

For the swift, who pounce like predators on every situation and every person, grabbing so violently at their hearts as to destroy the outer form of their bodies—for those swift men, the very reverse would be imperative: a slow diary in which the contemplated things gain a different aspect from day to day. This arduous constraint of not reaching the goal too quickly would have to give them a dimension that would otherwise by denied them.

Stendhal is one of those swift men. He does move in an extremely rich world, remaining open to it. Yet there are few themes in his diaries, and he kept going over them again and again. It is as though he occasionally wrote new diaries over his old ones. Since he cannot really be slow, he always keeps observing the same things. This is the process that eventually led to his great novels. Even the two that were completed and whose effect on others seems endless were not actually over for him. He is the very antipode of people who detach work after work from themselves with self-assurance and are able to tackle a new one only because the old one seems alien to them.

Kafka, the writer who most purely expressed our century and whom I therefore regard as its most essential manifestation, can readily be compared to Stendhal in that respect. He is never done with anything, it is always the same thing disquieting him from start to finish. He keeps turning it around, he circumscribes it, he goes through it with different paces. It is never exhausted, it could never have been exhausted, even if he had lived twice as long. Yet Kafka is one of the slow ones, just as Stendhal is one of the swift ones. It is the swift who tend to view their lives as happy. So Stendhal's work is dipped in the color of happiness, Kafka's in that of powerlessness. But the work of each develops out of a lifelong diary that keep going by questioning itself.

It must seem presumptuous to talk about one's own work after two such figures, who have come unscathed through the test of time. But a man can only give his own. And so, to be complete, I will list the themes that are the obsessions in my diaries and take up the most space in them. Next to many other things that remain ephemeral and scattered, these are the themes that keep getting varied to the point of exhaustion.

There are progress, regression, doubts, anxiety, and intoxication by a work that endured through the longest part of my life and from which I ultimately could hand over the crucial part with conviction. There is, further, the enigma of *metamorphosis* and its most concentrated utterance in literature, the drama, which has been haunting me since I first read Shakespeare at ten and since I encountered Aristophanes and the Greek tragedians at seventeen; thus I keep accounts of anything dramatic that I find, all dramas and myths, insofar as they still *are* dramas and myths, but also the things that are called that today, the shabby pseudo-myths. There are, further, the encounters with people from countries that I know either not at all or very well. There are the stories and destinies of friends whom I have lost sight of for a very long time and then suddenly find again. There is the struggle for existence waged by the people closest to me against illnesses, operations, perils lasting for decades, against the snuffing of their will to live. There are all traits of envy and avarice, which anger me—I have loathed them since childhood—but there are also generosity, goodness, and pride, which I absolutely idolize. There is jealousy, my private variety of power, a theme that Proust certainly exhausted, but that each man nevertheless must work out for himself. There is still any kind of madness: even though I tried to deal with it creatively at a very early time, it has never for an instant lost its fascination for me. There is the issue of faith, of faith per se, and in each of its manifestations to which I tend in accordance with my background, but to which I shall never commit myself so long as I have not puzzled out its nature. Finally, and most obsessively, there is death, which I cannot acknowledge though I never ignore it, which I have to hunt down into its very last hiding-place in order to destroy its attraction and its false charisma.

These themes, as we can see, are rather numerous, although I have named only the most urgent, and I wouldn't know how I could live with them and yet not continually justify them to myself. For what one considers valid and finally possesses in works that will not be unworthy of their readers is only a tiny fraction of the things happening every single day. Since these things keep going day after day, and should not cease, I shall never be one of those people who are ashamed of the inadequacies of a diary.

1965

REALISM
AND NEW REALITY

Realism, in a narrower sense, was a method of gaining reality for the novel. *Total* reality; it was important not to exclude anything from this reality, whether for aesthetic or for bourgeois moral conventions. It was reality as seen by a few unbiased and open minds of the nineteenth century. Even then, they didn't see everything, and this was properly thrown up at them by contemporaries who had set their hearts on other, seemingly eccentric practices. But even if we today were ready to admit with conviction that the few truly important realists did reach their goal, that they did succeed in gaining total reality for the novel, that their era was fully absorbed into their words— what would that signify for us? Could those of us who are after the same goal, though as people of our era, and who regard themselves as modern realists—could we employ the same methods?

One senses what the answer to that will be; but first, let us consider what has become of that past reality. It has changed so enormously that the very first inkling of it fills us with unparalleled helplessness. An attempt to overcome this helplessness will, I think, lead to distinguishing three essential aspects of the change. There is an *increasing* and there is a *more precise* reality; and then there is the reality of the *future*.

It is easy to see what is meant by the first of these aspects, *increasing* reality: a lot more exists now, not only numerically, there are many more people and things; but a far greater immensity exists in quality as well. The old, the new, and the different flow in from everywhere.

The old: more and more past cultures are dug up. History and prehistory keep reaching further and further back. An early art of enigmatic perfection has forever destroyed our arrogance about our own art. The earth is once again being populated with its most ancient dead. They have been resurrected from their bones, utensils, and cave paintings to live in our imagination as the Carthaginians and Egyptians lived for the people of the previous century.

The new: well, many of us were born before man could fly, and yet we take our flight to Vienna for granted. The younger people among us may be rocketed as tourists to the moon and may even be embarrassed to publish a description of something that banal after their return. Just as I am now embarrassed about enumerating other "new" things. In my childhood, they appeared as a few, single miracles: my first electric light, my first telephone call; today, tens of thousands of new things swarm in on us like mosquitoes.

Aside from the old and the new, I have also mentioned the different, flowing in from everywhere, the easy-to-reach foreign towns, countries, continents, the second language that just about everyone learns next to his own, sometimes even mastering a third and fourth. The precise exploration of foreign cultures, exhibits of their arts, translations of their literatures. The investigation of the still living primitive peoples: their material ways of life, their social structures, their creeds and rites, their myths. The number of totally different things, of excitingly rich finds by anthropologists, is immense, and all those things cannot possibly be measured by the same yardstick—as people generally assumed in the past, as some people would still like to assume today. *This* increase of reality means the most to me personally because acquiring it takes more effort than the banal new, which is evident to anybody. But this increase also very healthily reduces our arrogance, which puffs up with the promiscuously new. You see, one recognizes, among other things, that everything was already invented in myths, they are very ancient notions and wishes that we nimbly realize today. But as for our ability to invent new wishes and myths, we are in a lamentable state. We reel off the old ones like noisy prayer-mills, and often we don't even know what their mechanical prayers mean. This is an experience that should give us as writers pause to think, for above all we are supposed to be inventing the new. Finally, I do not want to neglect the fact that the different, about which we are only just learning, does not refer purely to human beings. The life that animals have always led has a different meaning for us now. The increasing knowledge of their rites and

56

games, for example, proves that animals, whom we officially declared to be machines three centuries ago, have something like a civilization, comparable to ours.

The expansion of this age, its increasing reality, at a speed with no foreseeable goal, is also its confusion.

The second aspect, that of *more precise* reality, joins the foregoing directly. The roots of this precision are exposed for all to see: they are science, particularly natural science. The realistic novelists of the nineteenth century were already calling upon science for their major undertakings: Balzac wanted to investigate and classify human society as precisely as a zoologist does the animal kingdom. His ambition was to be a Buffon of society. Zola, in his *Manifesto on the Experimental Novel,* leaned heavily on the physiologist Claude Bernard, quoting pages and pages from his *Introduction à l'étude de la médicine expérimentale.* Systematic science, e.g. zoology, which entranced Balzac, no longer sufficed for Zola; he was convinced that the novelist should look upon experimental science as a model and believed quite earnestly that his work employed the methods of the physiologist Bernard. The naïveté of this ideology is obvious, we need not waste any time on it. (It would, incidentally, be dangerous to draw any conclusions from it as to the value of the works it generated.) We must, however, establish that people still keep adducing scientific methods or theories; in fact, they have never stopped doing so since that time. We may consider ourselves fortunate that there are so many and so diverse scientific disciplines and directions. The influence of William James did as little damage to Joyce as Bergson's influence did to Proust. And Musil, with the help of gestalt psychology, managed to defend himself against psychoanalysis, which would have killed his work. Precision is mirrored equally in the bent for completeness that characterizes Joyce; a single day, but totally, with every motion of those experiencing that day; no instant lost or omitted, the book is identical with the day.

But what I wish to stress here is the impact of scientific precision, of scientific methods on reality per se. It is also the technological processes as such that contribute to the precision of reality, the number of laboratories in which more and more people are employed. Many actions that belong to the daily routine can succeed only through the application of alert precision. The sector of "approximate" activity and knowledge is rapidly shrinking. It is being measured and weighed by ever tinier units. A growing portion of cerebral work is being taken over by apparatuses that are more reliable than we. The verifying control exerted on anything and everything lives from its exactness. An interest in machines is shown by practically all young people. The precision of the annihilating instruments determines whether they wipe out their goal rather than, prematurely, their place of origin. Even the peculiar and rather ancient area of bureaucracy is changing in the same direction. One may assume that officials everywhere will soon be using apparatuses to understand precisely and immediately, and to react precisely and immediately. Mounting specialization is going hand in hand with mounting precision. Reality is departmentalized, subdivided, and can be grasped down to its minutest units from many directions.

As a third aspect of reality, I named the *reality* of the *future.* The future exists quite differently from ever before, it is approaching more swiftly and it is being consciously brought about. Its dangers are our most intrinsic work; but so are its hopes. The reality of the future has split: on the one side, annihilation; on the other, the good life. Both are simultaneously active, in the world, in ourselves. This split, this double future, is absolute, and there is no one who could ignore it. Everyone sees a dark and a bright shape at once, approaching him at an oppressive velocity. One may hold either shape at bay to see only the other, but both are persistently there.

There is reason enough to keep one shape, the dark one, out of sight occasionally. Everywhere on earth, in the most diverse forms, utopias are about to come true. The age of mocking and scorning utopia is over. There is no utopia that could not be materialized. We now have ways and means of realizing anything, absolutely anything. The boldness of the utopian desire has so greatly increased that we now hesitate to acknowledge and we actually avoid the word in its old, somewhat belittling tinge. Utopias are sliced up into segments and then tackled as plans stretching over a given number of years. Whatever the political credo of a country, no state with any self-respect, no government that takes itself seriously, will operate without plans.

The power of these utopias is enormous; but at times they bog down in the present, and they could not do otherwise. That does not mean that, after a breathing-spell, they do not recollect themselves. A utopia, right in the middle of materializing, is confronted with the enormous sum total of reality that has come down to us. This confrontation takes place in the individual who is within the area of this enterprise. His optimism may slacken because of the huge scope of the utopian demand. The torment of this fatigue may be very great and afflicting for the man who has taken it all seriously. It may be necessary for him to hit out against the exorbitant demand with scorn and sarcasm.

But let us not forget that there are very different kinds of utopias and that all of them are active at the same time. Social, scientific-technological, national utopias strengthen each other and chafe each other. They protect the continuance of their realization by developing weapons to intimidate. One knows what these weapons are like. Their actual use would turn against the user with no less force. Everyone senses this dark side of the future, which may come true. The existence of such weapons is leading, for the first time in human history, to a consensus on the necessity of peace. But so long as this consensus has not produced a plan adequate to all dangers and carried out for all people, the dark side of the future will remain a crucial part of reality, its oppressively close, unrelenting threat.

It is particularly this double aspect of the future, actively wished and actively feared, that distinguishes our century's reality from that of the previous one. Its increase and its greater precision were already apparent, diverging now from the past only in their scope and speed. The aspect of the future is totally different, and one can say without exaggeration that we are living in a period of the world that does not have the most important thing in common with the period of our grandfathers: its future is not a whole thing anymore, it is split in two.

Presumably, one or several of the aspects of our reality, such as I have briefly described, must emerge in the novel of our times; otherwise, one could hardly call it realistic. It is now up to our conversation to determine the extent to which this has already happened or could still happen.

1965

KAFKA'S OTHER TRIAL
The Letters to Felice

I

So now they've been published, these letters of a five-year torment, in a volume of 750 pages. For many years the name of the fiancée was discreetly designated by F., similar to K., so that for a long time, people didn't even know what the name was and they often brooded about it, never guessing it among all the names they weighed, and it would have been quite impossible to hit upon it—and now this name is written in large letters on the cover. The woman to whom these letters were addressed has been dead for eight years. Five years before her death, she sold the letters to Kafka's publisher, and whatever one may think about it, Kafka's "dearest businesswoman" demonstrated, at the very end, the efficiency that meant a great deal to him and even aroused his tenderness.

It is true that he had been dead for forty-three years when these letters appeared, and yet one's first response (one owed it to the respect for him and his misfortune) was embarrassment and abashment. I know people who got more and more embarrassed while reading the book, who couldn't help feeling they had no right to force their way in here of all places.

I greatly respect them for that, but I do not share their sentiments. I was as moved by these letters as I have not been moved by any literary work for years. They now belong among those singular memoirs, autobiographies, correspondences on which even Kafka nourished himself. He, whose supreme quality was awe, never shied away from reading the letters of Kleist, of Flaubert, of Hebbel over and over again. In one of the most afflicted moments of his life, he clung to the fact that Grillparzer no longer felt anything when taking Kathi Fröhlich on his lap. Most people, luckily, are aware of the horror of life only sometimes; a mere few, however, appointed as witnesses by internal forces, are always aware of it. And there is only one comfort for that horror of life: aligning it with the horror of preceding witnesses. We therefore really have to be grateful to Felice Bauer for preserving and salvaging Kafka's letters to her, even if she did find it in her heart to sell them.

It would be too meager to speak of a document here, unless one used the same word for the testimonies of existence by Pascal, Kierkegaard, and Dostoievsky. For my part, I can only say that these letters passed into me like a genuine life, and now I find them as enigmatic and as familiar as if they had always belonged to me, ever since I first began totally absorbing people in order to keep understanding them anew.

Late in the evening of August 13, 1912, Kafka first met Felice Bauer in the home of the Brod family. Around that time, there are several utterances by him about this meeting. The first mention is in a letter to Max Brod, dated August 14. Kafka is talking about the manuscript of *Betrachtung* (Meditation), which he had brought to Brod the previous evening so that the two of them might finally put it in order:

"Yesterday, while arranging the little pieces, I was under the influence of Fräulein Bauer, it is quite possible that this produced some silliness, a sequence that is perhaps only secretly comical." He asks Brod to fix things up, and thanks him. The next day, August 15, saw the following line in the diary: "Thought a great deal about . . . what embarrassment at writing down names . . . F.B."

Then, on August 20, a week after the encounter, he tries to achieve some objective description of the first impression. He describes her appearance, he realizes he is slightly estranging himself from her by "getting too close for comfort" in that description. He took it for granted that she, a stranger, should be sitting in that circle. He accepted the fact immediately. "While sitting down, I scrutinized her for the first time; by the time I was seated, I had an unshakable verdict." The entry breaks off in the middle of the next sentence. Otherwise, all the more important observations would have followed, and it will soon be evident how many.

He first wrote to her on September 20, reminding her (after all, five weeks had passed since the meeting) that they had been at the

Brod home and he was the man who had handed her one photograph after another across the table and "eventually, this hand, which is now striking the keys, held your hand, with which you confirmed a promise to go on a journey to Palestine next year."

The quickness of this promise, the self-assurance she made it with were the things so greatly impressing him at first. He regarded this handshake as a *Gelöbnis* (pledge), the word *Verlobung* (betrothal) seems close behind it; and he, who is so slow to make up his mind, for whom, because of a thousand doubts, every goal towards which he would like to go moves away instead of approaching—he could only be fascinated by quickness. However, the goal of the promise is Palestine, and at that stage in his life there could hardly be a more promising word for him, it is the promised (*gelobte*) land.

The situation is even more meaningful when one recalls what kind of pictures he was handing her across the table. They were photographs of a "Thalian journey." In early July, five or six weeks before, he and Max Brod had been in Weimar, and very strange things had occurred for him in Goethe's house. He had noticed the custodian's daughter, a beautiful girl, in the *Goethehaus*. He had managed to converse with her; he had gotten to know her family, he had photographed her in the garden and in front of the house, they invited him back, and thus he went in and out of the *Goethehaus*—not just during normal visiting hours. He also ran into her frequently in the streets of the small town, he sorrowfully observed her with young men, he made an appointment with her, which she didn't keep, and he soon realized she was more interested in students. The whole thing took place in a few short days, the movement of travel, when everything happens more swiftly, had helped the encounter. Right after that, Kafka, without Brod, spent a few weeks in the Harz mountains at the Jungborn *Naturheilanstalt* [a sanatorium using natural remedies]. There are wonderfully rich jottings from those weeks, free of "Thalian" interests, of reverence towards the places of great poets. However, he did get friendly replies to the postcards he sent to the beautiful girl in Weimar. He copied one full reply in a letter to Brod, adding the following remark, which was optimistic for his frame of mind: "For if I am not disagreeable to her, I am still as unimportant to her as a pot. But then why does she write just as I want her to? Could it be that one can bind a girl by writing?"

Thus, this encounter in the *Goethehaus* gave him heart. It was the pictures of the trip that he handed Felice across the table that first evening. The memory of that attempted acquaintanceship, of his activity during that time—which did at least produce the photos that he could now show—was transferred to the girl sitting opposite him, Felice.

It must also be mentioned that during this trip, which began in Leipzig, Kafka got to know Ernst Rowohlt, who had made up his mind to publish Kafka's first book. The writer had a great deal of trouble putting together the brief pieces from his journals for *Die Betrachtung.* He wavered, the pieces didn't strike him as good enough, Brod kept urging him and wouldn't stop. Finally it was all set; and on the evening of August 13, Kafka brought over the definitive selection, as already pointed out, to discuss its arrangement with Brod.

So, that evening, he was equipped with everything that could give him courage: the manuscript of his first book; the pictures of the "Thalian" journey, including the pictures of the Weimar girl, who had politely answered him; and an issue of the magazine *Palestine* in his pocket.

The meeting took place in a home where he felt comfortable. He always tried, as he tells, to prolong the evenings with the Brods, until finally they, wanting to go to bed, expelled him in a friendly manner. It was the family that drew him from his own family. Literature was not taboo here. The parents were proud of the young writer in the house, Max, who had already made a name for himself, and they took his friends seriously.

It was a time of diverse and precise writing for Kafka. This is revealed in the Jungborn journals, the finest of his travel diaries—and they are also the ones most immediately related to his own work, in this case *Amerika.*

How rich his memory was for concrete detail is demonstrated by his astonishing sixth letter to Felice, on October 27, in which he so accurately describes their first encounter. Seventy-five days have passed since that evening of August 13. Of the details he carries in his memory, not all have the same weight. He writes down some, one might almost say, mischievously, to show her that he noticed everything about her, that nothing eluded him. He thus turns out to be a writer in Flaubert's sense, a writer for whom nothing is trivial so long

as it is right. With a touch of pride, he presents it all, a double tribute, to her, because she was worth being grasped on the spot in every
detail; he partly also presents it to himself, for his all-seeing eye.

He notices other details, however, because they mean something to
him, because they correspond to crucial traits in his own nature, or
because they make up for things he lacks, or because they astonish
him and bring him physically closer to her with the aid of admiration. Only these features will be discussed here, for they are the ones
fixing her image in his mind for seven months; that's how long it
took him to see her again, and those seven months covered about
half of the huge correspondence between them.

She was earnest about looking at the pictures, those "Thalian" photographs, and she glanced up only when an explanation was given or
a new picture handed to her. She neglected her food because of the
pictures, and when Max made some remark about the meal, she said
that nothing was more repugnant to her than people who never stop
eating. (Kafka's abstinence in food matters will be discussed later.)
She told about being beaten a great deal as a little girl by brothers
and cousins, when she had been quite defenseless. She ran her hand
down her left arm, which, she said, had been black and blue in those
days. But she didn't seem at all like a crybaby, and he couldn't understand why anyone could have dared to hit her, even if she had only
been a little girl at the time. He thinks of his own weakness as a
child, but she hasn't remained a whiner like him. He looks at her
arm and admires her present strength, which in no way hints at the
earlier childhood weakness.

She casually remarked, while looking at something or reading, that
she had studied Hebrew. He gazed in wonder, though irked at how
exaggeratedly casual she was in mentioning it. And so he secretly
delighted when, later on, she couldn't translate Tel Aviv. But meanwhile, it turned out that she was a Zionist, and he was very glad
about that.

She said she enjoyed copying manuscripts and asked Max to send
her some. Kafka was so amazed he banged his fist on the table.

She was en route to a wedding in Budapest, Frau Brod mentioned a
lovely cambric frock that she had seen in Felice's hotel room. The
company then moved from the dining-room to the music room.
"When you stood up, one could see that you had Frau Brod's slippers

on, for your boots had to dry out. The weather had been terrible all day. These slippers probably confused you a bit, and you told me, at the end of the passage through the dark center room, that you were used to slippers with heels. Such slippers were new to me." The older woman's slippers embarrassed her, the description of her own kind, at the end of the passage through the dark room, brought her physically closer to him than his previous contemplation of her arm, which now had no more black and blue marks.

Later, when the company was breaking up, something else happened: "I simply couldn't get over the swiftness with which you whooshed out of the room at the end and then returned in boots." Here, it is the swiftness of her transformation that impresses him. His way of transformation is completely opposite. For him, it is nearly always a particularly slow process, which he has to materialize trait by trait before believing it. He builds transformations completely and accurately, like a house. But she was suddenly in front of him as a booted woman, and had only just whooshed out of the room in slippers.

Earlier, he had mentioned—casually—that he had an issue of *Palestine* along. The trip to Palestine was discussed, and she took his hand "or rather, I lured out [your hand] by dint of a brainstorm." Brod's father and he then saw her to her hotel. On the street, he lapsed into one of his "dreamy states" and behaved awkwardly. He learned that she had forgotten her umbrella in the train, a detail enriching her portrait for him. She was to leave early the next morning. "The fact that you still hadn't packed and yet also wanted to read in bed made me nervous. The previous night, you had read until four A.M." Despite his concern about her early departure, this feature must have made him feel closer to her, for he himself wrote at night.

On the whole, the picture of Felice is that of a definite person, who faces all kinds of people quickly and openly, and talks unhesitatingly about anything.

Their correspondence (only his letters are extant), which would intensify into daily letters, from him at once and from her soon, had some quite amazing aspects. The most conspicuous for an unbiased observer are Kafka's complaints about physical states. Such complaints already begin in the second letter, though somewhat veiled. "What moods take hold of me, Fräulein! A rain of irritabilities is coming down upon me uninterruptedly. What I want at one moment, I don't want at the next. When I reach the top of the stairs, I don't yet know what I will feel like when I enter the apartment. I have to accumulate uncertainties in me until they become a small certainty or a letter. . . . After all, my memory is very poor. . . . My halfheartedness. . . . Once . . . I even got out of bed to write down what I had been thinking for you. But then I got right back into bed because (this is another of my ailments) I reproached myself for the foolishness of my disquiet . . ."

One sees that the first thing he describes here is his indecisiveness, and his courtship begins with that description. But everything is already being connected to physical states.

His fifth letter starts right in with his insomnia and ends with the disturbances in the office, where he is writing. From now on there is literally almost no letter without complaints. At first they are balanced by his interest in Felice. He asks a hundred questions, he wants to know everything about her, he wants to picture exactly what things are like in her office, in her home. But that sounds all too general, his questions are more concrete. She ought tell him when she comes to the office, what she has had for breakfast, what view she has from her office window, what kind of work she does, what the names of her friends are, male and female, who wants to ruin her health with gifts of candy—that is only the initial list of questions, eventually followed by countless others. He wants her to be healthy and secure. He wants to know as much about the spaces she moves in as about her schedule. He won't take no for an answer and he demands explanations on the spot. The precision he asks for matches his precision in describing his own states.

A number of things are still to be said about them; with no attempt to understand them, nothing can be understood. But for now, let us merely establish what is obviously the deeper purpose during the first period of this correspondence: a link, a channel between her efficiency and health and his indecisiveness and weakness. Across the distance, from Prague to Berlin, he would like to cling to her robustness. The weak words he is allowed to say to her return from her with a tenfold strength. He writes her two or three times a day. Very much in contrast to assertions of his weakness, he wages a dogged, even relentless struggle for her replies. In this one respect, she is moodier than he, she is not under the same compulsion. But he does manage to impose his own compulsion upon her; before long, she too is writing him once, sometimes even twice a day.

His struggle for that strength, which her regular letters give him, does have a meaning; it is no idle correspondence, no end in itself, no mere self-gratification, it serves his *writing.* Two nights after his first letter to her, he writes down *The Judgment,* at one swoop, through one night, in ten hours. One could say that this story establishes his self-confidence as a writer. He reads it to his friends, its absoluteness manifests itself, he never again moves away from it as from so many other things. During the following week, he writes *The Stoker,* and in the course of two months, five more chapters in *Amerika,* making six altogether. During a two-week interruption in the novel, he writes *Metamorphosis.*

Thus it is a great period, not just as viewed from our later stand-point; there are very few comparable times in his life. To judge by the results—and by what else can one judge a writer's life—Kafka's behavior during his first three months of corresponding with Felice was just the right thing for him. He felt what he needed: a security in the distance, a source of energy, which did not confuse his sensitivity by too close a contact, a woman who was there for him without expecting more than his words, a sort of transformer whose possible technical defects he knew and controlled well enough to be able to repair immediately by mail. The woman thus helping him should not be exposed to his family, from whose proximity he greatly suffered; he had to keep her away from them. She must take seriously everything he had to say about himself. He, a man of few words in speech, should be able to fully expose himself to her in writing; complain relentlessly about anything; hold back nothing that bewildered him in his writing; report on every detail of the importance, continuation, and hesitations of his writing. During this time, his diary stops, the letters to Felice are his expanded journal, it has the advantage of his really keeping it every day, of his being able to repeat himself frequently, thus satisfying a basic need of his nature. The things he writes to her are not unique, set down for all time, he can correct himself in subsequent letters, he can confirm or retract, and even a jumping about, which such a conscious mind does not like to permit itself within the individual entry of a journal because of the disorderliness, is quite possible in the sequence of a letter. However, the greatest advantage, as already indicated, is beyond any doubt the possibility of repetitions, a veritable "litany." If anyone realized the need for and function of "litanies," it was Kafka. Of all his very pronounced features, it is the one that contributed most to the "religious" misinterpretations of his oeuvre.

But if this correspondence was so crucial as to exert its effect for three months and lead to such unique creations as *Metamorphosis*—why did his writing suddenly halt in January 1913? One cannot be satisfied with general statements about productive and unproductive spells in a writer. All productivity is conditional, and one must take the trouble to find the disturbances interfering with it.

Perhaps it should not be overlooked that the letters of the first period to Felice, no matter how little they appear to have of love letters in the usual sense, do contain something that quite specifically belongs to love: It is important to Kafka that Felice *expect* something from him. At that first meeting, which sustained him for so long, on which he built everything, he had the manuscript of his first book with him. She had made his acquaintance as a writer, not just as a friend of a writer whom she has read a bit of, and the claim he makes on her letters is based on her regarding him as a writer. The first tale to satisfy him, "The Judgment," is *hers,* he owes it to her, it is dedicated to her. Of course, he is not sure of her judgment in literary matters and tries to influence it in his letters. He asks for a list of her books, which he never receives.

Felice was an uncomplicated person, the sentences quoted by him from her letters, although not very numerous, quite adequately prove that. His dialogue—if one may apply such a standardized word to something so complex and unfathomable—his dialogue with himself through her might have easily gone on for a long time. But it was confused by her craving for culture, she read other writers, naming them in her letters. He had as yet brought forth almost nothing of what he felt as a gigantic world in his mind; and, as a writer, he wanted her all to himself.

On December 11, he sends her his first book, *Betrachtung*—it has just come out. He writes: "Listen, be kind to my poor book! These are those few pages you saw me arranging on our evening. . . . Can you tell how far apart in age the individual pieces are? One of them, for instance, is certainly eight or ten years old. Show the whole thing to as few people as possible so that they won't spoil your pleasure in me."

On the thirteenth, he mentions his book again: "I am so happy to know that my book, as much as I have to criticize in it . . . is in your dear hand."

On December 23, there is the following single line about it: "Ah, if only Fräulein Lindner [who worked in Felice's office] knew how hard it is to write as little as I do!" This refers to the small size of *Betrachtung* and can only be viewed as an answer to an evasiveness in Felice's letters.

That is all until his big fit of jealousy on December 28, seventeen days after he sent her the book. The letters during that time (and we only have his, as we have said) take up forty closely printed pages and deal with a thousand different things. It is clear that Felice never gave an earnest opinion of *Betrachtung*. His outburst, however, is directed at Eulenberg, whom she is mad about:

"I am jealous of all the people in your letter, whether named or not, men and girls, businessmen and writers (and, of course, especially the latter) . . . I am jealous of Werfel, Sophocles, Ricarda Huch, Lagerlöf, Jacobsen. My jealousy is childishly delighted that you called Eulenberg Hermann instead of Herbert. Whereas Franz is no doubt stamped upon your mind. You like *Schattenbilder?* You find it terse and clear? The only thing I know in its entirety is *Mozart,* Eulenberg . . . gave a reading of it here, but I couldn't stand it, a prose full of breathlessness and impurity. . . . But naturally, there can be no doubt that I am doing him a great injustice in my present frame of mind, *but you should not read* Schattenbilder. But now I see that you are 'quite mad' about it. (Just listen, everyone, Felice is mad about it, absolutely mad, and I rage against him in the middle of the night.) But other people appear in your letter, I would like to fight with all of them, all of them, not to do something bad to them, but merely to drive them away from you, to get you free of them, to read letters which are only about you, your family . . . and naturally! and naturally! about me."

The next day, he gets an unexpected letter from her (unexpected because it is Sunday), and he thanks her: "Dearest, this is once again

69

a letter making one hot with quiet joy. None of those many friends and writers are standing around in it . . ."

That very same night, he finds the explanation for the previous day's jealousy: "Incidentally, I have a more precise idea of why yesterday's letter made me so jealous: You like my book as little as you liked my picture that time. That wouldn't be so bad, because most of the things in the book are old . . . I feel your presence so strongly in everything else that I am quite willing to kick the little book away *first* with *my own* foot. . . . But the fact that you won't tell me, that you won't tell me in even two words that you don't like it! . . . It would be very understandable if you couldn't relate to the book at all. . . . After all, no one will be able to relate to it, that is and was clear to me—the effort and money that the spendthrift publisher sacrificed and that are totally lost torment me too. . . . But you said nothing, you did once announce that you would say something, but you didn't say it. . . ."

In late January, he comes back to *Betrachtung*. The Viennese writer Otto Stoessl, whom he greatly admires and also likes personally, has written him a letter about it. "He also writes about my book, but with such total misunderstanding that for a moment I believed my book was really good since it could be so misunderstood by such a perceptive man as Stoessl, who is so experienced with books." He copies the entire passage in the letter, a rather long passage. It contains astonishing things. "An inward directed humor . . . just as a man, after a good night's sleep, after a refreshing bath, freshly dressed, welcomes a free, sunny day with cheerful expectation and an inconceivable feeling of strength. A humor of a good frame of mind." A blunder of monstrous proportions, every word precisely wrong, Kafka cannot get away from the "humor of a good frame of mind," and he quotes this line again later on. But he adds: "The letter, incidentally, fits in very well with an excessively lauding review that appeared today and that finds only sadness in the book."

It is obvious that he has not forgotten her disregard of *Betrachtung,* his unwonted thoroughness in discussing these reactions to his book conceals a reprimand. He wants to teach her a lesson, she's made things too easy for herself, and he thereby reveals how greatly she has hurt his feelings with her complete lack of reaction.

70

His worst outbursts against other writers occur during the first half of February. Felice asks about Else Lasker-Schüler, he writes: "I cannot stand her poems, I feel nothing but boredom at their emptiness, and distaste because of the artificial expenditure. Her prose annoys me too for the same reasons, it shows the workings of the promiscuously twitching brain of an overwrought city-dweller. . . . Indeed, she's badly off, her second husband has left her, so far as I know, they're collecting money for her here too; I had to come up with five crowns though not feeling the slightest sympathy for her; I don't know the real reason, but I always picture her as a drunkard, dragging about the coffeehouses at night. . . . Away with you, Lasker-Schüler! Darling, come! Let no one get between us, no one around us."

Felice wants to go to the theater and see *Professor Bernhardi*. "A solid rope ties us together," writes Kafka, ". . . if you go to *Professor Bernhardi*, dearest, then you'll be pulling me along on that indubitable rope, and we'll both be in danger of landing in poor literature, which is what Schnitzler largely represents to me." So that same evening, he goes to *Hidalla*, in which Wedekind and his wife are acting. "For I do not like Schnitzler at all and I scarcely respect him; he certainly has some talent, but his big plays and his big prose are filled, for me, with a simply staggering mass of the most repugnant hackwork. One cannot put him down deeply enough. . . . It is only when looking at his portrait, at that false dreaminess, at that tenderheartedness, which I would not even touch with my fingertips—it is only then that I can understand how he could develop in that way from some initial works that were partly excellent (*Anatol, La Ronde, Lieutenant Gustl*). I will absolutely not speak of Wedekind in the same letter.

"Enough, enough, let me get rid of Schnitzler right away, he wants to get in between us just as Lasker-Schüler did before."

His jealousy of writers, in regard to Felice, has the powerful characteristics of jealousy in general, one is amazed and relieved to find such a natural unbroken aggressiveness in him. For one can still hear his attacks on himself in every one of the countless letters, the reader is familiar with them, as though his voice were speaking. But the unusual tone of these attacks on other writers, the murderousness, the brutality, which are really foreign to him, are symptoms of a change in his relationship to Felice. It took a tragic turn because of her lack of sympathy for his own writings. She, whose strength he needs for his writing like an incessant nourishment, is incapable of realizing whom she is nourishing with herself, that is to say, her letters.

His situation in this respect is made particularly difficult by the nature of his first book publication. He is too sensible and too serious to overestimate the weight of *Betrachtung*. It is a book in which some of his themes are struck. But it is pieced together, it is somewhat whimsical and artistic, it betrays outside influences (Robert Walser), and it especially lacks coherence and inevitability. It has meaning for him because he was carrying the manuscript the first time he saw Felice.

But six weeks after that evening, hard upon his first letter to Felice, he had become totally himself in "The Judgment" and in "The Stoker." It appears even more important, in this connection, that he was fully aware of the value of these two pieces. The correspondence with Felice continued, he kept writing his pieces night after night, within eight weeks he reached the pinnacle of his mastery in *Metamorphosis*. He wrote something he could never surpass because there is nothing that could surpass *Metamorphosis,* one of the few great and perfect literary works of this century.

Four days after he finished *Metamorphosis, Betrachtung* came out. He sends this first book to Felice and waits seventeen days for her to say something about it. Letters go back and forth every day, he waits in vain, having already written *Metamorphosis* and a good portion of *Amerika.* Even a rock would be moved to pity. He now learned that the nourishment of her letters, without which he couldn't possibly have written, had been given blindly. She didn't realize whom she was nourishing. His doubts, always at work, became overwhelming, he was no longer sure of his right to her letters, which he had extracted from her in the good time, and his own writing, which was his real life, began to flag.

A secondary consequence (though conspicuous by its vehemence) of this catastrophe was his jealousy of other writers. Felice read; and she deeply injured him with the names promiscuously pushing to the fore in her letters. They were all writers in her eyes. But what, in her eyes, was he?

Her boon for him was thus at an end. With his immense tenacity, the amazing reverse of his weakness, he clung to the form of the es-

72

tablished relationship, gazing back nostalgically to the paradise of those three months, which could never come again; the equilibrium they had given him was destroyed.

Certainly, during those days, other things happened, contributing to this disturbance. There is the engagement of Max Brod, his best friend, who more than anyone else had urged him, egged him on, to write. Kafka fears the change in this friendship, a change striking him as inevitable by the mere presence of a wife for his friend. It is also the time of preparations for his sister Valli's wedding. He experienced everything belonging to these preparations, experienced them up close, in his parents' home, which was also his home. He is saddened by the thought of his sister's departure, it makes him feel the crumbling of the family, whom he does hate after all. But he has settled into this hatred and needs it. The many unwonted events, which take up an entire month prior to the wedding, only disrupt him. He wonders why he is suffering in this peculiar way from these engagements, as though some misfortune were assailing him, momentarily and immediately, while the main participants themselves are unexpectedly happy.

His repugnance at marriage as a way of life, for which such vast preparations are being made, is now more acute, and he gives free rein to his reaction in an area where this form of life might be expected of him: he begins to sense Felice as a danger, his lonely nights are threatened, and he makes her feel it.

But prior to an account of how he defended himself against this danger, it is necessary to find out the exact nature of his sense of being threatened.

"My life is focused entirely on writing. . . . Time is short, strength is small, the office is a horror, the apartment is loud, and one has to worm one's way through with tricks if a fine, straight life doesn't work." Thus writes Kafka in an early letter, his ninth, to Felice on 1 November 1912. He then explains his new schedule to her, a schedule allowing him to sit down and write at 10:30, night after night, sticking to it until one, two, three A.M., depending on strength, desire, and luck.

But even earlier, in the very same letter, he has made a statement that one can scarcely ignore, it is monstrous at this point: "I am the skinniest person I know, which is saying something, since I have been in a lot of sanatoriums. . . ." This man, wooing for love (for naturally one first assumes he is wooing for love), and instantly calling himself the *skinniest* person! Why does such an utterance, at this time, seem so unsuitable, nay, almost unpardonable? Love requires weight, it's a matter of bodies. They have to be there, it is ludicrous when a non-body woos for love. Great agility, courage, impact can pinch-hit for weight. But they have to be active, present themselves, virtually always keep promising. Instead, Kafka offers one thing, his very own: the wealth of what he sees, the things he sees around the person he is courting; this wealth is *his* body. But that can work only with a person having a related wealth, it escapes anyone else or strikes him as eerie.

When he talks about his skinniness right away and with such a strong emphasis, it can only mean that he greatly suffers from it: he feels a compulsion to tell about it. It is as though he had to say about himself: "I am deaf," or "I am blind," since hiding such a fact would make him a swindler.

One doesn't have to hunt through his diaries and letters for long to be convinced that this is the core, the root of his "hypochondria." On November 22, 1911, his diary has the following entry: "It is certain that one chief hindrance to my progress is my physical condition. With such a body, nothing can be achieved. . . . My body is too long for its weakness, it has no fat whatsoever for creating a beneficial warmth, for maintaining an inner fire, no fat from which the mind could some day nourish itself beyond its daily need without damaging the whole. How shall the weak heart, which has often wrenched me of late, manage to push the blood through the entire length of these legs . . ."

On January 3, 1912, he makes a detailed list of what he has sacrificed to writing: "When it became obvious in my organism that writing was the most profitable direction of my nature, everything pushed towards it, leaving idle all faculties mainly directed at the joys of sex, of eating, of drink, of philosophical reflection, of music. I lost weight in all these directions. That was necessary because my strength was altogether so meager that it had to be collected in order to even halfway serve the purpose of writing . . ."

On July 17, 1912, he writes to Max Brod from the Jungborn Sanatorium, already mentioned: "I have the silly idea of fattening myself up and thereby curing myself in general, as though the second or even just the first were possible."

The very next statement about his skinniness is the one already quoted from the letter to Felice on November 1, of the same year. A few months later, on January 10, 1913, he writes to Felice again: "How was the bathing? I must unfortunately suppress a remark (it refers to my appearance in the bath, to my skinniness). When bathing, I look like an orphan boy." Then he tells how, as a small boy, at a summer resort on the Elbe, he stayed away from the very small, crowded bathing place because he was embarrassed about his appearance.

In September 1916, he decides to see a doctor, something highly unusual for him since he distrusts doctors, and he tells Felice about this visit: "The physician I went to . . . was very agreeable to me. A calm, somewhat comical man, but arousing confidence with his age, his physical mass (how you could feel trust for such a long, skinny thing like me is something I will never understand): . . ."

I will quote a few more passages from the last seven years of his life when he had finally terminated his relationship to Felice. It is important to note that this idea of his skinniness remained potent in him until the very end, coloring all memory.

In the famous "Letter to the Father," 1919, there is a further passage about childhood swimming: "For instance, I recall the way we often undressed together in a cabin. I, skinny, weak, small, you strong, big, wide. Even in that cabin I already felt lamentable, and not just in front of you, but in front of the whole world, for you were the measure of all things for me."

The most moving passage is in one of the first letters to Milena, in 1920. Here too, he feels compelled to present himself very soon in his skinniness to a woman he is courting (and he courts Milena passionately): "A few years ago, I spent a lot of time in a rowboat on the Moldau, I rowed upstream and then, all stretched out, I floated back down with the current, under the bridges. My skinniness must have made it look very funny to anyone watching from the bridges. An official from my office, who once saw me like that from the bridge, formulated his impression after sufficiently emphasizing the comic aspect: he said it looked like Doomsday. It looked like that moment when the coffin tops are already off, but the dead are still lying motionless."

The figure of the emaciated man and the figure of the dead man are seen as one: in connection with the image of the Last Judgment, the picture of his physicality is bleak and fateful beyond any imagining of it. It is as though the emaciated man or the dead man, who are one here, had just barely enough life to float with the current and appear at the Last Judgment.

During the final weeks of his life in the Kierling Sanatorium, Kafka was advised by doctors not to speak. He answered questions by writing on small slips of paper, that have come down to us. He was asked about Felice, and he gave the following reply: "I was once supposed to go to the Baltic Sea with her (and her friend), but I was too embarrassed because of my skinniness and other anxieties."

The pronounced sensitivity to everything connected with his body never left Kafka. It must have already appeared during his childhood, as is obvious from the statements quoted. His skinniness made him aware of his body at an early time. He became accustomed to noting everything his body *lacked*. His body was an object of observation that he never lost, that could never elude him. Here, whatever he saw and whatever he felt was close to him, one could not be separated from the other. Starting with his emaciation, he became unshakably convinced of his weakness, and it may not even be so important to know whether it actually always existed. For what did exist was a sense of looming danger, a feeling based on that conviction. He feared the invasion of enemy forces into his body, and to prevent that, he vigilantly traced the path they might take. Gradually, he became preoccupied with individual organs. A special sensitivity to them began to develop until he finally watched over each one separately. But this multiplied the dangers—there were countless symptoms to which a distrustful mind must pay heed once it is aware of the special character and vulnerability of the organs. Pains here and there remind us of the organs, it would be arrogant and unforgivable not to notice them. The pains announce dangers, they are harbingers of the enemy. Hypochondria is the small change of fear; it is fear that seeks and finds names by way of distraction.

His sensitivity to noise was like an alarm, it announced superfluous, as yet unarticulated dangers. One could avoid them by avoiding noise like the devil—there were enough familiar dangers, whose well-mounted attacks he warded off by *naming* them.

His room was a shelter, it became an external body, one might call it the "forebody." "I have to sleep alone in a room. . . . It is only anxiety pleading: one cannot fall if one sleeps on the floor, and likewise, nothing can happen to one who is alone." Visitors in his room are unbearable to him. Even living together with his family in one apartment is tormenting. "I cannot live with other people, I absolutely hate all my relatives, not because they are my relatives, not because they are at all bad . . . but simply because they are the people living closest to me."

Most of all, he complains about insomnia. Perhaps this is nothing more than an alertness for his body, a watchfulness that cannot be halted, that perceives threats, waits for signals, interprets and connects them, designs systems of countermeasures, and has to reach a point at which they appear secure: the point of the equilibrium of the dangers, all balancing out, the point of repose. Sleep then becomes a salvation, in which his sensitivity, that indefatigable torture, finally releases him and vanishes. He has a kind of worship of sleep, he views it as a panacea, the best thing he can recommend to Felice when her condition worries him is: "Sleep! Sleep!" Even the reader can hear this advice as an evocation, a blessing.

The dangers to the body include all poisons going into it: as breath; as food and drink; as medicaments.

Bad air is dangerous. Kafka often talks about it. Just recall the attic offices in *The Trial,* or the painter Titorelli's overheated studio. Bad air is seen as a misfortune, leading to the brink of catastrophe. The travel journals are filled with the cult of good air: his letters reveal how much he expects of fresh air. Even in the coldest winter nights, he sleeps with the window open. Smoking is not permitted; heating uses up the air, he writes in an unheated room. He regularly does exercises naked in front of an open window. The body offers itself to the fresh air, so that it may caress the skin and pores. But real air is out in the country; rustic life, to which he encourages his favorite sister Ottla, subsequently becomes his own for long months.

He looks for food that he can convince himself is not dangerous. He is a vegetarian for long stretches at a time. At first, this attitude doesn't seem like asceticism; in response to a worried question from Felice, he sends her a list of the fruits he partakes of every evening. He tries to keep poisons and dangers away from his body. Naturally, he has forbidden himself coffee, tea, and alcohol.

There is something like frivolity and exuberance in his sentences when he writes about this aspect of his life, while his lines on insomnia always sound despairing. The contrast is so blatant that one feels tempted to explain it. The naturopaths attract him with their concept of the body as a unity; he fully appropriates their rejection of organic therapy. He, who comes apart into his separate organs during sleepless hours, listening for their signals, brooding over their stirrings—he requires a method prescribing unity for his body. He considers official medicine harmful for its dealing too specifically with the individual organs. To be sure, his rejection of medicine also contains a bit of self-hatred: he too finds himself hunting for symptoms whenever he can't sleep at night.

And so, with a kind of elation, he plunges into any activity demanding and restoring the unity of the body. Swimming, naked calisthenics, wild leaps down the stairs at home, running, long hikes out of doors where one can breathe freely—all these things animate him, making him hopeful about escaping the degeneracy of the white night for once or even for a while.

By late January 1913, Kafka has finally abandoned his novel after repeated attempts at writing it, and so the accent in his letters shifts more and more to complaints. One could say that from now on the letters only serve his lamenting. Nothing can balance his dissatisfaction; the nights in which he found himself, his justification, his only true life, now belong to the past. Nothing holds him together anymore but complaint; instead of writing, complaint becomes his—by far inferior—unity. Yet without it, he would fall silent and collapse into his fragmented pains. He is accustomed to the freedom of letters, in which he can say anything; at least, they loosen his taciturnity in dealing with other people. He needs the letters from Felice, who still tells him about her life in Berlin; and if he cannot cling to a fresh word of hers, then he feels "as if he were in a vacuum." For despite the uncertainty "that haunts the failure to write like his evil spirit," he always remains his own object of observation. And when one has managed to accept the litany of complaint as a kind of language, in which everything else is salvaged, one can hear the strangest things about him in this never-silent medium—statements of a precision and truth such as are granted to few people.

There is an inconceivable measure of intimacy in these letters, they are more intimate than the complete depiction of happiness could be. There is no comparable account by a vacillating man, no self-revelation of such fidelity. A primitive man could scarcely read this correspondence, it would have to strike him as the shameless spectacle of mental impotence. For it contains everything belonging to that: indecision, anxiety, emotional coldness, a thoroughly depicted lack of love, a helplessness so vast as to be made credible only by an over-exact portrayal. Yet everything is framed in such a way that it instantly becomes law and knowledge. Slightly incredulous at first, but then rapidly convinced, one comes to realize that nothing of this can ever be forgotten, as though it were written into one's skin, like "In the Penal Colony." There are writers—very few, to be sure—who are so totally themselves, that anything one presumed to say about them would sound barbaric. Such a writer was Franz Kafka. Hence, at the risk of seeming unfree, one must adhere as closely as possible to his own statements. One is certainly embarrassed when one starts by invading the intimacy of these letters. Yet they themselves remove this embarrassment. For they make us realize that a tale like *The Metamorphosis* is even more intimate, and we finally know what distinguishes it from any other story.

The important thing about Felice was that she existed, that she was not invented, and that she, as she was, could not have been invented by Kafka. She was so different, so active, so compact. As long as he gravitated around her from afar, he idolized and tormented her. He plied her with his questions, his requests, his fears, his tiny hopes in order to force letters out of her. Any love she addressed to him, he said, coursed as blood through his heart, he had no other blood. Didn't she notice, he asked, that he did not really love her in his letters, for he would then have to think only about her and write only about her; he really simply worshipped her, he said, and expected something like help and blessing from her in the most absurd things. "Sometimes, Felice, I think that you have such power over me; turn

79

me into a man who is capable of the things people take for granted."
In a good moment, he thanks her: "What a feeling to find refuge
with you from this terrible world, which I can cope with only in
nights of writing."

He feels in himself the slightest wound of the other. His cruelty is
that of the non-combatant, who feels the wound *beforehand*. He shies
away from the clash, everything cuts into *his* flesh, and nothing happens to the foe. If a letter of his contains anything that might offend
Felice, he draws her attention to it in the next letter, pushes her to it,
repeats his apology, she notices nothing, she usually doesn't even
know what he's talking about. Thus, in his own way, he treated her
as an enemy.

He succeeds in summing up the essence of his indecisiveness in just
a few words: "Have you ever known . . . uncertainty, seen how
various possibilities here and there open up as though for you alone,
regardless of others, and thereby something else arises, a ban against
your stirring at all . . ."

The significance of these various possibilities opening here and
there, the fact that he sees them all simultaneously, cannot be over-
rated. They explain his actual relationship to the future. For a good
portion of his work consists of tentative steps towards ever-different
possibilities of a future. He does not recognize *one* future, there are
many, their multitude paralyzes him and weighs down his feet. It is
only when writing, when hesitatingly trudging towards one of them,
that he can focus on that one and leave out the rest; but he cannot
recognize more of it than the next step allows. The concealment of
anything further away is his true art. It is probably this continuation
in one direction, the separation from all other possible directions,
that makes him happy when he writes. The measure of accomplishment is the walking itself, the clarity of the steps that succeed, and
the fact that no step is skipped. that no step, once taken, remains dubious. "I cannot . . . really tell a story, indeed, almost not even
talk; when I narrate, I usually feel as small children might feel during
their first attempts at walking."

He always keeps complaining and describing with uncanny clarity
his difficulties in talking, his taciturnity with people: "Another un-
necessary evening with various people. . . . I bit my lips to go along
with it, but, for all my strenuous efforts, I wasn't there, yet I wasn't

anywhere else either; did I not exist during those two hours? That must be it, for had I been sleeping in my chair, my presence would have been more convincing. . . . I really believe I am lost for human intercourse." He even goes so far as to claim, surprisingly, that during all the weeks of traveling with Max Brod, he never had *one* long, coherent conversation with him that brought forth his entire being.

"I can best be endured in familiar spaces with two or three acquaintances; I am free then, I am not forced to be continually attentive and involved, and if I feel like it, I can, if I wish, refrain from participating, as long or as little as I wish, no one misses me, no one feels uneasy about me. If there is any stranger present who gets into my blood, all the better, I can get quite lively, apparently from borrowed strength. But if I am in a strange home, among several strangers, or people I feel as such, then the entire room weighs on my chest and I cannot stir . . ."

He always turns such descriptions into warnings against himself, and countless as they may be, he keeps reformulating them. "I just don't rest in myself, I am not always 'something,' and if I ever was 'something,' I pay for it with months of 'non-existence' ". He compares himself to a bird that is kept by some curse from its own nest, always soaring around this totally empty nest, never losing sight of it.

"I am a different man from what I was in the first two months of our correspondence; it is no new metamorphosis, but a change backward, and probably a lasting one. . . . My present state . . . is not exceptional. Do not yield to such delusions, Felice. You could not live with me for even two days. . . . After all, you *are* a girl and you want a man and not some soft worm on the ground."

One of the counter-myths he has set up for his own protection, trying to prevent Felice's physical approach and her invasion into his life, is the one about his dislike of children.

"I shall never have a child," he writes very early, on November 8, but he expresses it as envy of one of his sisters, who has just had a girl. He becomes more serious in late December, when his disappointment in Felice intensifies into more and more somber and hostile letters through four nights in a row. We know the first letter, that jealous outburst against Eulenberg; likewise the second, in which he reprimands her for her lack of any reaction to his *Betrachtung*. In the third letter, he quotes from a collection of Napoleon's sayings: "It is terrible to die without children." He adds: "And I have to prepare myself for taking that upon me, for . . . I could never dare expose myself to the gamble of becoming a father." In the fourth letter, on New Year's Eve, he feels as abandoned as a dog, and he almost hatefully portrays the noise of merrymaking on the street. At the end of the letter, in reply to her statement "we absolutely belong together," he says that it is true a thousand times over, and now, in the first hours of the new year, he would have no greater or more foolish wish "than that we could be indissolubly bound together by the wrists of your left and my right hand. I don't quite know why that occurs to me, perhaps because I have before me a book on the French Revolution with accounts by contemporaries, and because it is after all possible . . . that once a couple tied together in that way was taken to the scaffold. But then, all sorts of things are running through my head. . . . That's due to the thirteen in the number of the new year."

Marriage as a scaffold—the new year began for him with that idea. And despite all waverings and conflicting events, nothing changed in that respect for him throughout the year. The most tormenting thing about his idea of marriage must be the fact that one cannot vanish into something tiny, one has to be there. Fear of a superior power is central to Kafka, and his way of resisting it is transformation into something small. The hallowing of places and conditions, which operates so astonishingly in him as to seem compulsive, is nothing but the hallowing of man. Every place, every moment, every feature, every step is earnest and crucial and peculiar. One has to avoid violation, which is unjust, by vanishing as far away as possible. One becomes very tiny or changes into an insect to spare others the guilt they incur by lovelessness and killing; one "hungers oneself away" from the others, who will not leave one alone with their disgusting customs. There is no situation in which this withdrawal would be less possible than matrimony. A man always has to be there, whether he wants to or not, part of the day and part of the night, in a proportion corresponding to that of the spouse, a ratio that cannot be altered, otherwise it is not marriage. The position of smallness, however, which exists here too, is usurped by the children.

One Sunday, at home, he experiences "the insane, monotonous,

82

uninterrupted shouting and singing and clapping that always resumes with fresh vigor": it is his father entertaining a great-nephew in the morning and a grandchild in the afternoon. African dances are more comprehensible to him. But perhaps, he says, it is not the screaming that assaults him so much, it takes a great deal of strength to endure children in the apartment at all. "I cannot do it, I cannot forget myself, my blood refuses to flow, it is all congealed," and this desire of the blood, he says, is what makes up love for children.

Thus, it is also envy that Kafka feels in the presence of children, but a different kind of envy than one might expect, an envy coupled with disapproval. At first, the children seem to be usurpers of the smallness into which he himself would like to slip. But then it turns out that they are not the actual smallness, which would like to vanish as he does. They are the false smallness, prey to the noise and painful effects of the adults, the smallness that is egged on to get bigger, and then also wants to get bigger, in opposition to his deepest natural tendency: to grow smaller, quieter, lighter, until completely vanishing.

If one now seeks for Kafka's possibilities of happiness, or at least of well-being, one is almost surprised, after all the testimonies of discouragement, paralysis, and failure, to come upon possibilities having strength and definiteness.

There is, above all, the solitude of writing. In the middle of setting down *The Metamorphosis,* in his most fulfilled time, he asks Felice not to write him in bed at night, but rather to sleep. She should leave nocturnal writing to *him*—that small possibility of pride in night work; and to prove that night work belongs to men everywhere, even in China, he copies down a small Chinese poem for her, a poem he especially loves. A scholar, poring over his book, forgets to go to bed. His mistress, making a great effort to control her anger, finally grabs away his lamp and asks: "Do you know what time it is?"

That is how he sees his nightly labor, so long as it goes well; and when quoting the poem, he is not aware of any barb against Felice. Later, on January 14, with the situation changing, Felice having disappointed him, and his failure to write, he recalls the Chinese scholar. But this time, the scholar is used for keeping Felice at bay: "Once you said that you wanted to sit near me while I write; you

must realize I couldn't write in that case. . . . Writing means opening oneself to an excessive degree. . . . That is why one cannot be
too alone when one is writing, that is why it cannot be quiet enough
when one is writing, the night is insufficiently night. That is why
one doesn't have enough time, for the roads are long, and one easily
goes astray. . . . I have often thought that the best life for me would
be with paper and pen and a lamp inside the innermost room of a
vast, locked cellar. Food would be brought and placed far from my
own room behind the outermost door of the cellar. The walk to the
food, in my housecoat, through all the cellar vaults, would be my
sole promenade. I would return to my table, eat slowly and deliberately, and then resume writing immediately. What things I would
then write! From what depths would I tear it out!"

One has to read this splendid letter all the way through, never has
anything purer and stricter been said about writing. All the ivory
towers in the world collapse in the face of this basement dweller, and
that abused and vacuous expression, the writer's "solitude," has suddenly regained weight and meaning.

This is the only true and valid happiness for him, and every fiber in
his being yearns for it. A second and quite different situation that satisfies him is to stand on the sidelines, watching the joys of others who
leave him out and expect nothing of him. Thus, he likes to be among
people who are eating and drinking everything that he denies to himself. "When I sit at a table with ten acquaintances and they are all
drinking black coffee, I feel something like happiness at this spectacle. Meat can be steaming around me, beer mugs can be emptied in
huge draughts, those juicy Jewish sausages . . . can be sliced up by
all my relatives around me—all these and far more irksome things do
not repel me in the slightest, on the contrary, they make me feel
thoroughly good. It is certainly not malicious glee . . . it is really a
relaxing calm, the totally unenvying calm of watching other people
enjoying themselves."

Perhaps these two situations of well-being are the kind one would
expect of him, even if the second is more strongly accentuated than
one might have imagined. But it is truly surprising to find that he
also has the happiness of reaching out, namely in *reading aloud to
others*. Whenever he tells Felice about reading his things to others,

the tone of his letters becomes altogether different. Kafka, who cannot weep, has tears in his eyes when he finishes reading "The Judgment." The letter of December 4, following hard upon this reading, is positively amazing in its wildness: "Dearest, I simply . . . love reading to others, shouting into the expectant and attentive ears of listeners is so good for the poor heart. And I certainly shouted at them with a vengeance, and the music from the adjoining rooms, which tried to hinder my effort in reading—I simply blasted it away. Do you know, commanding people or at least believing in one's ability to command—there is no greater delight for the body." Just a few years ago, he continues, he liked to dream of having an auditorium filled with people, to whom he would read the entire *Education sentimentale* (the Flaubert book that he loved most of all) in French, without interruption, for as many days and nights as necessary: "And the walls would ring!"

It is not really "commanding" (he is not expressing himself clearly because of his exaltation), it is a *law* that he would like to proclaim: a law secure at last, and if it is Flaubert, it is like God's law for him, and he would be its prophet. But he also feels the liberation and entertainment in this kind of expansion; in the middle of his wretchedness during February and March, he suddenly and tersely writes to Felice: "A fine evening at Max's. I read myself into a rage with my story." (He probably means the concluding portion of *Metamorphosis*.) "We then had a good time and laughed a lot. When one locks the doors and windows against this world, one can occasionally create the semblance and almost the beginning of a beautiful existence."

Towards the last of February, Kafka receives a letter from Felice, which frightens him, it sounds as if he hasn't said anything against himself, as if she's heard nothing, believed nothing, understood nothing. He doesn't immediately deal with the question she asks him, but he does answer later with unusual curtness. "You recently asked me . . . about my plans and prospects. I was amazed at your question. . . . I naturally have no plans whatsoever, no prospects whatsoever, I cannot walk into the future—plunge into the future, roll into the future, stumble into the future, those things I can do, and the best thing I can do is to remain lying. But I really have no plans or prospects at all; if things are going well, I am utterly filled with the present; if things are going badly, I curse the present, not to mention the future!"

It is a rhetorical answer, not a precise one: as proven by the totally implausible way he depicts his relationship to the future. It is a panic defense; a few months later, we experience other rhetorical outbursts of this nature, they contrast very powerfully with his usual just and balanced manner.

But with this letter, he begins solidifying the idea of a visit to Berlin, which he started toying with some weeks earlier. He wants to see Felice again in order to frighten her away with his person, since his letters have failed to do it. He chooses Easter for the trip, he has two days off. His way of announcing the visit is so characteristic of his indecisiveness that the letters from the week before Easter have to be quoted. It is the first time in over seven months that they are to see one another, their truly first meeting after that one evening.

On March 16th, the Sunday before Easter, he writes: "To ask you straight out, Felice, would you have any hour whatsoever free for me during Easter, that is, Sunday or Monday, and if you did have a free hour, would it be all right if I came?"

On Monday, he writes: "I don't know if I'll be able to come, it's still uncertain today, tomorrow it may be certain. . . . By ten A.M. Wednesday, you will know for sure."

On Tuesday: "Actually, the obstacle to my trip still exists and will, I fear, keep existing, but as an obstacle it has lost its meaning, and so, to the extent that this can be taken into account, I could come. I just wanted to tell you this in haste."

On Wednesday: "I am going to Berlin for no other reason than you, who have been misdirected by letters, I want to tell you and show you who I really am. Will I make it clearer personally than I was able to do in writing? . . . . Where can I meet you Sunday morning? In case my trip is held up, I would telegraph you by Saturday at the latest."

On Thursday: ". . . and along with the old threats, new threats of possible hindrances for the small trip. Now, at Easter, there are usually—I hadn't thought of it—congresses of all kinds of associations . . ." He might have to take part in a congress as a representative of his insurance company.

On Friday: ". . . It is still not certain whether I am going: it won't be decided until tomorrow morning. . . . If I do come, I will very likely stay in the Askanischer Hof. . . . But I really have to get a good night's sleep before I show up."

This letter is only mailed on Saturday morning, March 22. On the envelope, as the latest news, he writes: "Still undecided." But then, that same day, he hops the train for Berlin and arrives late in the evening.

On Easter Sunday, the twenty-third, he writes to her from the Askanischer Hof: "What's happened, Felice? . . . I'm in Berlin now, I have to leave by four or five this afternoon, the hours are passing and no word from you. Please send me an answer with this boy. . . . I'm sitting and waiting in the Askanischer Hof."

Felice—and this was understandable after the conflicting announcements during that week—had scarcely believed he was still coming. He lay on the couch in his hotel room for some five hours, waiting for her possible call. She lived far away, he finally did see her, she had little time, they met twice in all for just a couple of moments. That was their first meeting in over seven months.

But Felice seems to have used even these few minutes well. She takes all responsibility upon herself. He has, she says, become indispensable to her. The most important outcome of this visit is the decision to meet again at Whitsuntide. Instead of seven months, this separation is to last only seven weeks. One has the impression that Felice has now set a goal for both of them and is trying to imbue him with strength for a decision.

Fourteen days after his return home, he surprises her with the news that he has worked with a gardener out in a suburb of Prague, in the cool rain, wearing only a shirt and trousers. It did him good, he says. His main goal was to free himself "from self-torment for a couple of hours, in contrast to the ghostly work in the office . . . to do some dull-minded, honest, useful, silent, lonesome, healthy, strenuous work." And he also wants to earn a better sleep for the night. Shortly beforehand, he had enclosed a letter from Kurt Wolff, who had asked for "The Stoker" and *The Metamorphosis*. It would revive his hope to be appreciated as a writer by her.

But he had also written her a completely different letter on April 1, one of those counter-letters he always announces in advance to underscore their finality. "My real fear—probably nothing worse can be said and heard—is that I can never possess you. . . . That I shall sit next to you and, as has already happened, feel the breath and life of your body at my side and yet basically be more remote from you than now in my room. . . . That I shall remain forever excluded from you, even if you bend down so deeply towards me as to expose yourself to danger . . ." This letter hints at a fear of impotence, but one should not set too much store by it, it can be understood as only one of his many bodily anxieties, which have already been thoroughly discussed. Felice does not react, it is as if she did not understand what is meant, or as if she knows him well enough by now not to even want to understand.

But for ten days, which she spends at a Frankfurt exhibit for her firm, he has little news from her, postcards perhaps and a telegram from the festival hall. Likewise, after she returns to Berlin, her letters are briefer and rarer. Perhaps she has realized that this is the only way she can influence him; and her withdrawal of letters drives him closer to the decision she expects of him. He shows alarm. "Your most recent letters are different. My affairs are not so important to you anymore, and, what is even worse: you no longer care to write me about yourself." He discusses the Whitsuntide trip with her. He wants to meet her parents, an important step. He entreats her not to pick him up at the station in Berlin, he always arrives in a dreadful state.

On May 11 and 12, they meet again in Berlin. This time, he sees more of her than at Easter, and he is received by her family. Shortly thereafter, he writes her that the family had a look of total resignation in regard to him. "I felt so tiny, and they all stood around me so gigantic, with such a fatalistic expression in their faces. It all fitted in with the circumstances, they possessed you and therefore were big, I did not possess you and therefore was small. . . . I must have made a very ugly impression on them . . .!" The bizarre thing about this letter is the translation of power and possession into physical smallness and largeness. Tininess as powerlessness is familiar to us from his works. The antipodes are in the gigantic and—for him— overpowering members of the Bauer family.

But it is not just the family, especially the mother, who terrifies and paralyzes him; he is also unnerved by the way he affects Felice:

". . . You're not I, after all, your essence is action, you are energetic, you think fast, notice everything, I saw you at your home.
. . . I saw you among strangers in Prague, you always took part and yet you were confident—but you slacken towards me, you look away or into the grass, you let my stupid words and my far more justified silence wash over you, you do not seriously want to find out about me, you suffer, suffer, only suffer. . . ." No sooner is she alone with him than she behaves like him: she lapses into silence, she becomes uncertain of herself, morose. Of course, he most likely has not properly grasped the reason for her lack of confidence. She cannot seriously want to find out anything about him, for she knows *what* she would find out: further and very eloquent doubts, which she could not oppose with anything but her sheer resolution to be engaged. It is striking, apropos, how greatly his image of her is still determined by that one evening in Prague "among strangers." Now it may be obvious why there was such a thorough discussion initially about that first meeting.

But whatever new qualms may have arisen through her behavior in his presence, he promises to write a letter to her father, which he will first submit to her judgment. He announces it on May 16, then again on the eighteenth; on the twenty-third, he specifies what he will write in the letter, but the letter never arrives, he never succeeds, he cannot write it. Meanwhile, she uses her sole weapon: silence; he doesn't hear from her for ten days. Then comes "the ghost of a letter," which he complains about bitterly and quotes: "We are all sitting here together in the restaurant by the zoo after sitting in the zoo a whole day. I am now writing here under the table while discussing travel plans for the summer." He begs her for letters as before: "Dearest Felice, please write me about yourself again as in earlier days, about the office, about your girlfriends, about your family., about walks, about books, you have no idea how badly I need that to live." He wants to know whether she finds any meaning in "The Judgment." He sends her "The Stoker," which has just come out. Once, she writes in greater detail, this time expressing doubts of her own. He prepares an "essay" by way of reply, but it is not yet finished; after this news from him, her letters stop again. On June 15, despairing over her silence, he writes: "Just what do I want from you anyway? What drives me after you? Why don't I stop, why don't I follow any sign? Under the pretext of trying to free you of myself, I become importunate . . ." Then, on June 16, he finally sends her the "essay," on which he has been working haltingly for a week. It is the letter in which he asks her to become his wife.

This is the strangest of all marriage proposals. He piles up all the difficulties, he says countless things about himself which would stand in the way of a marital life together, and he asks her to consider all of these things. Letters following this one add further difficulties. His resistance to living with a wife finds very clear expression. But it is equally clear that he fears solitude and is thinking of the strength he might have from someone else's presence. He makes basically unfulfillable conditions for a marriage and he reckons with a refusal that he wishes and provokes. But he also hopes for a strong, unswerving feeling in her, which would sweep away all difficulties and cope with him no matter what. The moment she says yes, he realizes he should never have left the decision up to her. "The evidence against it is not over, it could go on forever." He accepts her "yes" as though seemingly and takes her as his "dear fiancée": "And I instantly . . . say that I have an absurd fear of our future and of the misfortune that can develop through my nature and guilt from our living together and that would have to strike you first and fully, for I am basically a colder, more unfeeling, more self-seeking person, despite all the weakness, which conceals rather than mellows that."

And now begins his relentless struggle against the engagement, a struggle lasting through the next two months and ending with his flight. The above quoted passage is characteristic of this struggle. While he used to depict himself—one might say: more honestly, a rhetorical note now enters his letters along with the mounting panic. He becomes an advocate against himself, working with any means, and it cannot be denied that some of them are shameful. At his mother's prompting, he hires a detective in Berlin to make inquiries about Felice's reputation, and then he describes the "both horrid and hilarious concoction. We'll have a chance to laugh at it." She seems to take it calmly, perhaps because of the humorous tone, whose falseness she does not see through. But right afterwards, on July 3, his thirtieth birthday, he tells her that his parents have expressed a desire to make inquiries about her family as well, and he has gone along with it. However, this deeply hurts Felice, she loves her family. He defends his step with sophistic arguments, he even cites his insomnia, and although not owning to doing wrong, he asks her forgiveness for hurting her feelings, and he withdraws his agreement to his parents' inquiries. This whole affair so greatly contradicts his usual character that it can be explained only by his panic at the consequences of the betrothal.

When it is a matter of saving himself from the marriage, all he has left is eloquence against himself. It is recognizable as such on the spot, its chief trait is his disguising his own anxieties as worry about Felice. "Have I not been twisting for months in front of you, like something venomous. Am I not now here and then there? Are you not yet sick of the sight of me? Can you still not see that I have to remain locked up inside myself if unhappiness, yours, your unhappiness, Felice, is to be prevented?" He asks her to play the devil's advocate against him with her father, even by exposing his letters: "Felice, be honest with your father, even though I wasn't; tell him who I am, show him letters; with his aid, climb out of the accursed circle into which I, dazzled as I was and am by love, have pushed you with my letters and pleas and entreaties." The rhapsodic tone here is almost like Werfel's, he knew him well and felt drawn to him in a manner that appears inexplicable today.

There can be no doubt as to the authenticity of his torture, and when he leaves Felice out of the picture, making her seem like a mere mirage, he says things about himself that cut into one's heart. His insight into his constitution and nature is ruthless and dreadful. Of many sentences, let me cite one, which strikes me as the most important and most terrible: he says that along with indifference, *angst* is his basic feeling towards others.

That would explain the uniqueness of his work, with its total *lack* of most of the emotions that literature chattily and chaotically teems with. If we think about it courageously, ours has become a world dominated by *angst* and indifference. Kafka, expressing himself without indulgence was the first to offer a picture of *this* world.

On September 2, after two months of endlessly mounting torment, Kafka quite suddenly informs Felice of his flight. It is a long letter, and it is written in both languages, the rhetorical one and the insightful one. For her, "the greatest human happiness" (which it is not for him, of course), which he is renouncing in favor of writing. For himself, the lesson he has learned from his models: "Of the four men whom I feel to be my very own blood relatives, Grillparzer, Dostoievsky, Kleist, and Flaubert, only Dostoievsky got married, and perhaps only Kleist found the right way out when he shot himself in the dilemma of inner and outer crises." He says he is leaving for Vienna on Saturday to attend the International Congress for First Aid and Hygiene. He will probably remain until the following Saturday and then go on to a sanatorium in Riva, where he will remain, perhaps taking an excursion to Northern Italy during the last few days. He tells her to use the time to calm herself. For the sake of her calm, he is willing to give up letters altogether. This is the first time that he does not ask her for letters. He too will not really write her. Perhaps it is tact that makes him conceal his real reason for going to Vienna: the Zionist Congress; a year earlier, they had discussed a joint trip to Palestine.

He spent bad days in Vienna. The Congress and the many people he saw were unbearable for him in his desolate condition. He vainly tried to pull himself together by making some entries in his diary, and he traveled on to Venice. In a letter to Felice from that city, his rejection of a tie to her seems more decided. Then came the days in a Riva sanatorium, where he met the "Swiss girl." He got close to her very quickly, a love developed, which he never denied, despite his delicacy and discretion; the love did not last for more than ten days. It seems to have released him from his self-hatred for a while. During six weeks, between the middle of September and the end of October, the connection between Kafka and Felice was broken off. He did not write her, anything was more endurable to him than her insistence on an engagement. Not hearing from him, she sent her friend Grete Bloch to Prague to mediate between them. By way of a third person, a new and very odd phase of their relationship commenced.

As soon as Grete Bloch came on the scene, Kafka underwent a schism. The letters he had been writing to Felice a year earlier were now addressed to Grete Bloch. She is now the one about whom he wants to know everything, and he asks the same old questions. He wants to picture the way she lives, her work, her office, her travels. He wants instant answers to his letters, and since they sometimes come late, albeit slightly, he asks her for a regular correspondence, which she rejects. He is interested in questions of her health; he wants to know what she reads. In some ways, he has an easier time than he had with Felice, Grete Bloch is more flexible, more receptive, more passionate. So she gives in to his suggestions; even if she doesn't immediately read what he recommends, she does register it and comes back to it later. Although unhealthier and living a less orderly life than Felice, she does think about his advice in these matters, weighs it in her replies, and thereby eggs him on to more decisive suggestions; he needn't feel that his influence is totally fruitless. He is more self-confident in these letters; if it were anyone else, one might be tempted to call him domineering. The abridgement of that earlier correspondence is naturally easier for him than the original was; it is a keyboard on which he has practiced amply. There is something playful about these letters, which the earlier ones seldom were, and he quite blatantly curries her favor.

But two things are essentially different from before. He complains a lot less, he is almost sparing with laments. Since Grete Bloch soon opens up to him and tells him about her own problems, he is touched by her sadness and consoles her, she becomes something like a fellow sufferer, even an alter ego eventually. He tries to fill her with his own dislikes, e.g. his distaste for Vienna, which he has hated ever since that miserable week the previous summer and where she receives his letters. He does all he can to get her out of Vienna, and he succeeds. Withal, she has the good fortune of being quite a businesswoman, or at least he thinks so; it is the only thing she has in common with Felice, and once again he can draw strength from that.

The main topic of these letters, however, is Felice. Grete Bloch first came to Prague as her emissary. From the very start, he can openly talk to her about everything happening to him in this matter. She knows how to keep feeding the original source of his interest in her. In their very first conversation, she tells him things about Felice that repel him: the story of her dental treatment, for instance, and a great deal more will be heard about the new gold teeth. But she also mediates when he is afflicted; and when nothing else works, she succeeds in getting Felice to send him a postcard or some other news. His gratitude increases his liking for Grete Bloch, but he makes it very clear that his interest in her is not merely connected to her relationship to Felice. His letters grow warmer and warmer in regard to Grete, but he depicts Felice with irony and detachment.

This detachment, gained through the correspondence with Grete Bloch, combines with the effect of his conversations with the writer Ernst Weiss, his new friend, who does not like Felice and counsels Kafka against marrying her. All these things merely strengthen Kafka's obstinacy: he courts her anew. He is now resolved to make the engagement and the marriage come true and he struggles for his goal with an unerring precision that one would never have expected after his earlier behavior. He is certainly aware of his guilt of the previous year when he suddenly jilted Felice in the last minute before a public betrothal and hurried off to Vienna and Riva. In a huge forty-page letter at the end of 1913 and the start of 1914, he tells Felice about the Swiss girl and once again asks for her hand in marriage.

Her resistance is no less stubborn than his courtship; after her experience with him, one could hardly blame her. But this very resistance makes him more self-confident, more obstinate. He puts up with humiliations and painful blows because he can describe them to Grete Bloch; everything is immediately and thoroughly reported to her. A very considerable part of his self-torture turns into an accusation of Felice. Reading the letters, which were often written on the same day in immediate succession to Grete and Felice, one cannot doubt whom he really loves. The words of love in the letters to Felice sound false and implausible; whereas one feels them all the more strongly, though usually tacit, between the lines, in the letters to Grete Bloch.

Felice, however, remains adamant and indifferent for two-and-one-half months. He has said so many painful things about himself during the previous year, and now they all come back to him, reduced to her primitive sentences. Usually, though, she doesn't say anything. When he pays her a sudden visit in Berlin, he has his deepest humiliation during a stroll in the *Tiergarten*. He degrades himself before her "like a dog," but achieves nothing. The account of this humiliation and its effect on him, doled out over several letters to Grete Bloch, is significant, even aside from the context of the betrothal. Kafka's description makes it obvious how terribly he suffered when humiliated. To be sure, his peculiar gift was to turn himself into something small, but he applied this talent to reducing humiliations, and the successful reduction was what he enjoyed. This greatly distinguishes him from Dostoievsky; in contrast to him, Kafka is one of the proudest of men. Since he is saturated with Dostoievsky and often expresses himself in the latter's idiom, one is sometimes led to misunderstand him in this point. He, however, never sees himself as a worm without hating himself for that.

Then comes the loss of Felice's handsome brother, whom she so greatly admires and who is forced by an unpleasant financial matter to leave Berlin and migrate to America. His loss makes Felice uncertain of herself, and her defenses crumble. Kafka promptly sees his advantage, and after another four weeks he finally succeeds in getting her to become his fiancée. Easter 1914, in Berlin, brings the unofficial betrothal.

Right after his return to Prague, he writes about it to Grete Bloch: "I know of nothing that I have ever done with such resoluteness." But there was something else that he couldn't wait to tell her: "My engagement or my marriage will not change one iota in our relationship, which contains lovely and quite indispensable possibilities for me at least." He again requests a meeting with her, which he has often depicted for her before; he would prefer Gmünd, halfway between Prague and Vienna. Earlier he wanted them to meet alone in Gmünd on a Saturday evening, with each then returning home on Sunday evening; but now he is thinking of a joint meeting with Felice.

His warmth for Grete increases after the Easter engagement. Without her, he could never have brought about the betrothal, he knows it. She has given him strength and a detachment from Felice. But now that things have come this far, Grete becomes even more indispensable for him. His requests for prolonging the friendship become stormy—for him. She asks for her letters back, he refuses to give them up. He dotes on them as though they were his fiancée's. Although never enduring anyone in his room or home, he urgently invites her to spend the winter in his and Felice's apartment. He begs her to come to Prague and then travel to Berlin with him, in lieu of his father. He continues to take a perhaps even more intense part in her most personal affairs. She tells him about visiting the Grillparzer

Room in the Vienna Museum, which he has been urging her to do for a long time. He thanks her for this news with the following lines: "It was lovely of you to go to the museum. . . . I needed to know that you had been to the Grillparzer Room, thereby producing a physical relationship between me and the room." She has a toothache, he reacts with many solicitous questions, whereby he describes the effect on him of Felice's teeth, which are "nearly all gold": "At first, to tell the truth, I had to lower my eyes from F.'s teeth, for I was so frightened by that glowing gold (a really infernal glow in that unsuitable place). . . . Later, if possible, I deliberately looked at them . . . to torment myself and ultimately to believe that it was all really true. In some heedless moment, I even asked F. if she wasn't ashamed. Naturally, and fortunately, she wasn't. By now, however . . . I have almost fully come to terms with it. I would not wish the gold teeth away. . . . I never really did wish them away. Only today they strike me almost as fitting, highly suitable . . . a very clear, friendly, always demonstrable human defect that can never be denied to the eyes, that perhaps brings me closer to F. than healthy, and in a certain sense, even dreadful teeth could do."

He was thus willing to marry Felice *with* her defects, which he now saw, and there were others besides the gold teeth. In the past year, he had presented himself to her with all his defects, in the most terrible manner. He had not been able to frighten her off with this picture of himself, but his truth had gained such power over him that he fled it and Felice, hurrying to Vienna and then to Riva. There, in his solitude and deepest misery, he met the "Swiss girl" and was able to love, despite his feeling of incapability. This shook his "construction" of himself, as he later termed it. I believe it was also a matter of his pride to make good his failure and win Felice's hand after all. But now he experienced the effect of his self-portrait as a tenacious resistance in her. A compromise was possible only if he took her in marriage—as she him—with all her failings, which he now greedily sought. But it wasn't love, although he told her otherwise. In the course of the very hard fight for Felice, he developed a love for a woman without whose help he could not have survived the struggle: Grete Bloch. The marriage was complete only if he thought of her as part of it. All his instinctive actions during the seven weeks between Easter and Whitsuntide go in this direction. He surely hoped for her assistance as well in the painful external situations in which he would soon find himself and which he dreaded. But he was also moved by the vaster notion that a marriage which he viewed as a kind of duty, as a moral achievement, could not succeed without love, and it was the presence of Grete Bloch, for whom he felt love, that would bring love into the marriage.

In this connection, it must be pointed out that for Kafka, who seldom felt free in a conversation, love could arise only in his written word. The three most important women in his life were Felice, Grete Bloch, and Milena. For each of them, his feelings arose through letters.

The expected then did happen: the official betrothal in Berlin terrified Kafka. At the reception given by the Bauer family on June 1, 1914, he felt (despite Grete Bloch's presence, which he so greatly desired) "as bound up as a criminal. If they had dumped me in a corner with real chains and put gendarmes around me and let me watch from there, it wouldn't have been worse. And that was my engagement, and they were all making an effort to bring me into life and, since they didn't succeed, to tolerate me as I was." This was the entry in his diary just a few days afterwards. In a letter to Felice nearly two years later, he describes another terror of those days, which he still felt in his bones: the way they had gone shopping in Berlin to buy "furnishings for a Prague official's apartment. . . . Heavy furniture, which, once in place, would seem almost impossible to move away. The very solidity was what you appreciated most. The sideboard crushed my chest, a perfect tombstone or a monument to the life of Prague officialdom. If a death knell had tolled somewhere in the vast space of the furniture storeroom while we were shopping, it would not have been unfitting."

By June 6, just a few days after that reception, when he was back in Prague, he wrote Grete Bloch a letter, which sounds terribly familiar to anyone who has read the previous year's correspondence: "Dear Fräulein Grete, yesterday was another day on which I was completely bound up, unable to stir, unable to write the letter to you, which every vestige of life within me urged me to write. Sometimes—you are the only one to find it out for now—I don't really know how I can take the responsibility of getting married as I am."

But Grete Boch's attitude towards him had changed radically. She was now living in Berlin, as he himself wanted, and she didn't feel as desolate there as in Vienna. She had her brother, whom she was very fond of, as well as other people from before, and she saw Felice. Her mission, which she *had* believed in, namely bringing about the engagement, had succeeded. But right up until moving to Berlin, she had been receiving Kafka's letters, which were barely concealed love letters to her; she had answered them, they shared secrets concerning Felice, and Grete most likely had developed a strong feeling for him too. The frock she was to wear at the betrothal was discussed in their letters; it was as though *she* were the fiancée. "Don't fix anything else on it," he writes about *her* dress, "whatever it may be like, it will be seen with the, well, with the most tender eyes." He wrote that letter to her one day before the trip and the betrothal.

The betrothal, at which she was not the bride after all, must have been a shock for Grete. Shortly thereafter, he complained in a letter to her that the wedding was still three months away, to which she replied: "You'll manage, I think, to live for three more months." This statement alone—we have so few from her—is proof enough of the jealousy she was surely suffering. Now living near Felice, she must have felt especially guilty. She could free herself of this guilt only by siding with Felice. Thus, she suddenly became Kafka's enemy, watching suspiciously to see how earnest he was about the wedding. He, on the other hand, kept writing to her trustfully, his letters showing more and more anxiey about the imminent marriage with Felice. Grete began badgering him, he defended himself with the old arguments of his hypochondria, and, since it was she, he explained himself more convincingly and more collectedly than in the previous year's letters to Felice. He managed to alarm Grete, she warned Felice, he was summoned to the "court" in Berlin.

The "trial" in the Askanischer Hof during July 1914 marked the crisis in Kafka's double relationship to the two women. The breaking of the engagement, to which everything in Kafka urged him, was seemingly forced upon him from the outside. But it was as if he himself had selected the members of the court, preparing them as no defendant had ever done. The writer Ernst Weiss, who lived in Berlin, had been his friend for seven months. Along with his literary qualities, he gave the friendship something of inestimable value for Kafka: his unshakable dislike of Felice; he had been against the engagement from the very first. Kafka had been courting Grete Bloch's love for that same length of time. He had enchanted her with his letters, drawing her over to his side more and more. In the period between the private and the official betrothal, his love letters had been addressed to Grete Bloch instead of Felice. She thereby found herself in a predicament, from which there was only one release: an about-face, in which *she* became his judge. She played the prosecution's points into Felice's hand; these were passages in Kafka's letters which she underscored in red. Felice brought her sister Erna along to the "trial," perhaps as a counterweight to her enemy Ernst Weiss, who was also present. The accusation, which was harsh and hateful, was presented by Felice herself; the sparse documents do not make it clear whether and how far Grete Bloch took a direct part. But she was there, and Kafka regarded her as the actual judge. He said no word, he offered no defense, and the engagement collapsed, just as he had desired. He left Berlin and spent two weeks by the sea with Ernst Weiss. His diary depicts the paralysis caused by the days in Berlin.

Retrospectively, it may also seem as if Grete Bloch had thus interfered with the engagement, of which she was jealous. It can also be said that Kafka directed her to Berlin in a sort of cautionary presentiment, making sure his letters to her there put her in a state in which she took over for him and saved him from the betrothal.

But the manner of the termination, its concentrated form as a "court" (he never called it anything else afterwards) had an overpowering impact on him. In early August, his reaction began to be formulated. The trial taking place between him and Felice during two years of letters changed into that other *Trial,* which everyone knows. It is the same trial, he practiced it thoroughly. The fact that he incorporated into it infinitely more than one might realize from the letters alone should not conceal the identity of the two trials. The strength he had previously sought in Felice was now given to him by the shock of the "court." At the same time, the world had its own judgment—World War I broke out. His repugnance at the accompanying mass events intensified his energy. In regard to the private events within him, he did not have that scorn which distinguishes hacks from great writers. The man who believes that it is given to him to separate his inner world from the outer world has absolutely no inner world from which anything could be separated. But with Kafka, the weakness he suffered from, the intermittent halting of his vital energy, permitted him to focus on and objectivize his "private" events only very sporadically. To achieve the continuity that he regarded as crucial, two things were necessary. One was a very powerful but yet somehow false shock like that "trial," which would mobilize his torments of precision for a defense against the outside world. The other was a linking of the external hell of the world with his inner one. That was the case in August 1914; he saw this connection himself and expressed it clearly in his way.

II

Two decisive events in Kafka's life, which he in his own manner would have liked to keep very private, had taken place so very publicly: the official betrothal in the home of the Bauer family on June 1; and, six weeks later, on July 12, 1914, the "trial" in the Askanischer Hof, which ended the engagement. It can be shown that the emotional contents of both events passed directly into *The Trial*, which he began committing to paper in August. The engagement became the arrest in the first chapter; the "trial" is the execution in the last chapter.

A few passages in the journals make this connection so obvious that one may be permitted to demonstrate it. This will not affect the integrity of the novel. If there were any need to heighten its importance, the knowledge of this volume of letters would be a means. Luckily, there is no such need. But in no event will the novel lose any of its ever-growing mystery because of the following reflection, intrusive as it certainly is.

Josef K.'s arrest occurs in an apartment that is well-known to him. It begins while he is still in bed, any person's most familiar place. Hence, what is happening on this morning is all the more incomprehensible, since a total stranger is standing in front of him and a second one rather promptly informs him of his arrest. This news, however, is merely provisional, the actual ritual act of arrest is performed in front of the inspector in Fräulein Bürstner's room, where none of the people present, not even K. himself, really belongs. He is admonished to dress solemnly for the occasion. Besides the inspector and the two guards in Fräulein Bürstner's room, there are also three young men, whom K. does not recognize—until much later: they are officials in the bank where he has a high position. Strangers peer over from the house across the way. No grounds for the arrest are given, and, strangest of all, even though the arrest has been announced, he receives permission to go to his job at the bank and he can otherwise move freely.

This freedom of movement after the arrest is what recalls Kafka's betrothal in Berlin. Kafka had the feeling that the whole matter did not concern him. He felt as if he were chained up and among strangers. The already quoted passage from the diaries which refers to that goes: "[I] was as bound up as a criminal. If they had dumped me in a corner with real chains and put gendarmes around me and let me watch from there, it wouldn't have been worse. And that was my engagement . . ." The awkward thing about both events is their public character. The presence of the two families at the betrothal (he had always had problems keeping his own family at arm's length) drove him into himself more than ever. The pressure they exerted on him made him see them as enemies. The guests included members of the Bauer family whom he really didn't know, and further strangers, for instance Grete Bloch's brother. He had seen some of the others once or twice casually, but he felt always ill at ease even with Felice's mother, with whom he had already spoken. As for his own family, he seemed to have lost the faculty of recognizing them because they were participating in something like an act of violence against him.

A similar mixture of strangers and acquaintances of various degrees can be observed at Josef K.'s arrest. There are the two guards and the inspector: totally new figures; the people across the way, whom he may have seen without their concerning him; and the young men from his bank, whom he does see every day; but during the arrest, in which they take part through their presence, they become strangers to him.

More important, however, is the location of the arrest, Fräulein Bürstner's room. Her name starts with a B like Bauer, but so does Grete Bloch's name. There are family photos in the room, a white blouse is dangling from the window latch. No woman is present during the arrest, but the blouse is a conspicuous proxy.

However, the intrusion into Fräulein Bürstner's room without her knowledge preys on K.'s mind as does the resulting disorder. Coming home from the bank that evening, he has a talk with his landlady, Frau Grubach. The morning's events notwithstanding, she hasn't lost her confidence in him. "It's a matter of your happiness, after all," she begins one of her comforting sentences. The word "happiness" sounds strange here, it is an intruder, it recalls the letters to Felice, in which "happiness" was always used ambivalently, sounding as if it simultaneously and chiefly meant "unhappiness." K. remarks that he would like to apologize to Fräulein Bürstner for making use of her room. Frau Grubach puts his mind at ease, showing him the room, where everything has been restored to order. "Even the blouse was no longer dangling from the window latch." It is late by now, and Fräulein Bürstner isn't home yet. Frau Grubach loses control of herself and makes inflammatory comments on Fräulein Bürstner's private life. K. waits for Fräulein Bürstner to come home, involves her, somewhat against her will, in a conversation about the morning's events, and, while still in her room, gets so vociferous with his description that a loud knocking resounds several times from the adjacent room. Fräulein Bürstner feels compromised and is unhappy, K. kisses her on the forehead as though to comfort her. He promises to tell the landlady it was all his fault, but Fräulein Bürstner will hear none of it and pushes him into the vestibule. K. "seized her, kissed her on the mouth and then all over her face, the way a thirsty animal laps greedily at the spring water it has finally found. At last, he kissed her on the neck, right on the throat, and there he let his lips rest for a long time." Back in his room, he falls asleep very promptly, "before dropping off, he thought a little about his behavior, he was satisfied with it, but surprised that he wasn't even more satisfied."

It is hard not to feel that in this scene Fräulein Bürstner stands for Grete Bloch. Kafka's desire for her is here, powerful and immediate. The arrest, deriving from that tormenting process of the engagement to Felice, has been shifted to the other woman's room. K., unaware of any guilt that morning, has made himself guilty by his conduct that night, with his assault on Fräulein Bürstner. For "he was satisfied with it."

Kafka's complex, almost inextricable situation at the betrothal has thus been exposed in the first chapter of *The Trial* with fascinating lucidity. He had deeply wished for Grete Bloch to be present at the engagement and even shown interest in the frock she would wear. It is not unlikely that this frock was transformed into the white blouse hanging in Fräulein Bürstner's room. Despite his efforts during the course of the story, K. does not succeed in talking to Fräulein Bürstner about the events. She skillfully eludes him, much to his annoyance, and the nocturnal assault remains their inviolable secret.

That too recalls Kafka's relationship to Grete Bloch. Whatever occurred between them remained a secret. Nor can it be assumed, and there are no signs for it, that this secret came out at the "trial" in the Askanischer Hof. Here, the topic was his dubious attitude to the engagement; the passages in his letters to Grete Bloch which openly admitted this referred to Felice and the betrothal, the actual secret between Grete and Kafka was not violated by either of them. The volume of letters, in its present state, lacks anything that might shed light on this matter: It is obvious that some of her letters were destroyed.

To understand how the "trial," which struck Kafka with an enormous impact, became the execution in the last chapter of his novel, one has to see certain passages in the diaries and letters. In late July, he tries to record the course of events quickly and provisionally, one might say from the outside.

"The court of law in the hotel. . . . F.'s face. She runs her hands through her hair, yawns. Pulls herself together suddenly and says well-considered things, long stored up, hostile. The way back with Frl. Bl. . .

"With parents. Occasional tears of the mother. I recite the lesson. The father grasps it correctly from all sides. . . . They say I'm right, nothing or not much can be said against me. Diabolical in all innocence. Apparent guilt of Frl. Bl. . .

"Why did parents and aunt wave goodbye to me like that? . . .

"Didn't go to parents the next day. Just sent a messenger with a letter of goodbye. Letter dishonest and arch. 'Do not remember me badly.' Speech from the place of execution."

Thus, as early as July 27, two weeks after the events, the "place of execution" had lodged in his mind. The word "court" brought him into the sphere of the novel. The "place of execution" foreshadowed its goal and ending. This earliest establishment of the goal is remarkable. It explains the sureness in the development of *The Trial*.

One person in Berlin was "inconceivably good" to him, and he never forgot it. That was Erna, Felice's sister. On July 28, the journal entry says the following about her: "I think of the distance that we, E. and

I., walked from the trolley to Lehrter Station. Neither of us spoke. I thought of nothing but that every step was a gain. And E. is darling to me; even believes in me—incomprehensible—though she saw me in court; I even occasionally felt the effect of this faith in me, without, however, fully believing in the feeling."

Erna's kindness and the engimatic waving of the parents after everything was over were concentrated into an absolutely wonderful passage, that no one who has read it could possibly ever forget. The passage occurs on the last page of *The Trial,* just before the execution:

"His glance fell upon the top story of the house adjacent to the quarry. Like a flashing light, the casements of a window flew apart, a man, faint and insubstantial at that distance and that height, leaned out with a jerk and stretched his arms out even further. Who was it? A friend? A good person? A sympathetic one? One who wanted to help? Was he alone? Was it all men? Was there any help?"

(A few lines later, the original version went: "Where was the judge? Where was the High Court? I have something to say. I am raising my hands.")

Kafka did not defend himself in the Askanischer Hof. He kept silent. He did not recognize the court and he stated this by his silence. The silence lasted a long time: for three months, there was no communication between him and Felice. But he sometimes did write to her sister Erna, who believed in him. In October, Grete recalled her original role as mediator and tried to make contact again. Her letter to him is not extant, but his answer has been preserved. "You say that I hate you," he writes, "but this is not so. . . . You did sit in judgment over me at the Askanischer Hof—it was awful for you, for me, for everyone—but it only looked that way; in reality, I was sitting in your place and I still have not left it."

It would be easy to view the end of this remark as a self-accusal, that started long before and will never end. I do not believe, however, that this is its full meaning. What strikes me as far more important about it is that he is removing Grete Bloch from her seat of judgment, he has expelled her and occupied the arrogated place himself. There is no external tribunal that he recognizes, he is his own court, and very much so, his court will always be in session. As for her usurpation, he says nothing stronger than "it only looked that way," but his "seeing through" her usurpation makes it seem as if she had never really been sitting in judgment. Instead of forcing her out, he turns her into an illusion. He refuses to fight with her; but the nobility of his reply does not hide—as little as he concedes to her—even the hatred of struggle. He realizes he is conducting his own trial, no one else has the right to try him; and when he wrote this letter, he was far from being done.

Two weeks later, in his first, very long letter to Felice, he writes that his silence at the Askanischer Hof was not one of defiance—a not very convincing assertion. But then he goes on: "What you said was so unequivocal, I don't want to repeat it, but there were things that ought to have been almost impossible to say in private. . . . I don't want to say anything else against your bringing Frl. Bl. along; after all, I had practically degraded you in the letter to her, she had a right to be present. However, I didn't understand why you let your sister come, since I hardly knew her back then . . ."

The outcome of the matter, the broken engagement, was as he wished it to be, he could only feel relief. But what upset him, what so deeply embarrassed him was the public character of the incident. His embarrassment at the humiliation, whose gravity could be justly measured only by his pride, remained in him; it carried *The Trial* and flowed wholly into the final chapter. K. lets himself be taken almost silently, almost without resistance, to the execution. He suddenly and totally gives up the defense, whose stubbornness makes up the course of the novel. The passage through the city is like the synthesis of all earlier paths for his defense. "From a lower-lying street in front of them, Fräulein Bürstner climbed up a small stairway to the square. He was not quite sure it was she, but the resemblance was rather striking." He starts off and now *he* chooses the direction. "He determined it according to the path that the young woman was taking before them, not because he wanted to catch up with her, not because he wanted to see her for as long as possible, but merely not to forget the lesson that she represented for him." It is the reminder of his secret and the unuttered guilt. It is independent of the court of law, which has withheld itself from him, it is independent of the accusation, which he has never found out. Yet it strengthens him in giving up any resistance on his last mile. Still, the humiliation, previously discussed, persists further, until the very last lines:

"However, the hands of one gentleman were on K.'s throat, while the other thrust the knife into his heart and turned it twice. With breaking eyes, K. could still see the gentlemen close to his face, leaning on one another, cheek to cheek, observing the judgment. 'Like a dog!' he said; it was as if the shame must outlive him."

The final humiliation is the public nature of this death, which the two executioners, close to his face, cheek to cheek, are observing. K.'s breaking eyes bear witness to this publicity of his death. His last thought is about the shame, which would be strong enough to survive him, and his final utterance is, "Like a dog!"

In August 1914, as already mentioned, Kafka began writing. For three months, he succeeded in doing it daily, except for two evenings, which he notes in a subsequent letter, not without pride. His chief focus was *The Trial,* on which he spent his real impetus. But he also undertook other things; uninterrupted work on *The Trial* was evidently impossible. In August, he also began *Memoirs of the Kalda Railroad,* which he never completed. In October, he took two weeks' vacation to push the novel along, but instead he wrote "In the Penal Colony" and the last chapter of *Amerika.*

During this holiday, the women attempted to make contact with him again. First he got a letter from Grete Bloch; a part of his reply has already been quoted. This reply "seems adamant," he enters it in his diary and remarks: "I realize I am destined to remain alone." He thinks of his aversion at the sight of Felice "dancing, with severely lowered eyes, or running her hand over her nose and hair shortly before leaving the Askanischer Hof, and the countless moments of utter alienation." But nevertheless, he has played with the letter all through the evening, his work comes to a standstill, although he feels capable of writing. "It would be best for all of us if she didn't answer, but she will answer, and I will wait for her answer."

The very next day, both resistance and temptation have intensified. He says he has lived calmly without really communicating with Felice, dreamt about her as though she were dead and could never live again, "and now that I am offered a possibility of getting to her, she is once again the center of the whole thing. She also interferes with my work. When I thought of her recently, she did strike me as the most alien person I have ever known. . . . ."

The "center of the whole thing" is his real danger; she must never be the center, that is the reason he cannot marry, either her or any other woman. The home she always wants is she herself, the center. He can only be his own, always vulnerable center. The vulnerability of both his body and his head is the real precondition for his writing. Though he often looks as he were striving for protection and security against this vulnerability, all his efforts are deceptive, he needs his solitude as a state of *unprotectedness*.

Ten days later, a reply comes from Grete Bloch. "Completely undecided about answer. Thoughts so base that I cannot even write them down."

What he calls "base thoughts" coalesce for him into a resistance, whose strength cannot be underestimated this time. In late October, he writes a very long letter to Felice, announcing it by telegram. It is a letter of amazing detachment. It is scarcely lamenting; one can only find it healthy and aggressive, for Kafka.

He says, however, that he had no intention of writing to her—the Askanischer Hof made the worthlessness of letters and all written things far too clear. More calmly than in earlier letters he explains that it was his work which had to be defended against her as his greatest foe, defended with all possible strength. He describes his present life, with which he does not seem dissatisfied. He says he is living alone in his eldest sister's apartment (with her husband off in the war, she is living with his parents). He is alone, he says, in these three peaceful rooms, seeing no one, not even his friends. During the past three months, he has been writing daily. This is only the second evening that he hasn't worked. He is not happy, he says, certainly not, but still, he is sometimes content with doing his duty, as well as possible under these circumstances.

This is the kind of life-style, he continues, that he has always aspired to; yet the notion of such a life filled her with loathing for him. He lists all the occasions on which she betrayed this loathing, the final and decisive one being her outburst in the Askanischer Hof. It was his duty, he says, to watch over his work, he saw utmost danger for it in her loathing.

As a concrete example of the difficulties between them, he discusses in detail their disagreement over the apartment. "You wanted something that was a matter of course: a quiet, quietly furnished family-apartment, like those of the other families of your and also my social standing. . . . But what does your conception of that apartment mean? It means that you agreed with the others, but not with me. . . . These others, when they marry, are almost satiated, and marriage for them is merely the last, big, lovely morsel. But not for me, I am not satiated, I have not established any business that shall keep developing from matrimonial year to matrimonial year, I do not need a permanent home from whose orderly peace I will attend to this business—and not only do I not need such a home, but it actually frightens me. I have such a hunger for my work . . . yet my circumstances here are opposed to my work, and if I set up housekeeping in these conditions, according to your wishes, that would mean my attempting to make them lifelong—the worst thing that can happen to me."

At the end of the letter, he defends his correspondence with her sister Erna, to whom he says he will write the next day.

On November 1, Kafka's diary contains a highly unusual sentence: "Much self-contentment throughout the day." This feeling probably comes from that long letter, which he has most likely mailed by now. He had resumed contact with Felice though not yielding any ground. His position was now clear and hard, and though he sometimes expressed qualms about it, it would remain the same for a very long time. On the third, he wrote: "The fourth day on which I have not written anything since August. The letters are to blame, I shall try to write no letters or else only very brief ones."

Thus the interference comes from *his own* letters. This is a very important and plausible insight. As long as he is absorbed in dissociating *The Trial* from Felice, he can scarcely deal with her in such detail. The novel would have to get entangled, any precise scrutiny of their relationship would bring him back to the time before he started the novel: it is as though he were undermining its roots. So he now avoids writing to her; no letter of his has turned up from those next three months, until the end of January 1915. He tries to stick to his work with all his strength; he doesn't always succeed, but he never gives up. In early December, he reads "In the Penal Colony" to his friends and is "not entirely dissatisfied." The outcome of this day is: "Keep working absolutely, it has to be possible despite insomnia and office."

On December 5, he receives a letter from Erna about the situation of her family, which had greatly worsened because of the father's death just a few weeks ago. Kafka sees himself as the bane of the family, from which he also feels entirely cut off emotionally. "Only ruin has effect. I made F. unhappy, I weakened the resistance of all who now so greatly require it, I contributed to the father's death, put F. and E. at odds, and ultimately also made E. unhappy . . . . I was punished enough inside the whole thing, my very position with the family is punishment enough, I have also suffered so much that I will never recover . . . but for the moment I am suffering little from my relationship to the family, in any event less than F. or E."

This vast guilt that he ascribed to himself—the ruin of the entire Bauer family—had, as might be expected, a calming effect on him. There was no place in it for the particulars of his behavior towards Felice; all particulars were absorbed into the greater dynamics of the general destruction of the family. For six whole weeks, until January 17, neither Felice nor Erna nor any other member of the unhappy family crops up in his diary or letters. In December, he writes the chapter entitled "In the Cathedral" for *The Trial* and starts two new pieces: "The Giant Mole" and "The Assistant District Attorney." On December 31, his diary contains a summing up of his achievements during the past year. It is quite against his habit, one feels transposed into the diaries of Hebbel:

"Working since August, generally not little and not badly." Then, after a few qualifications and self-admonitions, which he cannot do without, there comes the list of six works he is busy with. Without a knowledge of the manuscript, to which I have no access, it is hard to determine how much of *The Trial* was on paper by this time. A very large part of it was surely already written. It is, in any event, a very impressive list, and one will not hesitate to call these five last months of the year 1914 the second great period in his existence as a writer.

On January 23 and 24, 1915, Kafka and Felice met in Bodenbach on the border. Something about this plan is noted in the diary only six days earlier. "I am seeing F. on Saturday. If she loves me, I don't deserve it. . . . I was very satisfied with myself lately and I had many arguments for my defense and self-assertion against F. . . ." Three days later, he writes: "An end to writing. When will it take me up again? In what a bad state I am meeting with F. . . . Inability to prepare myself for the meeting, whereas last week I could barely shake off important thoughts about it."

It was the first meeting with Felice since the "trial" at the Askanischer Hof, and she could scarcely have made a more annoying impression on him. Since by now *The Trial* had generally removed itself from her, he saw her with greater freedom and detachment. The traces left in him by the "court of law" turned out, nevertheless, to be ineradicable. He wrote down his impression of Felice: with some restraint in a letter to her, but unsparingly in his journal:

"Each privately says to himself that the other is unshakable and ruthless. I shall not give up my demand for a fantastic life that is calculated only for my work. Dull to all my mute pleas, she wants mediocrity, a comfortable apartment, interest in the factory, plenty of food, bed at eleven, a heated room, my watch had been one and a half hours fast for three months now and she sets it at the real time.

"We were alone in the room for two hours. Around me, only boredom and bleakness. We have not had a single good moment in which I could breathe freely. . . . I read aloud to her, the sentences got entangled repugnantly, no contact with the listener, who lay on the sofa with closed eyes, taking them in mutely. . . . My conclusion was correct and was acknowledged as being correct: each loves the other as he is. But he does not believe he can live with him as he is." Her most severe interference is with his watch. The fact that his watch runs differently from others is a tiny piece of freedom for him. She sets it to the real time, an innocent sabotage of this freedom, an adjustment to her time, the time of the office, the factory. However, the word "loves" in the last sentence sounds like a punch in the face, it could just as easily be "hates."

Now the character of the correspondence changes altogether. In no event does Kafka want to relapse into the old manner of writing. He makes sure not to involve her in the "trial;" almost none of its remnants belong to her. He resolves to write her every two weeks, but doesn't stick to that either. Of the 716 pages of letters in the present volume, 580 come from the first two years until the end of 1914. The letters from the years 1915–1917 together do not fill more than 136 pages. A few from this period have been lost; but even if they were extant, the ratio would not be essentially different. His messages become much rarer and also shorter; he starts using postcards—the correspondence of 1916 largely takes place on such cards. A practical reason was that they could more easily pass through the censorship existing between Austria and Germany during the war. The tone is altered: now it is Felice who often complains about his not writing, she is always the wooer now, he the repulser. In 1915, two years after the publication of his book, she actually reads—miracle of miracles— *Betrachtung.*

The encounter in Bodenbach can be seen as a watershed in Kafka's relationship to Felice. Once he was able to view her as ruthlessly as himself, he was no longer helplessly prey to his conception of her. After the "court of law," he had put aside his thoughts of her, knowing full well that they could spring forth at any time in a letter from her. But the courage he marshaled for a new confrontation with her provoked a shift in their power relationship. The new period could be designated as one of *correction;* he, who once drew strength from her efficiency, is now trying to remake her into a different person.

One may ask whether the story of a five-year withdrawal is so important as to earn such a detailed perusal. Interest in a writer can go very far, of course, and if the documents are as profuse as in this case, the temptation to study them and grasp their internal coherence can be irresistible; the observer's insatiability is heightened by the richness of the documents. Man, regarding himself as the measure of all things, is almost unknown. His progress in self-knowledge is minimal, every new theory obscures more of him than it illuminates. Only the unbiased, concrete study of individuals gradually brings us further along. Since this has been so for a long time, and the best minds have always known it, a man offering himself to investigation in such totality is a windfall without parallel. But with Kafka, it is more; and anyone approaching his private sphere can feel that. There is something deeply exciting about this obstinate attempt of a powerless man to escape power in any form. Before we depict the further course of his relationship to Felice, it seems advisable to show how absorbed he was with the one phenomenon that has become the most urgent and terrifying for our era. Of all writers, Kafka is the greatest expert on power. He experienced, and gave shape to, each of its aspects.

One of his central themes is humiliation; it is also the theme that most willingly offers itself to study. Even in "The Judgment," his first work to count for him, that topic can be grasped without difficulty. The story is about two connected humiliations, the father's and the son's. The father feels endangered by the son's alleged machinations. In his accusing speech, he stands up on the bed and, much bigger in proportion to him than he was originally, he tries to reverse his own degradation into its opposite, the humiliation of the son: he condemns him to death by drowning. The son does not recognize the legitimacy of the verdict, but he does execute it on himself, thereby admitting the measure of humiliation that costs him his life. The humiliation is strictly framed in its own terms; as absurd as it is, its effect makes up the strength of the tale.

The Metamorphosis concentrates the degradation in the body that suffers it: the object exists compactly from the start; instead of a son who feeds and maintains the family, a bug is suddenly there. This metamorphosis puts him inescapably at the mercy of degradation; an entire family feels challenged to practice it actively. The humiliation begins hesitantly, but it has time to expand and intensify. Gradually, all take part in it, almost helplessly and reluctantly. The act given at the beginning is performed again by them; it is the family who transforms Gregor Samsa, the son, irretrievably into a bug. Within the social context, the bug becomes a vermin.

The novel *Amerika* is full of degradations, although not such unheard-of or irreparable ones. They are contained in the very notion of the continent, whose name figures as the title of the book: Rossmann's raising by his uncle and his equally sudden plunge can suffice as examples of many other things. The harshness of living conditions in the new land is balanced by the great social mobility. Expectation always stays alive in the degraded man; each plunge can be followed by a miracle of raising. Nothing that happens to Rossmann has the fatality of something final. Thus this book is Kafka's most hopeful and least bewildering.

In *The Trial,* degradation comes from a superior authority, which is far more complex than the family in *Metamorphosis.* The court of law, once it has made itself perceptible, degrades by retreating; it shrouds itself in secrecy that will not give in to any efforts. The tenacity of these efforts demonstrates the absurdity of the attempt. Any clue that is pursued appears irrelevant. The question of guilt or innocence, which would be the true basis for the court's existence, remains peripheral; in fact, it turns out that the relentless strivings to get to the court are what produce the guilt. However, the fundamental theme of humiliation, as occurring between man and man, is also varied in individual episodes. The scene with Titorelli the painter, starting with the confusing scorn of the little girls, ends with the presentation and purchase of the same paintings over and over, while K. feels he is about to suffocate from the lack of air in the tiny studio. K. also has to witness the humiliation of others: he watches Block, the businessman, kneel down at the lawyer's bed and change into a kind of dog; even this, like everything else, is ultimately in vain.

(We have already discussed the conclusion of *The Trial,* the shame of the public execution.)

The image of the dog in this sense keeps recurring in Kafka's writings, and in his letters, too, where it refers to events in his own life. Thus, in a letter to Felice, he says about that event in spring 1914: ". . . When I run after you in the *Tiergarten,* you always about to go away altogether, I about to throw myself down; . . . in this humiliation that no dog suffers more deeply." At the end of the first paragraph of "In the Penal Colony," the image of the prisoner in his many chains is summed up in the following sentence: "In any case, the condemned man had a look of such doglike submissiveness that it seemed as if one could let him run about freely over the slopes and, at the start of the execution, one need only whistle for him to come."

The Castle, belonging to a much later period in Kafka's life, introduces a new dimension of vast space into his oeuvre. Even more than through landscape, the impression of vastness comes through the world he presents, a world that is more complete and more populated. Here too, as in *The Trial,* power is *evasive:* Klamm, the hierarchy of officialdom, the castle. One sees the powers that be, without, however, being certain of having seen them; the actual relationship between the powerless people, dwelling at the foot of the castle mountain, and the officials is that of *waiting for superiors.* The question as to the *raison d'être* of this superiority is never asked. But the thing coming from it and spreading among the ordinary people is humiliation by the authorities. The sole act of resistance against these authorities, Amalia's refusal to give in to one of the officials, ends with the expulsion of her entire family from the village community. The writer's emotions favor the lower ones, who wait futilely; he loathes the superiors, who rule in the mass orgies of their files. The "religious" aspect, that so many people claim to find in *The Castle,* may be there, but it is *naked,* an unquenchable and incomprehensible yearning towards the "above." No clearer attack against the subjugation to the above, whether one interprets it as a higher or merely an earthly power, has ever been written. For *all* authority has become one here, and it appears abominable. Faith and power coalesce, both seem dubious; the resignation of the victims, who never even dream of any possibility of alternate ways of life, would have to infuriate and arouse even the man who is totally untouched by the usual rhetoric of ideologies, a number of which have failed.

From the very beginning, Kafka sided with the humiliated. Many people have done so, and, in order to have an effect, they have allied themselves with others. The feeling of strength coming from this alliance soon relieved them of the acute experience of humiliation, whose end cannot be foreseen; it continues daily and hourly everywhere. Kafka kept each of these experiences apart from similar ones, but also from those of other people. It was not given to him to get rid of experiences by sharing or communicating them; he guarded them with a kind of obduracy, as though they were his most important possession. One could call this obduracy his true talent. People of his sensitivity are perhaps not so infrequent; a greater rarity is the slowing-down of all reactions which one finds so peculiarly stamped in him. He often speaks of his poor memory; but in reality, he retains everything. The precision of his memory is revealed in the way he corrects and fills out Felice's inaccurate recollections of the previous years. His failure to have his memory freely at his disposal all the time is another matter. His obduracy refuses him his memory; he cannot play irresponsibly with memory as other writers do. This obduracy follows its own harsh laws, one could say that it aids him in husbanding his defensive energy. Thus, it enables him to refuse to obey orders on the spot, yet to feel their stings as though he had obeyed, and then to use the stings for strengthening his resistance. But when he eventually does obey, the orders are no longer the same, for he has detached them from their temporal context, weighed them thoroughly, weakened them with his reflection, and thereby stripped them of their dangerous character.

114

This process would require a more precise study as well as concrete examples. Let me cite just one: Kafka's obstinate resistance to certain foods. He lived with his family for a very long time, but never gave in to their food habits, which he treated as orders to be rejected. Hence, though at his parental table, he sat in his own food world, which provoked his father's profound loathing. His resistance, however, gave him the strength of holding his own on other occasions and also against other people. In the struggle against Felice's obnoxious ideas of marriage, the emphasis on his peculiarities played a cardinal role. Blow by blow, he defended himself against the conformity she expected of him. But scarcely was the engagement broken when he permitted himself to eat meat again. In a letter to his Prague friends, from that Baltic resort where he stayed soon after the Berlin "trial," he describes, not without disgust, his debauchery in eating meat. Even months later, he is gratified to report in a letter to Felice that right after the termination of the betrothal he and her sister Erna went to dine on meat. If she, Felice, had been present, he would have ordered sugar-coated almonds. Thus, when no longer under her pressure, he carries out orders that no longer signify submission.

Kafka's taciturn ways, his secrecy, even with his best friends, have to be viewed as necessary practices of this obduracy. It is not always true that he is aware of what his silence conceals. But when his characters, in *The Trial* or particularly in *The Castle,* lapse into their sometimes garrulous speeches of defense, one feels that his own floodgates are opening: he finds a way to speak. As little as his obduracy usually allows him to talk, it does grant him a sudden freedom of speech here, in the apparent disguise of the literary character. These are not like the confessions we are familiar with in Dostoievsky; the temperature is different, nowhere as high. Nor is anything amorphous; it is really volubility on a clearly defined instrument, that is capable of only certain sounds: the fluency of a finicky, but unmistakable virtuoso.

The story of his resistance to his father, which cannot be dealt with in the usual banal interpretations, is also the early history of this obduracy. Many things have been said about it, most of them off target; one might have expected that Kafka's sovereign attitude toward psychoanalysis would have contributed at least to removing him from its confining precinct. The fight against his father was essentially never anything but a fight against superior power. His hatred was aimed at the family as a whole, the father being merely the most powerful part of this family. When the danger of a family of his own began to loom, the struggle against Felice had the same motive and the same character.

It is worth recalling once again the silence at the Askanischer Hof, the most revealing instance of his obduracy. He did not react as another might, he did not retort with counter-accusations. Given his great sensitivity, one can hardly doubt that he took in and felt everything said against him. Nor did he—and the term suggests itself— "repress" it. He stored it in his mind, but was quite conscious of it; he thought of it often; it surfaced so often that one would have to call it the very opposite of repression. What he blocked was any external reaction that could betray the inner effect. Whatever he stored in this way was as sharp as a knife, but neither hatred nor resentment, neither anger nor vindictiveness ever pushed him to any misuse of the knife. It remained separate from the emotions, an autonomous entity. But by refusing to join the emotions, it withdrew him from power.

We would have to apologize for the naive use of the word "power," if Kafka himself, in the teeth of all ambivalence, did not employ it dauntlessly. The word crops up in the most disparate contexts. His aversion to "big," overfilled words prevented him from writing a single "rhetorical" opus. He therefore will never become less readable; the continuous emptying and refilling of words, a process that makes nearly all literature age, will never touch him. Yet he never felt an aversion to the words "power" and "powerful"; both are among his unavoided, his inevitable words. It would, indeed, be worthwhile tracking down their every occurrence in his works, letters, diaries.

It is, however, not just the word, it is also the thing itself, in its infinity of aspects, that he formulates with peerless courage and clarity. For, by fearing power in any guise, by seeing the goal of his life as escaping it in any guise, he senses, recognizes, names or depicts it wherever others would take it for granted.

A sketch in the volume *Wedding Preparations in the Country* portrays the animal nature of power, a monstrous cosmic picture in eight lines:

"I was helpless in regard to the figure, it sat quietly at the table, gazing at the tabletop. I circled it and felt choked by it. A third person circled me and felt choked by me. A fourth person circled the third and felt choked by him. And thus it went on until the movements of the stars and beyond them. All felt the grip on the throat."

The threat, the grip on the throat, comes from the inmost center, there it springs forth, a gravitational force of choking which holds together one circle around the other, "until the movements of the stars and beyond them." The Pythagorean harmony of the spheres has become a violence of spheres, with human gravity preponderant and each individual making up a sphere of his own.

He feels the threat of teeth, so greatly that they even "hold" singly, and not just when the two rows are clenched:

"It was an ordinary day; he bared his teeth at me; I too was held by teeth and could not wriggle free; I did not know with what they were holding me, for they were not clenched; nor did I see them in the two rows, just a few here, a few there. I wanted to hold fast to them and vault over them, but I failed."

In a letter to Felice, he comes up with the staggering expression: "the fear of standing upright." He interprets a dream that she has told him about; his explanation makes it fairly easy to guess the content:

"Instead, let me interpret your dream for you. If you hadn't been lying on the ground among the animals you would not have been able to see the sky and the stars and you would not have been redeemed. You might not have survived the fear of standing upright. Nor is it any different with me; that was a joint dream which you dreamt for both of us."

One has to lie down among the animals in order to be redeemed. Standing upright is man's power over the animals; but this obvious position of his power is precisely what makes him exposed, visible, vulnerable. For this power is also guilt; and it is only by lying on the ground, among the animals, that one can see the stars, which redeem one from this fearful power of man.

This human guilt towards animals is testified to by the *loudest* passage in Kafka's works. The following paragraph occurs in "An Old Manuscript" in the *Country Doctor* collection:

"Lately the butcher thought he could at least spare himself the trouble of slaughtering, and so he brought a live bull the next day. He should not do that again. I must have been lying for something like an hour, at the back, flat on the floor of my workshop, and I had piled all my clothes, blankets, and pillows on top of me, just so as not to hear the bellowing of the bull, whom the nomads pounced upon from all sides, ripping out pieces of his warm flesh with their teeth. There had been silence for a long time before I dared to go out; like drinkers around a vat of wine, they lay wearily around the remains of the bull."

"Silence for a long time . . ." Do we have the right to say that the narrator was escaping the unbearable, that he found silence again, since there is no such thing as silence after that bellowing? It is Kafka's own position, but not all the clothes, blankets, and pillows in the world would be capable of muffling out that bellow forever. If he did escape it, then only to hear it again, for it never stopped. Of course, the word "escape" is highly inaccurate in regard to Kafka. In his case, it means that he sought silence in order to hear nothing else, nothing, that was less than fear.

Confronted as he was with power everywhere, his obduracy sometimes offered him a possibility of delay. But when it was insufficient or failed, he would practice *disappearing*. This reveals the helpful aspect of his skinniness, which he often, as we know, also despised. By physically diminishing, he withdrew power from himself, thereby taking less of a part in it; this asceticism too was directed against power. The same penchant for vanishing is shown in his relationship to his name. In two of his novels, *The Trial* and *The Castle*, he reduces it to an initial, K. In the letters to Felice, his name keeps getting smaller, finally disappearing altogether.

Most amazing of all is another device which he mastered as sovereignly as only the Chinese did: transformation into something small. Since he loathed power, but didn't feel he had the strength necessary to fight it, he magnified the distance between the stronger adversary and himself by becoming smaller and smaller in regard to that strength. This shrinking brought him two things: he eluded the peril by becoming too tiny for it, and he freed himself from any vile uses of power; the small animals into which he preferred to change were harmless.

A very clear light is shed on the genesis of this unwonted gift by an early letter to Brod. It was written in 1904, when Kafka was twenty-one. I call it the Mole Letter and I am quoting something

118

that seems necessary for understanding Kafka's metamorphosis into small things. But let me preface it with a line from a letter to his boyhood friend Oskar Pollak, one year earlier: "One should venerate the mole and its ways, but not make it one's patron saint." That still isn't much, but nevertheless: the mole has appeared for the first time. There is already a particular stress on "its ways," and the warning not to "make it one's patron saint" plainly announces its later significance. The letter to Max Brod says the following:

"We burrow through like a mole and emerge all blackened and velvet-haired from our buried vaults of sand, stretching up our poor red little paws for tender sympathy.

"During a walk, my dog came upon a mole that was trying to run across the road. He kept jumping on it and then letting it go, for he is still young and timid. At first, I was entertained and I especially enjoyed the mole's excitement, it was altogether desperately and vainly seeking to find a hole in the hard ground of the street. But suddenly, when the dog struck it with its stretching paw, it shrieked. 'Ks, kss,' that's what it shrieked. And then I thought—No, I did not think anything. It merely deluded me, because my head drooped down so heavily that day that I was amazed to notice in the evening that my chin had grown into my chest."

It must be added that the dog chasing the mole was Kafka's dog, Kafka was his master. But the master did not exist for the mole, which, in its deadly fear, was looking for a hole in the hard road; the animal was afraid only of the dog, its senses were alert only to the dog. Kafka, however, so above it all because of his upright position, his height, and his ownership of the dog, which could never threaten him—he laughs only at the desperate and futile movements of the mole. The mole doesn't realize it could turn to the man for help; it has never learned to pray, and all it can do is emit tiny shrieks. They are all that reach the god, for here the man is the god, the supreme being, the pinnacle of power, and God is even present in this case. "Ks, kss," shrieks the mole, and that shriek turns the spectator into the mole; and without having to fear the dog, which is his slave, he feels what it's like being a mole.

The unexpected shriek is not the only vehicle for metamorphosis into something small. A further device is the "poor red paws,"

119

stretching out like hands for pity. The fragment, *Memoirs of the Kalda Railroad* (August 1914) contains a related attempt at approaching a dying rat by way of its "small hand."

"For the rats, who sometimes attacked my food, my long knife was enough. During the early time, when I seized curiously upon everything, I once skewered such a rat and held it up on the wall at eye-level. One sees smaller animals accurately only when holding them at eye level; if one bends down to the ground for them and looks at them there, one gets a false and incomplete idea of them. The most conspicuous thing about these rats were the claws, big, slightly hollow, and yet sharp at the end, they were very suitable for digging in. In the final struggle in which the rat hung before me on the wall, it extended its claws stiffly, apparently against its living nature, they were like a small hand stretching out to someone."

One has to have smaller animals at eye-level to see them accurately: it is as though one were making them one's equal by raising them. Bending down to the ground, a kind of condescension, offers a false, incomplete idea of them. The raising of small animals to eye-level recalls Kafka's habit of magnifying such creatures: the bug in *Metamorphosis*, the molelike creature in "The Burrow." The transformation into something small is made more graphic, more palpable, more credible by the animal's cooperation, its increase in size.

Anything comparable to Kafka's interest in very small animals, especially insects, can be found only in the life and literature of the Chinese. One of their favorite animals, very early in their history, is the cricket. In the Sung Period, it was customary to keep crickets as pets, they were trained and used in cricket-fights. They were worn on the chest in walnut shells, which were appointed with furniture for their living needs. The owner of a renowned cricket let mosquitoes suck blood from his own arm, and when they were full, he would chop them up and serve this hash to his cricket for increasing its lust for battle. People used special brushes for egging the crickets on to attack and then, squatting or lying prone, they would watch the combat. A creature that excelled in unusual bravery was honored with the name of a general in Chinese history, under the assumption that the general's soul had come to reside in the cricket's body. Because of Buddhism, most Chinese took the belief in transmigration for granted, and so such an honor had nothing bizarre about it. The search for suitable crickets for the imperial court extended all over the empire, and very high prices were paid for promising candidates. It is said that during the time the Sung empire was being overrun by the Mongols, the Chinese commander-in-chief was flat on his belly, watching a cricket fight, when he received the news that the capital was surrounded by the enemy and that they were in utmost danger. He just couldn't tear himself away from the crickets, he first had to see who the winner was. The city fell, and the reign of the Sungs was over.

Much earlier, in the Tang Dynasty, crickets were kept in small cages for their chirping. But whether the Chinese held them aloft to better observe their chirping from close up or wore them on their chests because of their value and then removed them in order to take special care of their dwellings, they did lift the crickets to eye-level, as Kafka recommended. They looked at them as equals, and when the crickets had to fight, the Chinese would crouch down or lie on the floor. Their souls, however, were those of famous generals, and the outcome of their fights could appear more crucial than the fate of a great empire.

Stories in which small animals play a part are very widespread in China, especially ones about crickets, ants, bees who take in a human being and act like human beings toward him. Martin Buber's *Chinese Ghost and Love Stories* contains a few such tales, but whether Kafka actually read this book is not quite clear from the letters to Felice. Still, the book is mentioned by him with praise, and, to his annoyance—it is the time of his jealousy of other writers—it turns out that Felice has already bought it. In any event, some of Kafka's stories could put him right into Chinese literature. Themes from China have been picked up by European writers since the eighteenth century. But the only essentially Chinese writer to be found in the West is Kafka.* In a note, which could derive from a Taoist text, Kafka himself summed

---

* In favor of this opinion, I would like to mention that it is also shared by Arthur Waley, the best modern expert on Eastern literature, and has been discussed in many conversations. Most likely for this very reason, Kafka was the only German prose writer that Waley passionately read, he was as familiar with him as with Po Chü I and the Buddhist monkey novel, which he himself translated. Our conversations often dealt with Kafka's "natural" Taoism, and, so that no aspect of the Chinese might be lacking, with the special tone of his ritualism. Outstanding examples of this, for Waley, were "The Refusal" and "While Building the Great Wall of China"; and further tales were also mentioned in this connection.

up what "smallness" means for him: "Two possibilities: to make one-self infinitely small or to be infinitely small. The latter is perfection, that is, inactivity; the former is beginning, that is, action."

I fully realize that we have touched only upon a very small portion of what might be said about power and metamorphosis in Kafka. Anything more thorough or complete would require a larger book; and all we are after here is to finish the story of Kafka's relationship to Felice, three years of which are still left.

Of all the dry spells in this relationship, the year 1915 was the worst. It was overshadowed by Bodenbach. Whatever Kafka put into words, whatever he wrote down, had a lasting effect on him. At first, as a result of the clash, but at greater and greater intervals, Felice still received a few letters. Kafka complained about the slowdown in his writing (it had really come to an end again), about the noise in the new rooms he had moved into; that was the topic he was most de-tailed about, and those are the most gripping passages. He had more and more trouble coming to terms with his life as an official; of the reproaches he unsparingly heaped upon Felice, the harshest was that she had desired to live with him in Prague. This city was unbearable to him; and in order to get out, he toyed with the idea of joining the army. The thing he suffered from most in the war was not taking part in it. But he said it was not impossible for his turn to come. His physical was imminent, he pointed out, and she ought to wish that they would induct him, as he wanted. But despite repeated attempts, nothing did come of it, and he remained in his Prague bureau "as desperate as a trapped rat."

She sent him *Salammbô* with a very dismal inscription. It made him unhappy to read it; and for once he tried to send her a comforting let-ter. "Nothing is over, no darkness, no cold. You see, Felice, the only thing that's happened is that my letters have grown less frequent and different. What was the outcome of the more frequent and different letters. You know it. We have to start again. . ."

Perhaps it was that inscription which prompted him to meet her and Grete Bloch at Whitsuntide in Bohemian Switzerland. For both, it was the only bright spot that year. Grete Bloch's presence may have contributed to the smooth course of the two days. Something of the rigid terror of the "trial" that the two women had put him through must have dissipated on this occasion. Felice had a toothache, he was permitted to get aspirin and "love her face to face in the corridor." She should have seen him, he wrote her, right after his return to Prague, seeking the memory of her and her room in the lilacs, throughout that long journey. At no other time did he ever take anything similar along on a trip, he did not care much for flowers. And the next day, he wrote that he was worried about having stayed too long. Two days, he said, were too much: One can easily let go after one day; but two days create ties, and letting go hurts.

Just a few weeks later, in June, there was a further meeting in Carlsbad. This time it was brief, and everything went poorly. Details are unknown, but a subsequent letter talks about Carlsbad and the "truly repulsive trip to Aussig." It must have been especially horrible after the good days at Whitsuntide, for Carlsbad is on his list of the worst moments, right next to the *Tiergarten* and the Askanischer Hof. From now on, he almost never wrote, or else he rebuffed her complaints about his silence. "Why don't you write?" he said to himself. "Why do you torture F.? Her cards make it obvious that you *are* torturing her. You promise to write and you don't write. You wire 'letter en route,' but there's no letter en route, it's only written two days later. Something like that should only be done perhaps once, by girls, and only by way of an exception. . . ." The reversal is blatant, he is doing to her the very same thing that she did to him years ago, and his mention of girls' being allowed to do it does not exactly indicate that he is unaware of it.

From August to December, she heard nothing from him; and if he did write now and then later on, it was nearly always to ward off her suggestion that they meet. "It would be nice to get together, but I don't think we ought to. It would be only something provisional, and we have suffered enough from provisional things. . . . Taking one consideration with another, it would be better if you don't come." . . . "So long as I am not free, I do not want to be seen, I do not want to see you." . . . "I am warning you and me against a meeting, think hard about earlier meetings, and you will not wish for any more. . . . So, no meeting."

The last quotation is from April 1916, and sounds a lot harsher, given the context of the letter. His resistance had strengthened during one and one half years, aside from the meager Pentecostal intermezzo in 1915, and one cannot see how it could ever change again. But it was precisely in this April that the word Marienbad cropped up for the first time, in a postcard, recurring regularly from then on. He was planning a vacation, hoping to spend three quiet weeks in Marienbad. Postcards now came more frequently. In mid-May he really did visit Marienbad during an official trip, and from there he instantly wrote her a long letter and a postcard.

". . . Marienbad is incomprehensibly beautiful. I should have followed my instinct a lot earlier when it told me that the fattest people are also the wisest. For one can thin down anywhere, even without worshipping a mineral spring; but this is the only place where one can wander about through such woods. Of course, the beauty is now intensified by the stillness and emptiness and by the receptivity of all animate and inanimate things, yet scarcely impaired by the dismal, windy weather. I think that if I were Chinese and went home right away (basically, I *am* Chinese and I am going home), I would soon make sure of coming here again. You'd like it so much!"

I have quoted this postcard almost in its entirety, for it contains so many of Kafka's most essential feelings and qualities in the smallest space; his love for the woods, his penchant for stillness and emptiness, the issue of skinniness and his almost superstitious awe of fat people. Stillness and emptiness, the dismal, windy weather, the receptivity of all animate and inanimate things recall Taoism and a Chinese landscape, and thus we have the only passage, to my knowledge, in which he says of himself: "Basically, I *am* Chinese. . ." The concluding line, "You'd like it so much!" is his first real attempt at approaching Felice in years, and it bursts with the days of happiness in Marienbad.

The negotiations (one cannot use any other term) over the joint holiday dragged out for another month, enlivening the correspondence in quite an astonishing way. Felice, for his sake, even suggested a sanatorium. Perhaps she dimly recollected the one in Riva, where, three years earlier, the presence of the "Swiss girl" had been a boon to him. But he didn't like this suggestion, a sanatorium being almost "a new office in the service of the body." He preferred a hotel. From July 3 to 13, Kafka and Felice spent ten days together in Marienbad.

He left the Prague office in exemplary order, he was blissful at leaving it. Had it been for good, he would have "been willing to kneel down and scrub every step of the stairway from attic to basement in order to show his gratitude at the farewell." In Marienbad, Felice picked him up at the station. He spent the first night in an ugly room facing the courtyard. But the next day, he moved to an "extraordinarily lovely room" in the Hotel Balmoral. There he lived next door to Felice, each had the key to the other's room. Headaches and insomnia were bad; during the first few days, especially at night, he was tortured and despairing, his diary indicates how wretched he felt. On the eighth, he and Felice took an outing to Tepl in miserable weather; but then the afternoon grew "mellow and beautiful," and that was the turning point. Now came five happy days with her, one might say one for every five of their years. His diary said: "I was never intimate with a woman, except in Suckmantel. And then with the Swiss girl in Riva. The first was a woman, I was innocent; the second was a child, I was totally confused. I was intimate with F. only in letters, and personally only for the past two days. It's not all that clear, doubts remain. But how lovely the gaze of her soothed eyes, the opening of female depth."

On the eve of Felice's departure, he began a long letter to Max Brod, not ending it until later on, after she was gone:

". . . But now I saw a woman's gaze of confidence and I could not shut myself off to it. . . . I have no right to resist it, even less so since, if what happens did not happen, I would willingly bring it about myself merely to receive that gaze again. After all, I did not know her; along with other qualms, of course, I was hindered back then by a fear of the reality of that woman writing her letters; when she came towards me in the large room to take the betrothal kiss, a shudder went through me; the betrothal expedition with my parents was a torture for me, every step of the way; there was nothing I was so frightened of as being alone with F. before the wedding. Now, things are different and good. Our contract is in brief: To marry soon after the war's end, rent two or three rooms in a Berlin suburb, each person taking care of his or her own domestic needs. F. will work again as before, and I, well I—I can't say as yet. . . . Nevertheless—there is peace in it now, certainly, and hence a possibility of life. . .

". . . Since the Tepl morning, we had such lovely and mellow days, such as I would never have dreamt I could experience. There were darknesses in between, of course, but the lovely and mellow parts outweighed the others. . ."

Kafka had brought Felice to Franzensbad on the last day of her vacation so that they might visit his mother and one of his sisters there. By the time he returned to Marienbad that evening, planning to spend another ten days alone, his hotel room, which was particularly quiet, had been rented to other guests, and he had to move into Felice's room, which was much noisier. Thus, after her departure, his postcards are again filled with complaints about noise, headaches, and poor sleep. But after five more days, he was used to her room, and now, with his habitual slow reaction, tenderness and a sense of happiness spread throughout his cards to her—cards that will move the reader at least for their rarity. It must be seen as a windfall that he remained in the same places after she left. He walked along the same paths in the woods of Marienbad, ate the prescribed foods for gaining weight, had his meals in the same restaurants. At night, he sat on her balcony, at the same table, writing to her by the light of the lamp that was familiar to both of them.

Everything was on postcards, he sent her one every day, sometimes two. The first calls her "My poor darling," for he still feels bad; whenever he calls her "poor," he means himself, he is the poor one. "I am writing with your pen, your ink, sleeping in your bed, sitting on your balcony—that would not be bad, but there is only a single door, and through it I can hear the noise from the corridor and the noise of the double tenants to the right and the left." The noise still drowned out everything here, otherwise he would hardly have used words like "that would not be bad" to describe the result of what went on before. The card ends with the sentence: "I am now going to the Dianahof to think about you while leaning over the butter dish."

In a later card, he tells her he is getting fat despite insomnia and headaches, and he transmits the whole of "yesterday's menu." It includes, precisely bound to their times of day, the things one would expect of him: milk, honey, butter, cherries, etc. But at twelve noon (one can scarcely believe one's eyes): "smoked pork, spinach, potatoes."

Thus, he had actually given up part of his resistance to her: the menu was important in this love. He was growing "fat," he was also eating meat. Since he was otherwise eating only things he had approved of earlier, the compromise between them was in the amount of those things and in the "smoked pork." So, during their days together in Marienbad, they had also grown closer and been reconciled through mutual food. The routine of life in the spa put Kafka at ease and allayed his fear of routine per se. After her departure, he kept eating the same things in the same places and told her about it in something like a declaration of love.

But he also paid her a less intimate, a more elevated tribute: "Just look, we didn't even meet the most sublime guest at Marienbad, i.e. the one in whom the greatest human trust is placed; the Rabbi of Belz, now probably the chief representative of Chassidism. He's been here for three weeks. Yesterday, for the first time, I was among the dozen people in his retinue during the evening walk. . . . And how are you, my sublime Marienbad guest? I haven't any news yet, I'm content with the stories of the old paths, e.g., today, the promenade of sulks and secrets."

Once, after getting no news from her for two days, he wrote: "One was so spoiled by being together, two steps to the left and one could have news." On another day, the second card said: "Darling—am I overwriting as I used to in earlier times? By way of apology: I am sitting on your balcony, at your side of the table, it is as though the two sides of the table were the two pans of a scale; the equilibrium existing on our good evenings seems disturbed; and I, all alone on the one pan, am sinking: sinking because you are far away. That's why I'm writing. . . . There is almost the stillness here that I want: The nightlight is burning on the small table on the balcony, all the other balconies are deserted because of the cold, there is only the steady murmur coming from *Kaiserstrasse* and it doesn't bother me."

At that moment, he was free of fear. He sat on her side of the table, as though he were she, but the scale pan sank because she was far away, and he was writing to her. It was almost the stillness he wanted, the nightlight was burning only on his balcony, and it was not feeding on indifference. All the other balconies were cold and empty. The steady murmur from the street was not annoying.

There was a line from the time when he did not really know Felice: namely, that fear, along with indifference, was his basic feeling towards other people. But that sentence was now invalid. Enjoying the freedom of the nightlight, he also felt love: "Someone has to stay awake, it is said. Someone has to be here."

Any life that one knows well enough is ludicrous. When one knows it even better, it becomes serious and dreadful. Kafka, returning to Prague, tackled an enterprise that can be viewed from both sides. His image of Felice before Marienbad was unbearable to him, and he devoted himself to the Herculean task of changing it. He had already been seeing her clearly for a long time, even since Bodenbach, and he had been mercilessly rebuking her for the things in her that tormented him. Yet he had done so only sporadically and without hope, for there was nothing he could do to change her. In Marienbad, they had happened to talk about the Jewish People's Home in Berlin, which cared for refugees and refugee children, and Felice had spontaneously said she wanted to work there in her spare time. He had told her about it with no expectation or intention, and he was glad that she "so freely and so well understood the idea of the home." From that instant on, he felt hope for her; and with a tenacity that supplanted strength in him, he now reminded her, in every letter to Berlin, of her plan to get in touch with the Jewish Home. For three or four months, until early November, he wrote her almost daily, and the most important if not only topic in his letters was the People's Home.

Felice reluctantly sought information, she feared that perhaps only students were permitted to work at the Home. He, in his reply, did not understand why she thought so. "Naturally, students, as the—on the average—most selfless, most decisive, most restless, most demanding, most hardworking, most independent, most farsighted people, did begin the thing and are in charge of it, but any living person can equally well be part of it." (One would be hard put to find so many superlatives in any other passage of Kafka's.) He told her that putting herself at the Home's disposition was infinitely more important than the theater, than Klabund, or whatever. It was also, he said, one of the most selfish of matters. One was not helping, one was seeking help, there was more honey to be gleaned from this work than from all the flowers in the forests of Marienbad—he was downright greedy for news of her participation. As for Zionism, he added, which he did not sufficiently know, she need not fear. The Home was bringing out other aptitudes of hers, which were much more crucial to him.

In Marienbad, he had read a book on the life of Countess Zinzendorf, he admired her attitude and her "almost superhuman labor" in directing the Moravian Church. He speaks of her often; and with every suggestion he now makes, he thinks of her as an admittedly quite unattainable model for Felice. "When the countess, after her wedding at twenty-two, came to her new Dresden home, which Zinzendorf's grandmother had furnished for the young couple in a way that was affluent by contemporary standards, she burst into tears." Then comes a pious statement by the young countess about her innocence in regard to this trumpery and her plea that God's grace may hold her soul fast and avert her eyes from all foolishness of the world. Kafka added the following: "To be engraved in a tablet and mounted over the furniture store."

In the course of time, Kafka's attempt at influencing Felice grew into an all-out campaign, and it was clear what he was after. He wanted to wean Felice from her bourgeois habits, as it were, exorcise the furniture, which, for him, embodied all that is horrible and hateful in bourgeois marriage. She was to learn how little the office and the family mean as the life form of selfishness, and he contrasted them with the humble work of helping in a home for refugee children. But his way of pestering her revealed a measure of parsonical tyranny that one would scarcely have expected from him. He demanded an account of her every step bringing her closer to the Home and then every detail of her activity there once she was accepted. There is a letter in which he asks her some twenty questions, he becomes more and more insatiable, he can never hear enough about it. He egged her on, criticized her, took part in working on a talk she was to give in the Home, to which end he studied Friedrich Wilhelm Förster's *Apprenticeship of Youth*. He selected things to read for the children in her Home, even sending her—from Prague—the juvenile editions of some works that he considered especially suitable. With meticulous pendantry, he kept coming back to the topic over and again in his letters, he asked Felice for pictures of her among her children, whom he wanted to get to know from afar by carefully studying the photographs. He praised Felice rhapsodically when he was satisfied with her, and this praise sounded so intense, that she had to regard it as love; it always came when she did what he told her to do. Bit by bit it did come to be a sort of submission and obedience that he expected from her. Correcting his image of her, changing her character, without which he could not imagine a future life with her—it all gradually turned into controlling her.

Thus he took part in her activity, for which, as he put it in a letter, his own devotion would be lacking; what she did, she did in lieu of him. He, in contrast, needed more and more solitude, which he got on Sunday strolls in the environs of Prague, at first in the company of his sister Ottla, whom he admired like a fiancée. An acquaintance from his office, who met them together, even mistook Ottla for his fiancée, and Kafka did not hesitate to tell Felice about it.

He now had a new pleasure in his free time: lying in the grass. "Recently, I was lying . . . almost in the road ditch (but this year the grass is high and thick even in the ditch), when a rather distinguished gentleman, with whom I sometimes have official dealings, drove past in a carriage and pair on the way to a even more distinguished festivity. I stretched out and felt the joys of . . . being declassé." While strolling with Ottla near Prague, he discovered two wonderful places, both "as quiet as paradise after the expulsion of man." Later, he also walked alone: "Do you really know the joys of being alone, walking alone, lying alone in the sun? . . . Have you ever walked far alone? The faculty for that requires a great deal of past sorrow and also a great deal of happiness. I know I was alone a great deal as a boy, but I was forced to be alone, it was seldom a voluntary happiness. Now, however, I run towards solitude like water towards the sea." Another time, he wrote: "I walked very far, for about five hours, alone and not alone enough, in deserted valleys, yet not deserted enough."

Thus the inner premises developed for a country life, which he later shared with Ottla in Zürau. At the same time, he tried to bind Felice more and more strongly to the community in the Jewish People's Home. During the week, he continued his life as an official, though it filled him with mounting repugnance, so much that he still thought of escaping to the war; as a soldier, he at least would not be spared. Meanwhile, Felice justified him with her activity in the Home.

Still, his letters of this period often mention his writing as well. Since this was a time in which he did not feel capable of any new work, he usually told about the fate of earlier stories, about publications, and also about reviews. In September, he informed her of being asked to give a reading in Munich. He liked giving readings, felt like going, and wanted her to attend; but he refuses her suggestions to meet him in Berlin or Prague. Berlin frightens him with the memory of the engagement and the "trial," which, however, are seldom referred to in his letters, two years separate him from that time. But when place names in Berlin do stir up his recollection, he does not hesitate to show how keen the pains of those days still are. Prague frightens him with the thought of his family; he could not avoid letting Felice sit at his parents' table, and her inclusion would strengthen the family, that superior power which he incessantly resists with feeble strength. In keeping Felice away from Prague, he acted like a politician trying to prevent the union of two of his potential enemies.

Hence, he dwelt obstinately on the plan of meeting in Munich. They corresponded about it for two months. He knew that a reading would be a source of strength for him; Felice, too, as she was now, obedient and making an effort, likewise gave him energy. Both wellsprings would join together and increase one another in Munich. But it changed nothing in the peculiar manner of his *decisions*. Again, he went through his familiar waverings: the trip was probable but not yet definite, there were external threats that could ruin it. After two months of discussion, just five days before the trip, he wrote: "It is more and more probable every day. In any case, on Wednesday or Thursday, I'll send you a wire with the lovely words: 'We are going,' or the sad word 'No.' "—On Friday, he took off.

The absolute peculiarity of Kafka's state of mind is shown by his inability to learn from mistakes. Failure after failure are never multiplied into success for him. The difficulties always remain the same, as though their invincible nature had to be demonstrated. His countless reflections and calculations always consistently leave out the one thing that could spell success. The freedom to fail is always protected, as a kind of supreme law, it is meant to guarantee an escape at any new juncture; one might call it the freedom of the weak man, who seeks salvation in defeats. The prohibition of victories expresses his true uniqueness, his special relationship to power. All reckonings derive from powerlessness and lead back to it.

Thus, despite all his experience with the failures of brief encounters, he gambled the achievement of the four months: his control of Felice by means of the Berlin Jewish Home—gambled it on that one Saturday together in Munich. Everything in Munich was unfamiliar: the locales, the people, the course of the reading on Friday after a day in a train, the sequel on Saturday. But he did risk it, as though it contained a secret possibility of freedom. Eventually, in a "horrible *Konditorei*," they had a quarrel, about which no details are known. Felice, who had been striving for so long to oblige him in everything, seemed to have rebelled. Her sudden outbursts hardly excelled in subtlety, she accused him of being selfish, and it was an old reproach. He could not just take it; it struck him deeply, for, as he himself later wrote, it was correct. But his greatest selfishness, greatest by far, was his *obstinacy,* and this allowed only *his* reproaches of himself. "My sense of guilt is always strong enough, it requires no nourishment from outside, but my constitution is not strong enough to choke down such nourishment frequently."

Thus ended the second flowering of their relationship: this close rapport had lasted for four months. One can readily compare these four months with that first period from September to December 1912: both periods were marked by the hope and strength that Kafka drew from Felice. Yet that early period was an ecstatic time of writing, whereas the second period was devoted to the change in Felice's character and her adjustment to his values. His writing, during the first period, dried up because of his disappointment. This time, his estrangement from her had the reverse effect; it brought him back to writing.

He returned from Munich with new courage. The reading was a "huge failure"; he had read "In the Penal Colony." "I came with my story as a travel vehicle to a city that did not concern me except as a meeting place and a bleak childhood memory, I read my filthy story in total indifference, no empty hole in a stove could be colder, I was then together with strange people, which seldom happens here." The reviews were bad, he agreed with them, it was, he said, "fantastic arrogance" on his part to give a public reading after—as he exaggerated—not writing anything for two years. (However, in Munich, he had also found out that Rilke had a high regard for him, especially liking "The Stoker," which he preferred to *Metamorphosis* and "In the Penal Colony.") But this very arrogance—the public appearance, the fact that there were verdicts and chiefly negative ones, the defeat and the grandeur of the failure amid new people—actually exhilarated Kafka. If we add the quarrel with Felice, which gave him an inner detachment to her, without which he could not write, then his new courage after his return is understandable.

He immediately began looking for an apartment, and this time he was lucky: Ottla rented a small house for herself in *Alchimistengasse,* furnishing a room for him to write in. It was a very quiet room, and he soon made himself at home. He refused to see Felice at Christmas, and she complained about headaches for the first time in four years, she had taken them over from him. He was almost disdainful in mentioning the Home, which they had talked about so much in the past. It was now to do its job of holding her and fixing her, but that was all.

He had good moments at Ottla's. It was better than ever before during the last two years. "It is strange when one locks one's door in this narrow street under the starlight. . . . It's nice living here, nice wandering home around midnight down the old castle stairs to the town below." Here he wrote "A Country Doctor," "The New Advocate," "In the Gallery," "Jackals and Arabs," and "The Next Village," which were later included in the collection *The Country Doctor.* Here he also wrote "The Bridge," "The Hunter Gracchus," and "The Bucket Rider." What these tales had in common was spaciousness, transformation (no longer into smallness), and movement.

The final phase of his relationship to Felice is scarcely present in Kafka's letters. A letter from around New Year's Day of 1917 deals with the pros and cons of an apartment in the Schönborn Palace, he is very thorough and, as he himself would reproachfully term it, "calculating," with six points against and five for it. His letter presumes they will live together after the war. This apartment would be ready for Felice, who would then recuperate, at least for two or three months. However, she would have to do without a kitchen or bathroom. One cannot say that her presence is taken into account very convincingly; she figures in only one of the eleven points. But nevertheless, she does figure; and, even more important, she is to think everything over carefully and give advice.

No postcard or letter is extant from the year 1917, though he must have written to her at least occasionally until August; the first sign of life is in September. That February, Kafka had moved into the apartment at the Schönborn Palace. Here, he wrote further tales, which wound up in the *Country Doctor* volume, as well as very important things that were never published during his lifetime, for instance *While Constructing the Great Wall of China*. He was not quite unsatisfied with this period, as he stated in a letter to Kurt Wolff in July 1917.

Whatever happened between him and Felice during that same month of July can be gleaned only from other sources; hence, the presentation cannot be as precise as before. July was the month of the second official betrothal. The war was still going strong, and they seem to have jumped ahead with their original plan. Felice came to Prague; one might assume that she lived at the Schönborn Palace, but a few things speak against it. Kafka paid official betrothal visits with her to his friends. Brod records their rather stiff and slightly ridiculous visit in his home. They again went out to buy furniture and find an apartment; perhaps Felice was unhappy with the Schönborn Palace and insisted on a bathroom and kitchen from the very beginning. She carried 900 crowns about in her handbag, an unusually high sum. In a letter to Frau Weltsch about a temporary loss of this very bag, Kafka specifically mentions his "fiancée." He probably overdid the official actions and titles of this sort. It has already been said that it was not in his character to learn from earlier experience. But perhaps, without fully realizing it, he was aiming at the old kind of tribulations in order to *have* to escape. In the second half of July, he and Felice visited her sister in Arad, Hungary. There must have been some sort of falling-out during the trip. Perhaps the confrontation with a member of her family was necessary for hastening the rupture. In Budapest, he left Felice and went back alone, via Vienna, to Prague. The memoirs of Rudolf Fuchs, whom he saw in Vienna, contain some of Kafka's statements, which would indicate that a definite break with Felice had occurred or was intended. Kafka wrote her two letters from Prague, which are not preserved, and in which he probably went very far.

He was now truly resolved to break off with her, but since he didn't trust in his own strength, he had a hemorrhage two days after the second letter, on the night of August 9, 1917. A much later description would make it appear that he somewhat exaggerated the duration of his hemorrhage. But there is no doubt that he did lose blood from his lungs, quite suddenly late at night, and that this glaring event had very earnest consequences for him—if for no other reason than poetically, through the notion of a "blood wound." Even though he subsequently felt relieved, he consulted a physician, that Dr. Mühlstein, whose "bodily mass" put him at ease. The latter's reaction is not quite clear, but Kafka's account was enough to frighten Brod. It took him a few weeks to talk Kafka into seeking out a specialist. For Kafka, from the very start, was quite aware of the true reasons for his illness, and not even the prospect of freedom, more important to him than anything else, made it easy to surrender forever to official medicine, which he so obstinately distrusted. The visit to the specialist on September 4 launched a new period in his life. The pronouncement by this authority, whom he forced himself to recognize, rescued him from Felice, his fear of the marriage, and his hated job. But it tied him for all time to the disease of which he ultimately died and which may not even have been so serious at that moment.

Indeed, the earliest statement about the specialist's finding, in Brod's diary on the very same day, does not sound all so perilous. There was a double apicitis and a *danger* of tuberculosis. The fever, as it soon turned out, disappeared altogether. But the unusual medical arrangements focused on a plan to escape, which was indispensable for Kafka's spiritual salvation. It was decided that he should go to the country—at first, for three months. The place had been—it cannot be put any other way—prepared long ago: Ottla's farm in Zürau. During four weeks, Felice heard nothing about all that. It was only when the plan was irrevocable, on September 9, three days before his moving to Zürau, that he finally wrote her a first and very serious letter. Perhaps this letter should have expressly told her of his harsh decision to break off their relationship once and for all. But after her long silence following his two August letters, she had written to him again conciliatingly and as though there were no problem between them; and he had received her friendly letters, rather inopportunely for him, on September 5, the day after his visit to the specialist. "Today," he informed Brod, "two letters came from F., calm, friendly, with no resentment, just as I see her in my sweetest dreams. Now it is hard to write her."

But he did write her, on September 9, dramatically summing up the events concerning his lungs. He talks a great deal about blood and emphatically about tuberculosis. For his sake, they do not wish to retire him, he will remain on active duty and be given a leave of absence for at least three months. His parents are not to find out anything for the time being. The only thing she might view as a lasting threat to herself is the conclusion. He writes "poor, dear Felice," and the "poor," which we know so well in his correspondence, now strikes us for the first time, when he is writing about his ailment, as though it referred to her and not himself. "Shall it become the steady final word of my letters? It is not a knife that only cuts forward, it circles and also stabs back."

In a postscript, he adds that he has been feeling better than previously since that hemorrhage. This was true, but perhaps he merely wanted to prevent her from flying to him in sudden alarm.

The period in Zürau began on September 12. The very first letter to Brod sounded as if it came from another world. He couldn't write on the first day because he liked everything too much, nor did he care to exaggerate as he ought to have done. But even the next day, he wrote: "Ottla really carries me on her wings through the difficult world, the room . . . is excellent, airy, warm, and the house almost perfectly silent; everything I am supposed to eat is in abundance here . . . and freedom, above all freedom.

". . . . At any rate, today I relate to tuberculosis like a child holding on to its mother's apron strings. Sometimes I feel as if my brain and my lung had come to terms without my knowledge. 'Things can't go on like this,' the brain said, and after five years, the lung agreed to help."

And the next letter: "I am living in a good little marriage with Ottla; matrimony not on the basis of the usual violent short circuit, but with the current that goes straight ahead through small curvings. We have a nice household, which you people will, I hope, like." However, there is a shadow on this letter. "F. sent a few lines to say she was coming. I don't understand her, she's extraordinary. . ."

She came; her visit is mentioned in a diary entry, which I shall

136

quote in part: "September 21, F. was here, traveled thirty hours to see me. I should have prevented it. As I picture it, she bears an extreme misfortune, essentially because of me. I don't understand myself either, I am totally unfeeling, equally helpless, I think of the interference with my own comforts and my only concession is to playact."

The penultimate letter to Felice, the longest one, written ten days after her visit to Zürau, is Kafka's most disagreeable letter; it takes an effort to quote from it. Meanwhile, she had written to him twice; he at first did not open her letters, he let them lie about. He tells her this right at the start, and also that he finally did read them. He was ashamed by what they contained, but he sees himself even more sharply than she saw him, this has been true for some time, and he wants to explain the sight that he offers.

Now comes the myth of the two warriors in him, it is a false and ignoble myth. The image of struggle cannot capture his inner processes, it distorts them by virtually heroicizing his loss of blood, as though there had actually been a gory struggle. But even if this image were accepted, it instantly inveigles him into a falsehood: he claims that the better of the two warriors belongs to her, there is nothing he has been doubting less during the past few days. However, we know that this struggle, or whatever one may call it, ended long ago and that nothing belongs to her, especially during the past few days. Should we see this untruthful statement as a solace for her, something like chivalry towards the humiliated and rejected woman? Nevertheless, this is soon followed by a sentence which deserves being quoted as a sentence of Kafka's: "I am a mendacious person, I cannot maintain balance any other way, my boat is very leaky." He moves on to a long paragraph, which sums up his self-perception. The paragraph is successful, it merits a place in literature; he liked it so much that he copied it verbatim in a letter to Max Brod and once again in his diary. Let it remain there, but the reader will understand why we will do without it here. Then comes a long piece on the eventful destinies of the two warriors and the blood that was shed. He goes on to a line that occupies him seriously: "I secretly regard this disease as not being tuberculosis or at least not primarily tuberculosis but as my general bankruptcy." Still, the blood and the struggle are not yet over, and further inferences are drawn from them. All at once, he writes: "Do not ask why I put up a barrier. Do not humiliate me like that." Here he is quite firmly saying that he is ridding himself of her and that there is no explanation; and if the letter consisted of just those two lines, it would have the power of a Biblical utterance. He then softens it with an empty gesture, but suddenly finds himself face to face with the truth: "The real or alleged tuberculosis," he says, "is a weapon, next to which the almost countless ones used up earlier, from 'physical incapacity' up to 'work' and down to 'avarice' appear utterly practical and primitive."

Finally, he tells her a secret which he momentarily does not believe himself, but which must be true: he will never get well again. He thereby deadens himself for her and withdraws from her through a kind of future suicide.

Thus, the substance of this letter was dictated by a striving to escape further annoyances from her. Since he had no feelings whatsoever left for her, he had no real comfort for her either. The happiness in Zürau, a happiness of freedom, offered no airs of grief, not even airs of regret.

The last letter to Felice is dated October 16 and reads as though it were not meant for her. He pushes her far away, even though she is already remote, his glassy sentences do not contain her, they seem to be addressed to someone else. He begins by quoting a letter from Max Brod: Kafka's letters, his friend had written, testify to great calm, and he must be happy in his unhappiness. By way of confirmation, he describes Felice's last visit. This description may be accurate, it is certainly colder than ice. "You were unhappy about the senseless trip, my incomprehensible behavior, about everything. I was not unhappy." He felt the whole misery less when he saw and recognized it and calmly limited himself, in that acknowledgment, to keeping his lips firmly, very firmly closed. The body of the letter consists of an answer to Max Brod, quoted approximately; he had sent it four days earlier. His physical state is excellent, he hardly dares to ask about hers. With detailed reasons, he has asked Max, Felix, and Baum not to visit him—a warning to *her* not to return.

The final paragraph goes: "I do not know Kant, but the statement should probably only apply to the nations, it can scarcely be meant for civil wars, 'internal wars,' where the peace is only the kind that one wishes on the ashes."

He was thereby rejecting a wish for peace that Felice had dressed up in a line of Kant's. With the peace that one wishes on ashes, he withdrew even more emphatically behind death than at the end of the previous letter. His simultaneous and detailed correspondence with his best friends never once mentions ashes.

The fact that the illness, once a device, ultimately became true cannot be accepted as a rationale. The justification is to be found in that new series of jottings, the "Third Octavo Notebook," which he began two days after the final letter to Felice. His earlier diary breaks off for years. The next-to-last entry, virtually belated, contains the following lines: "I have not yet written down the decisive thing, I am still flowing in two directions. The work to be done is enormous."

1968

WORD ATTACKS

Address at the Bavarian Academy
of the Fine Arts

It would be presumptuous of me and it would certainly be pointless to tell you what we owe to language. I am only a guest in the German language, which I learned at the age of eight, and the fact that you are welcoming me in it today means more to me than if I had been born in its realm. I cannot even regard it as a credit that I held on to German when I came to England over thirty years ago and decided to remain. For continuing to write in German there was as much a matter of course as breathing and walking. I could not have done otherwise, another possibility was never even considered. Furthermore, I was the willing prisoner of several thousand books that I had been fortunate enough to bring along, and I do not doubt that they would have viewed me as an apostate from their midst had I made even the slightest change in my relationship to them.

But perhaps I can tell you something about what happens to language under such circumstances. How does it resist the unflagging pressure of the new environment? Does anything alter in its aggregate state, in its specific weight? Does it become more domineering, more aggressive? Or does it turn into itself and hide? Does it grow more intimate? After all, it might conceivably become a secret language, that one uses only for oneself.

Well, the first thing to happen was that one confronted it with a different sort of curiosity. One compared more, especially in the most everyday phrases, in which the differences were conspicuous and palpable. Literary confrontations turned into very concrete encounters in socializing. The earlier or chief language became odder and odder, namely in details. *Everything* about it was conspicuous, whereas earlier only a few things were that.

At the same time, one could sense a lessening of self-complaisance. For one personally saw cases of writers who had given up and gone over to the new country's language for practical reasons. They lived, so to speak, in the vanity of their new effort, which was meaningful only if it succeeded. How often did I hear both gifted and ungifted people say in almost silly pride: "I now write English!" Yet the man who clung to the earlier written language, and without any prospect of achieving some external goal, must have regarded himself as abdicating in terms of the public. He competed with no one, he was alone, he was also a bit ridiculous. He was in a predicament, it seemed hopeless, the people sharing his fate might consider him a fool, and the people in the host country, among whom he did have to live, viewed him for a long time as a nobody.

Under such circumstances, it can be expected that many things become more private and more intimate. One says certain things to oneself that one would otherwise never have let pass. The conviction that nothing will ever come of it, that it has to remain private—no readership is conceivable, after all—gives one a bizarre sense of freedom. Among all these people who speak their daily things in English, one has a secret language for oneself, which serves no outer purposes anymore, which one utilizes nearly alone, to which one clings more and more obstinately, the way people may cling to a faith that is taboo in their greater environment.

Well, that is the more superficial aspect of the matter; there is a further aspect, that one realizes only gradually. A man with literary interests tends to assume it is the works of writers that represent a language to one. To some extent, that is certainly the case; and ultimately, one does live on them. But the discoveries one makes by living in the realm of a different language includes a very special one: namely, that it is the words themselves that do not let one go, the individual words per se, beyond any larger intellectual contexts. The peculiar strength and energy of words can be felt most strongly when one is often forced to replace them with others. The dictionary of the hardworking student who has striven to learn a foreign tongue is suddenly reversed, everything wants to be named as it was named earlier and actually. The second language, which one hears all the time any-way, becomes banal, it is taken for granted; the first language, de-fending itself, appears in a special light.

I recall that in England, during the war, I filled page after page with German words. They had nothing to do with what I was work-ing on. Nor did they join together into any sentences, and naturally they did not figure in the notes I jotted down in those years. They were isolated words, never yielding any sense. It would suddenly take me by storm, and I would cover a few pages with words, as fast as lightning. Very often they were nouns, but not exclusively; there were also verbs and adjectives among them. I was ashamed of these attacks and concealed the pages from my wife. I spoke German with her; she had come with me from Vienna. I know of very little else that I ever concealed from her.

I viewed those word attacks as pathological and did not wish to make her uneasy; like all other people, we had enough things to make us uneasy and that could not be concealed. Perhaps I should also mention that it really goes against my grain to smash words or warp them in any manner, their form is inviolable for me, I leave it intact. Thus, one can hardly imagine a more foolish occupation than string-ing together unscathed words. When I sensed that such a word attack was imminent, I would lock myself in as though to work. I ask your forgiveness for bringing up such a private absurdity, but I must add that I felt extremely happy during such fits. Since then, there has been no doubt for me that words are charged with a special kind of passion. They are really like human beings, they refuse to be ne-glected or forgotten. However they may be preserved, they maintain their life; they suddenly spring forth and demand their rights.

Word attacks of that sort are certainly a sign that the pressure on language has gotten very great, that one not only knows—in this case—English well, but also that it very often forces itself upon one. A rearrangement has formed in the dynamics of words. The frequency of what one hears leads not only to one's noting it, but also to new inducements and suggestions, motions and countermotions. Many an old, current word freezes in the struggle with its adversary. Others rise above any context and radiate in their irreplaceability.

This is not a case—as must be stressed—of mastering a foreign tongue at home, in a room, with a teacher, backed up by all the people who speak as one is accustomed to hearing in one's own town, at all hours of the day. Actually, one is at the mercy of the foreign tongue in *its* precinct, where all people are on its side, and together and with a semblance of legality, they smash in on one with their words, heedlessly, steadfastly, and incessantly. Furthermore, one knows one remains, one does not go back—not after a few weeks, not after months, not after years. Hence, it is crucial to understand everything one hears; that, as everyone knows, is the hardest thing at first. Then one keeps imitating until it too is understood. In addition, something happens in reference to the earlier language: one has to make sure it does not intrude at the wrong time. So it is gradually repressed, one encloses it, one propitiates it, one puts it on a leash; and as much as one secretly fondles and caresses it, in public it feels neglected and rejected. No wonder that it sometimes takes revenge and ambushes one with swarms of words, which remain isolated, do not join into any meaning, and whose onslaught would be so ludicrous for others that it merely forces one to be even more secretive.

It may seem highly inappropriate to make such an ado about these private linguistic situations. In a time when everything is getting more and more enigmatic, when the existence of not just individual groups but literally all mankind is at stake, when no decision turns out to be a solution, for there are too many mutually contradictory possibilities, and no one is capable of even sensing most of them, because too much is happening, and we find it out too soon, and before we have even grasped it, we are already finding out the next thing—in a time that is swift, menacing, and rich, and developing more and more richly because of that menace, in such a time, if a man takes the liberty of thinking, one would expect something different from him than the tale of the agon of words, occurring independently of their meaning.

If, however, I *have* said a little about that, then I owe you an explanation. It strikes me that today's man, charged with more and more in his fascination with the universal, is seeking a private sphere, which is not unworthy of him, which is clearly distinct from the generality, yet is perfectly and more accurately reflected in it. What I mean is a kind of translation from one into the other, not a translation that one selects as a free game of the mind, but one that is both incessant and necessary, forced by the constellations of external life, and yet is more than a compulsion. For many years now, I have been involved in this translation; however, the private sphere in which I have settled now, albeit not comfortably, and in which things should be conscientious and responsible, is the German language. Whether I shall succeed in satisfying it in this fashion—I cannot say. But the honor which you have paid me today, and for which I thank you, is something that I shall take as a propitious omen that I might still succeed.

1969

HITLER,
ACCORDING TO SPEER
Grandeur and Permanence

Hitler's architectural plans are perhaps the most astonishing thing transmitted to us by Speer in his book. Since they are presented in pictures and stand in flagrant contrast to everything that modern architecture is striving for, they have caused the greatest sensation. They are unforgettable for anyone who has even casually glanced at them.

But one cannot be content with such cheap statements. There is no relying on the uniqueness of such phenomena. It is necessary to focus more carefully on them and to determine what they *consist* of, what they are really made of.

The first obvious thing is—as Speer himself emphasizes—the adjacency of construction and destruction. The plans for the new Berlin come from the time of peace. Their completion is slated for the year 1950. Even Speer, the miracle-worker, who gained Hitler's trust with the speed of his performance, would not have had an easy time meeting that deadline. The passion with which Hitler followed these plans makes it impossible to doubt that they were serious. But at the same time, he developed his plan to conquer the world. Step by step, and from victory to victory, he revealed the scope and seriousness of this goal too. It could not conceivably come true without war, and so war was taken into account from the very start. However strong the position that could be reached without war, a war was nevertheless inevitable. The *Reich,* which by stressing the Germans and perhaps all "Germanics" was ultimately to enslave the entire world, could operate only with terror; much blood *had* to flow. And so he consistently entangled himself in war. The simultaneity of this entanglement with the deadlines for completing the construction plans would make it seem that Hitler wanted the latter to hide his military aims. This is a possibility that Speer himself weighs, and yet he is not satisfied with it. One has to agree when he takes both sides of Hitler's nature for granted and does not subordinate one to the other. Both desires, construction and destruction, are acutely present, adjacent, and operative in Hitler.

Even the strong impression that the building projects make on the spectator today is determined by that fact. While poring over these plans, one is aware of the dreadful destruction of the German cities. One knows the ending; and now, suddenly, the beginning is presented in its full scope. This adjacency is what makes such a confrontation shattering. It seems enigmatic and inexplicable. Yet it is the most concentrated utterance of what makes us uneasy beyond Hitler. It is basically the one undeniable and recurrent outcome of all previous "history."

It compels us to thoroughly investigate that sudden focusing of history, as which one can regard Hitler's appearance. It is impossible to turn away in disgust and repugnance, which would be natural. Nor is it enough to accept the usual methods of historical inquiry. Their inadequacy is obvious. Where is the historian who could have offered a prognosis of Hitler? Even if a particularly conscientious historiography could now manage to remove forever its inherent admiration of power from its circulatory system, it would at best be able to warn against a new Hitler. But since he would turn up elsewhere, he would appear different, and the warning would be idle.

The full grasp of this phenomenon requires new methods. One has to perceive them, draw on them, and employ them wherever they are to be found. The method for such an inquiry cannot yet exist. The rigor of the disciplines turns out to be superstition here. The things that elude them are precisely the crucial ones. An integral contemplation of the phenomenon itself is the supreme requirement. Any arrogance of concept, wherever else it may have proved its value, is harmful.

Hitler's constructions are meant to attract and to hold the greatest crowds. The creation of such crowds is what brought him to power, but he knows how easily great crowds tend to fall apart. Aside from war, there are only two ways of preventing that. One way is their *growth,* the other their regular *repetition.* As an empiricist of crowds, such as few have existed, he knows both their forms and their methods.

On huge squares, so big that they are hard to fill, the crowd has the possibility of growing, it remains open. Its passion, which he is especially aiming at, increases with its growth. He and his helpers are quite familiar with everything involved in forming such crowds: flags, music, marching units, which operate as crowd-crystals, and especially a long wait for the appearance of the main figure. We need not describe these things in detail. The important thing is to point out the insight into the openness of the crowd, its possibility of growth, in terms of the kind of construction plans.

For the regular *repetition,* he wanted buildings of a cultic nature. Their model is the cathedral. The *"Kuppelberg,"* planned for Berlin, is to be seventeen times as large as St. Peter's. Ultimately, such buildings serve *closed* crowds. However large they are meant to be, once they are full, the crowd can no longer grow, it bumps into a limit. Instead of further growth, the aim here is regular repetition. The crowd, breaking up when leaving such a space, should confidently look ahead to the next time it forms.

At sporting events, the crowd appears as a closed—or also half-closed—ring; countless people sit facing one another, the crowd *sees itself* while following the events that occur in its midst. As soon as two parties form, a two-crowd system arises, egged on by the struggles being presented. For this system, the models come from Roman Antiquity.

A different form of crowd, which I have called the *slow* crowd, forms in processions, parades, and marches. I do not want to repeat what I have said about this form in *Crowds and Power.* But Hitler was quite cognizant of its importance. It is especially served in his plans by a splendid boulevard that is 120 meters wide and five kilometers long.

These edifices and areas, which are so large as to seem cold and standoffish even on paper, are filled—in their builder's mind—with crowds that behave differently according to the nature of the vessel holding them, according to the nature of their delimitation. One would expect a precise picture of the events here, but that would require describing the course of a crowd occurrence in each single one of these places from start to finish. That cannot be our task now; it should suffice to generally emphasize the way those buildings and areas would be animated.

It is an animation that continues beyond the death of the builder. "Your husband," he says solemnly to Speer's wife on the first evening they meet, "will erect buildings for me such as have not arisen for four thousand years." He is thinking of Egypt, particularly the pyramids, because of their size, but also because they have always existed during these four thousand years. They could not be concealed in any way and were not covered by anything, no event could do anything to them; it is as though they had stored up their millennia, for which they were meant, as permanence. Their public character and their permanence have deeply impressed him; the fact that the way they were built makes them serve as crowd symbols may not have been clear to him; but with his instinct for everything connected to crowds, he must have sensed it. For these constructions, whose parts were dragged together and joined together through the efforts of countless people, are the symbol of a crowd that cannot crumble.

His buildings, however, were not pyramids and were to take over only their size and permanence. They contained space that was to be refilled by the living crowds of every generation. They were to be constructed of the most resistant stone, for one thing because of permanence, but also to join the tradition of the edifices that had lasted until his time.

There are no problems in understanding these tendencies in terms of the builder's mind. Naturally, the issue of permanence per se is a precarious thing and would have to be well thought out in regard to its nature and its value. But assuming that man is inspired with an urge for permanence, in a heedless way that prohibits asking about its sense or senselessness, one can readily comprehend that the urge will find utterance in such plans.

The crowds through whose arousal he came to power are to be rearoused, over and over again, even when he is no longer here. Since his successors will not be able to achieve that end in his fashion, for he is unique, he leaves behind the best kinds of assistance, well-prepared places of any kind that serve the tradition of crowd arousal. The fact that they are his buildings gives them a special aura: he hopes to live long enough to dedicate them and to imbue them with himself for several years. The memory of his very own crowds, whom he has aroused himself, shall aid his weaker successors. It is possible, and even probable, that they do not deserve this legacy; but nevertheless, the power he has acquired through his crowds will thereby survive.

For of course, the crux is ultimately power. Next to the "crowd containers," there is also something that one might call courtliness, the seat of power: his *Reichskanzlei* or chancellery—his palace—and not too far away the seats of the ministries, which draw their power from him. For his special whim, he thinks of preserving the old Reichstag building. This aim may be inspired by the difference in size. How small the old Reichstag will look next to the new colossuses!

His scorn for the Weimar period, whose sole purpose was to help his rise, will impart itself to all who notice the Reichstag dwarf in the shadow of his giant monuments. We were so small, and he has made us so big. But reverence for his history is involved. Many important things for him took place in that Reichstag, and so it has to be included among the places of his cult.

However, he has a superstitious veneration for his own rise. It is not enough for him that every phase has been officially recorded, which he takes for granted from a servile historiography; he also speaks about it himself, within the circle of his larger and smaller court. He talks about it for hours, over and over again. The stories of his difficulties and the changes in his fortune are so familiar to his listeners that they could continue each tale were he to lapse into silence. Sometimes he does lapse into silence and falls asleep.

He has a special liking for the town of his youth, Linz. He can forget nothing and so he also remembers with what scorn Linz was treated by the Viennese government. He still bears a deep grudge against Vienna, he had a very bad time there; not even his triumphal entry there in March 1938 could reconcile him with Vienna, and the only thing that interests him now as ever is the Ring with its splendid edifices. He cannot forgive the city for letting the Danube flow to its left. In contrast, Linz is to become a second Budapest, with grand buildings along both shores of the Danube. It will be the place for his old age, and that is where he wishes to put up his tomb. Linz will ultimately become more important than Vienna, and the imposing new buildings will avenge the humiliations of his early time. A pet notion of his is to have Linz *outdo* Vienna.

Since this word has now cropped up, it would seem to be time to say something about the role of *outdoing* in Hitler. It may offer the best opportunity of getting close to the mechanisms of his mind. Each enterprise of his and even his deepest wishes are dictated by a compulsion to outdo: One may go so far as to say that he is a *slave of outdoing.* But he is by no means alone in that. If we had to sum up the essence of our society in a single feature, we sould simply point out: the compulsion to outdo. In Hitler, this obsession has reached such proportions that one cannot help running into it all the time. Conceivably, it explains something of his inner emptiness, about which Speer, towards the end of his book, finds remarkable words.

Everything competes, and all people compete in struggle, and the person who outdoes is a never-ending winner. The idea of the indispensability of fighting and the legitimation of all demands by victories is so deeply rooted in Hitler that, while never taking into account a defeat for himself, he nevertheless approves of destruction and annihilation for his own side in case it should ever be defeated. The stronger is the *better,* the stronger deserves to win. So long as it is possible, he achieves bloodless victories by outwitting his opponents. He regards those victories as strengthening the real decision, which must be bloody, nothing is truly valid without bloodshed. He laughs till tears come at the quickly broken treaties that Ribbentrop has concluded and feels so proud of. He cannot take treaties seriously, if for no other reason than that they cost no blood; and he considers the other side's politicians decadent because they rely on treaties and fear war.

But wars alone do not show his delight in competing and outdoing. He is simply infested with it, competitiveness is practiced incessantly and in every way, it is applied as a kind of panacea to everything. He sees it as crucial to entrust one and the same task to two different people, so that they will try to outdo each other.

There is nothing conspicuous anywhere on earth that would not arouse Hitler's competitiveness. Napoleon is doubtless the figure who challenges him the most. The Champs-Elysées, leading to the Arc de Triomphe, is two kilometers in length: his splendid avenue will not only be wider but stretch for five kilometers. The Arc de Triomphe is fifty meters high, his Triumphbogen will be 120 meters high. Napoleon's aim was to unify Europe: *he* will succeed in that and his unification will last. His Russian campaign is prescribed by Napoleon. The energy he produced for this undertaking, the stubborn hold on the conquered positions that could not be held anymore, a stubborn hold despite all advice and better knowledge, can also be explained by a compulsion to surpass Napoleon. He wants to hold the Caucasus as a base for pushing on to Persia, whereby he identifies with Napoleon's plans for India. The fact that Napoleon, in turn, felt spurred by Alexander the Great shows that the only historical tradition to seem unextinguishable is that of the men who keep trying to outdo their past models.

There are more trivial achievements that stick in his mind. The tribune of honor in Nuremberg is crowned by a figure that outstrips the Statue of Liberty by fourteen meters. The Grand Stadium in the same city will hold two or three times more people than the Circus Maximus in Rome. Todt designs a suspension bridge for Hamburg which will surpass San Francisco's Golden Gate Bridge. The Zentralbahnhof in Berlin should rout New York's Grand Central Station. The dome of the enormous Meeting Hall ought to contain Washington's Capitol Building, Rome's St. Peter's, and a few other places as well. Speer in no way disguises his own part in these "overtrumpings." He was, as he points out, intoxicated with the thought of creating stone witnesses to history. "I also excited Hitler when I could prove to him that we had 'beaten' historically outstanding constructions at least in their dimensions." Clearly, he was infected by Hitler's megalomania and incapable of resisting Hitler's increasing trust in him. But back then, he made a remark whose full import perhaps struck him only later: "His passion for edifices for eternity left him completely uninterested in traffic structures, residential areas, and open green spaces: he was indifferent to the social aspect."

The mad notion of outdoing is linked, as I have shown in *Crowds and Power,* to the illusion of *further growth.* This, in turn, is taken as a guarantee of *further life.* Hence, in reality, these plans, stretching over many years, must be viewed as a way of prolonging his life. During this period, he often voices doubts as to his longevity. "I won't be living much longer. I always thought I could take time to carry out my plans. I have to carry them out myself!" These anxieties, with their special tinge, are characteristic of a paranoid nature. The seeming or real vulnerability of the body expresses other dangers, which are connected to the indomitable claim to greatness. In the Schreber case (see *Crowds and Power*), the paranoia was much further developed, and the above connection could be plausibly demonstrated. Such fears certainly do not mean that even the slightest claim to greatness is given up. But there is a "useful" interchange between fears and claims. The plans, about whose execution one is worried because the given time often seems too brief, maintain their greatness or increase in order to *force* a prolongment of life. He *has* to stay alive until 1950, when the plans for the new Berlin are fully carried out, and for another few years, so that he can charge the buildings for his weaker successors, i.e. make them eternal for their function.

The effect of such intense goals in time is quite astonishing, even in regard to less ambitious people. Had it not been for the war, which brought on the catastrophe in Hitler's fate, one can assume that, despite all anxieties and vulnerabilities, he would have lived to see his new Berlin in the year 1950.

THE ARCH OF TRIUMPH

Of all the constructions Hitler plans for Berlin, the Arch of Triumph is closest to his heart (except perhaps for the big domed hall). He designed the Arch as early as 1925; Speer used the design to build a model almost four meters high as a surprise for Hitler's fiftieth birthday in April 1939. A few weeks earlier, his troops had marched into Prague. It seems like a very good time for an arch of triumph. Hitler is profoundly moved by this gift. He is drawn to it over and over again, he gazes at it for long stretches, shows it to his guests; a photograph of it, indicating his delight, is included in Speer's *Memoirs*. Hardly a present has ever struck a deeper chord in the recipient's heart.

Previously, Hitler and Speer had often discussed this Triumph-bogen. It was to reach a height of 120 meters, i.e. twice that of Napoleon's Arc de Triomphe in Paris. "That will at least be a worthy monument to our dead in the World War. The name of every one of our 1,800,000 casualties will be carved in granite!" Those are Hitler's words as recorded by Speer. There is nothing else so tersely summing up Hitler's nature. The defeat of World War I is not acknowledged, it is transformed into a victory and celebrated by a triumphal arch that is twice as big as the one granted to Napoleon for all his victories together. The goal of outdoing Napoleon's victories is thus clearly announced. Since the arch is meant to last for all eternity, it has to be made of hard stone. But actually, it consists of something far more precious: 1,800,000 dead Germans. The name of each single one of these casualties will be carved in granite. They are thereby honored, but are also close together, closer than they ever could be in a crowd. In this enormous number, they constitute Hitler's arch of triumph. They are not yet the corpses of his new war, planned and desired by him, they are the casualties of the first war, in which he himself served like anyone else. *He* survived it but he has remained true to it and has never denied that war. In the awareness of those dead, he has gathered the strength of refusing ever to recognize the outcome of the war. They were his crowd before he had any other; he feels they are the crowd that helped him to achieve power. Without the dead of World War I, he would never have existed. His aim of bringing them together in his Triumphbogen is an acknowledgment of this truth and of his debt to them. Yet it is *his* arch of triumph and it will bear *his* name. Hardly anyone will read many of the other names. Even if 1,800,000 names can actually be carved in, the overwhelming majority will be ignored. Their number is what will lodge in memories, and that enormous number belongs to *his* name.

The feeling for the crowd of the dead is decisive in Hitler. It is his *real* crowd. Without this feeling, he cannot be understood, nor can his beginning, nor can his power, nor what he meant with this power, nor what his undertakings led to. His obsession, which was sinisterly alive, is: those dead.

Victories! Victories!

Victories! Victories! If there is any disastrous feature in Hitler that overrides the others, it is his faith in victories. Once the Germans stop winning, they are no longer his people; and without further ado, he takes away their right to live. They have proven themselves to be the weaker, he can do without them, he wishes their annihilation, which they deserve. Had they kept winning, as was customary under him, they would be a different nation in his eyes. The fact that so many still believe in him, even though their cities lie in ruins and almost nothing can protect them against enemy air attacks, makes no impression on him. Göring's failure, after so many empty promises (he realizes it, for he rants at him about it), is ultimately blamed on the crowd of Germans, for they are no longer able to win.

He actually resents the army for every piece of conquered terrain that it yields. So long as he can, he balks at giving up anything, no matter how many victims it may cost. For he views everything that has been conquered as a piece of his own body. His physical degeneration during the past few weeks in Berlin, which Speer so grippingly describes and which arouses his pity despite everything that he tries to do to obstruct him, is nothing but the shrinking of his power. The paranoiac's body is his power, with which he thrives or shrinks. Until the end, he concentrates on preventing the enemy's desecration of his body. He does order the final battle for Berlin, in order to go under in a struggle, a cliché from the historical plunder that fills his mind. But "I will not fight," he says to Speer, "there is too great a danger that I would only be wounded and fall into the hands of the Russians alive. And I do not want my foes to play havoc with my body. I have ordered my cremation." Without fighting himself, while the others fight, he shall perish; and whatever happens to the others fighting for him, his concern is that nothing should happen to his dead body, for that body is identical for him with his power, the body contains the power.

On the other hand, Goebbels, who dies in his immediate proximity, succeeds in outdoing him even in death. He forces his wife and children to die with him. "My wife and children shall not survive me. The Americans would merely train them to make propaganda against me." Those are his words, as transmitted by Speer. The latter is not permitted to say farewell *alone* to Goebbels' wife, with whom he is friendly. "Goebbels remained at my side persistently. . . . It was only at the end that she indicated what was really moving her: 'How happy I am that at least Harald [her son by her first husband] is still alive.' " The last act of Goebbels' power consists in preventing his children from outliving him. He fears they could be trained in his very own profession—propaganda—against him. The fact that, in the end, he obtains the satisfaction of *this* survival should not be misunderstood as atonement for his activities: they culminate in that.

Hitler's indifference to the fate of his nation, whose greatness and prosperity he claimed so long as the true meaning, as the goal and substance of his life, is obvious in Speer's description—obvious in a way that probably has no comparable example. It is Speer who now suddenly takes over Hitler's earlier alleged role: he tries to save whatever can be saved for the Germans. One cannot help respecting the doggedness of his struggle against Hitler, who has decided upon the total annihilation of the Germans and who still has the power and authority to force that annihilation. Hitler makes absolutely no bones about his intention. "If the war is lost," he tells Speer, "then the people will be lost too. It is not necessary to take into account the foundations that the German people requires for its most primitive survival. On the contrary, it is better to destroy even these things. For the people has proven to be the weaker, and the future belongs exclusively to the stronger Eastern people. All that will be left after this fight will be the inferior sort, for the good have fallen!"

Here the victory is explicitly declared to be the supreme authority. He himself has driven his nation into war, but since it has turned out to be the weaker, even those who are still left shall not survive. The deeper motive is that he does not want to be survived. He cannot prevent the victorious enemies from outliving him. But he *can* destroy the remnants of his own people. He declares them as inferior according to a tried-and-true pattern, "for the good have fallen." Those still alive are in a fair way of becoming vermin in his eyes. But it is not even necessary to push the process of devaluation to its end; it suffices to designate them as inferior, like all the mentally ill before. All the people he has exterminated are awake in him. *The crowd of the murder victims is calling for its increase.*

It is the huge size of their number that he is well aware of; that the fact and the manner of their annihilation were kept secret and were only known to those involved strengthens their effectiveness in him. They have become the biggest crowd available to him, and they are his secret. Like any crowd, they desire increase. Since he cannot add any foes to them—for his foes have gained the upper hand—he feels compelled to add his own people. As many as possible before him and as many as possible after him are to die. Without knowing the inner connections of these events, some of which were still hidden from him, Speer could feel only profound horror at the statements betraying them. It was perfectly blatant what Hitler's destruction orders meant. But their *rationale,* in case of resistance, prompted Speer to wish his death. Today, it is difficult to comprehend that not every German who heard about these orders felt and reacted in the same way.

But all of us, both Germans and non-Germans, have become distrustful of orders after learning about those things. We *know* more, that most dreadful of examples is still close enough to us, and even those who can still believe in orders would turn them over twice before obeying them. In those days, Germans were trained precisely by Hitler, to blindly carry out every one of his orders and to see that as the greatest virtue. There was no value superior to that; Hitler had so quickly and so sinisterly succeeded in dismantling all values which were recognized as universal after so many millennia. One can certainly say that the awareness of that fact united mankind in the most amazing coalition against him. By scorning these values, by underestimating their significance for men of all kinds, Hitler demonstrated a blindness without parallel. Even if he *had* won, which is inconceivable, his power would have very swiftly crumbled for that very reason. There would have been rebellions in every part of his Reich, and his own followers would ultimately have been infected by those rebellions. He, who drew his confidence from Napoleon's victories, was incapable of learning from Napoleon's defeats. His deepest urge was to outdo Napoleon's victories. It is, as already observed, unlikely that Hitler would have insisted on conquering Russia if Napoleon had not foundered there. Hitler's mind was helplessly at the mercy of all victories in mankind's past. But he had to transform his models' defeats into victories for himself—if for no other reason than to outdo them.

He had emerged from Versailles and the defeat of World War I. The struggle against Versailles had won him his first crowds and ultimately the power in Germany for him. Step by step, he succeeded in abolishing the effects of Versailles. From the instant of his victory over France, which signified the reversal of Versailles, he was *doomed*. For now he was convinced that he could turn *any* defeat, even Napoleon's Russian campaign, into victory.

The Relish of the Leaping Number

He believes himself capable of anything, the more difficult the better; if *he* does it, it has to succeed. There are decisions, surprises, concealments, demands, threats, solemn promises, broken treaties, temporary non-aggression, ultimately wars; but there is also a kind of omniscience and particularly one in specialized fields.

His memory for numbers is an astonishing case. Numbers play a greater role for him than for other people. They have something of crowds that grow by leaps and bounds. His most vehement passion is for the number of Germans, who will all come together in his Reich. The relish for the jumping numbers throughout his speeches is striking. The most powerful way of arousing the crowds is to pull the wool over their eyes in regard to their growth. So long as the crowd feels itself increasing, it does not have to crumble. The higher the number that is dangled as attainable, the greater its impact on the crowd. But one also has to give it an acute sense of how to reach that number. One soars up with greater and greater excitement. Sixty, sixty-five, sixty-eight, eighty, one hundred million Germans! It wouldn't work without millions, he has personally experienced the effectiveness of that number. He will succeed in bringing them all together. The crowd, struck by these numbers, experiences them as instant growth. Its intensity thereby reaches its highest conceivable measure. No one affected by it will ever be rid of it internally. It becomes his indomitable addiction to find his way back into that condition externally as well.

The other devices offered for such occasions are familiar. We need not discuss them. Still, it is remarkable to see what a good instinct Speer revealed at the start of his career when he designed enormous flags and special arrangements for them.

As for Hitler's sense of huge numbers, it was transferred from people to many other things. He enjoys the thought of the enormous expense for his Berlin constructions, he wants them to be as big as possible. He is not intimidated by the example of Ludwig II of Bavaria; on the contrary, it attracts him. He imagines that some day American tourists will be lured with the cipher of one billion, the cost of his *Kuppelberg,* and he is entertained by the idea that for their sake, the amount could be raised to one billion and a half. He particularly likes noting numbers that surpass something, those are his favorites.

The turning-point of the war forces him to deal with other numbers. Since his men cannot conceal anything from him (he reserves any overview and any decision for himself), his ministers have the duty to inform him of his enemies' production rates. In their precipitous increase, they are awfully similar to his own numbers, as he used to employ them for his own purposes. He fears them and refuses to take note of them. He is all too familiar with the liveliness of leaping numbers. Now that they turn against him, he feels their enmity and tries to escape their infection by looking the other way.

Visits Denied

As the great German cities sank into ruins one by one, Speer was not alone in feeling that Hitler's visits to these cities was advisable, even necessary. Churchill's example was in everyone's mind. The English prime minister always *faced* those war victims who were not directly involved in the fight. He proved not only his fearlessness to them, but also his sympathy. Despite the tasks that he was overburdened with, he found time for those people and demonstrated with his presence how important they were to him, how much they counted. He demanded a great deal more from the civil population, but he also took them seriously. It is possible that without this behavior of Churchill's, the morale of the English would have suffered to a dangerous extent during the year when they were alone in confronting an opponent who was stronger and who was winning everywhere.

Hitler, in contrast, persistently refused to be seen in the bombed-out cities. One can hardly assume that he lacked the physical courage for such a decision—at least during the earlier stages of these events. His troops were occupying a good portion of Europe, and he never dreamt of admitting defeat. But aside from the people who expected immediate orders from him, and the very few others making up his inner court, he was accustomed solely to facing crowds, and very specific crowds to boot.

He had mastered *accusations;* during the years of his rise, they were his basic device for arousing people into a crowd. Once the crowd had helped him attain power, he did his best for some years to fulfill the expectations of that crowd and to assure its enthusiastic devotion. It was the period of his triumphant travels through Germany, in an atmosphere of spontaneous jubilation that was no longer merely arranged. Speer has described the feedback effect of that atmosphere on Hitler: he regarded himself as the most popular man in all German history. He felt that there had been no one since Luther to whom the peasants spontaneously streamed everywhere. From that and from his organizational preparations, Hitler drew the strength to move toward an attack against the outside world. He began the series of easy victories, which were taken as even greater miracles for being won without bloodshed. He was considered a triumphator before a single shot was fired, and he remained a triumphator when the first shots *were* fired. It was natural for him to face the acclamation as a victor. It merely continued the manner and constellation of the crowd to which he was accustomed from the very outset. The crowd that thanked its Führer had grown stronger, but it was the very same kind of crowd that he had created, that he had always operated with.

His self-image was determined by it, and he was incapable of facing any other kind of crowd. For one thing, he did not care to, he regarded it as harmful to alter or expand his public image. After all, he was very careful about what photographs of him went out, he kept Eva Braun's existence a secret so as not to forfeit the devotion of German women to the unattached man; and likewise, he did not want to appear in connection with destroyed German towns. The picture of the constant victor would have suffered, and his ability to achieve ultimate victory would have become less credible. He preferred keeping his image intact, untouched by any destruction within his Reich, not communicating with anything like it.

It is not easy to decide whether he was wrong from his limited point of view. The faith in miracle weapons, which helf fast until the very end, may be connected to his unscathed image as a constant victor. So long as he refused to acknowledge the destruction in Germany, so long as he did not let it reach him personally, Germany, which, in his delusion, was embodied in his person, did not seem beaten.

But one must add that he would not have been capable of visiting people who had true grounds for grief and lament. What words could he have addressed to them? He had no pity for anyone, except for himself in the final stages: to whom could he have plausibly expressed sympathy? He was not even capable of play-acting, much less having, "weaker" feelings, which he scorned. Hitler cannot be imagined among lamenting people. The lack of anything that truly makes up a human being—emotions towards other, even unknown, people, emotions that are disinterested, uncalculating, unaware of success or influence—that total lack, that dreadful vacuum, would have made him appear helpless and powerless. He certainly did not for even one instant consider putting himself into such a situation.

Secrecy and Singularity

Hitler's circle in Obersalzberg, a few people with whom he spends much of his time, is astonishingly meager. It consists of the tried-and-true photographer, the chauffeur, the male secretary, the mistress, two female secretaries, the diet cook, and finally a very special sort of man, his personal architect. All of them, except for the latter, have been selected according to the principle of the most primitive usefulness. They are not only fully dependent on him, they are in no way capable of any opinion of him. Among them, he is always sure of his immense superiority. They know nothing of what really imbues him, of his plans and decisions. He can live in secrecy with no interference whatsoever: the security of his secret is his utmost existential need. It is the secret of the grand state, which he alone rules, and he can certainly justify to himself the necessity of absolute secrecy. He remarks often enough that he trusts nobody, especially women, and since he permits no thinking women to be near him, he has no problem clinging to his scorn for them. In this milieu, in which no one can get to him, he feels good, he lives unscathed as the Only One, as which he regards himself. Since no one has any claim to him, he feels protected from pleas for mercy that might reach him. He sees his integrity in his hardness. He never deviates from his notion of power, he has absorbed all the power of his historic models and sees the reason for his successes in his consistent maintenance of power.

Yet he fully realizes he cannot exercise power without the few people who helped him to rise and who have proven themselves. He permits them a great deal, so long as they serve him and accept each decision uncontradictingly. He has a keen eye for any weaknesses of theirs, which go as far as corruption. So long as he *knows* them, so long as nothing is hidden from him, he puts up with them. Omniscience in regard to them too is one of his cardinal demands. He makes sure of reserving that omniscience for himself by keeping the power areas of others strictly apart. *He,* however, must be informed about everything, which no one else is allowed to be. He considers himself a master in this separation of what he assigns to each of his helpers. He makes sure not to pull them constantly into his proximity, because they could thereby find out more than he wishes them to.

In this, he demonstrates a correct instinct—in his terms—for the one man who is always near him, Bormann, and who in his position as secretary does find out a great deal, thereby truly achieves power.

One has the impression that Hitler simply *needs* the weaknesses of those to whom he has delegated partial power. Not only does he more effectively control them, but he does not have to cast about for reasons to dismiss them. He maintains a feeling of moral superiority towards them. He needs to be able to tell himself that he is free of ordinary foibles like greed, lechery, vanity, anything belonging to common, petty life. When he supervises his image for the public, he can rationalize it politically. He is worried about gaining weight, but that has nothing to do with vanity: a Führer with a paunch is impossible. His gigantic structures are to impress other potentates, making them pliable. Chiefly, however, they are meant for eternity: to fortify his nation's self-confidence when he is no longer here. Everything he undertakes, no matter how immense, serves his mission, and since he is richly endowed with the paranoiac's gift for *reasons,* he find nothing about himself that he could not convincingly justify to others and to himself.

In his harmless inner circle, he can ride all over his accomplices, he never holds back, and it is both amusing and informative to read about that in Speer. Hitler mocks Göring about his passion for hunting: it is so easy to shoot animals from a distance. Killing animals is a butcher's job. He makes no statements about killers of human beings. Can he truly regard it as more dangerous in every case? Rosenberg's *Philosophy of the Twentieth Century* is incomprehensible to him. He has no respect for it, but one feels that he resents the popularity, the enormous editions of the book. Of course, those of his own book are much, much higher. But he dislikes anything that comes near him in any area, threatening his singularity even from afar. Himmler's Teutonomania gets on his nerves. Should they remind the world that the Teutons lived in clay huts at the time of the Roman Empire? He seems ashamed of these ancient Teutons, who lived without art or culture. He, who has an eye for Grützner and Vienna's Ringstrasse, feels way above them. He is quite sharp in his comments when Himmler calls Charlemagne the slaughterer of Saxons. He *approves* of the Saxon massacres, for the reign of the Franks brought culture to Germany. It is virtually an omen of his later indifference to the fate of the Germans that he approves of the butchery of Germanic Saxons. He brooks no criticism of Charlemagne, if for no other reason than because he views him as his precursor. At bottom, he respects the Teutons only since the Holy Roman Empire; the attraction of empires on a man about to establish *his* own worldwide empire is not to be resisted.

His relationship to Speer is intrinsically different from any other. As Speer himself realizes, Hitler sees his own youth in him. Not only will that man perfectly fulfill the architectural ambitions of Hitler's own youth—in dealing with him, he regains some of the enthusiasm that imbued his solitude back then. Perhaps he also has an inkling of the relative purity of those early years of zealous but hopeless sketches, a purity that expressed admiration for *something else,* which already existed. Most likely, he admired nothing so much as "grand" architecture. But he would not be capable of admitting that these sketches, by being realized, destroy the one valuable element in this admiration, its character of dreaminess and veneration. All "materialization" has now gained a kind of rabid power over him, and he subjugates to it any emotion that he has preserved.

Destruction

The twofold delight in permanence and destruction, characteristic of the paranoiac, is thoroughly treated in *The Schreber Case.* The threat to his own person, acutely felt as though constantly present, is opposed in two directions: through an extension over vast spaces, which are virtually incorporated into his person, and through the attainment of "everlastingness." The formula of the "thousand-year Reich" could not be called immodest for a fully developed paranoia. Anything that he is not himself is wiped out or subjugated, with the latter as merely a temporary solution, that can easily turn into total extermination. Any resistance in his own sphere of power is considered unbearable: resistance, says Speer, could make Hitler go white-hot with fury. He is more accommodating only when he hasn't achieved absolute power, for he is still in the process of attaining it. In its vast scope, the Reich is his own person, which is finally no longer endangered, and so long as he does not reach across the entire world, he cannot truly relax. The plan for permanence is taken for granted; there is no lack of testimony to both in Speer's *Memoirs.*

An eagle is supposed to be put on top of Hitler's Kuppelberg in Berlin, at a height of 290 meters. In early summer of 1939, he talks about it to Speer. "Here, the eagle shall no longer stand over the swastika, it will rule the entire globe! The crowning of this biggest building in the world must be the eagle over the globe!"

Two years earlier, in 1937, during a discussion of the Great Stadium, he had said almost casually: "In 1940, the Olympic Games will once again take place in Tokyo. But after that, they will take place in Germany for all time."

The books he most carefully studies deal with war or architecture, they are his favorite reading. In these areas, he even surprises experts with his precise knowledge; his memory makes it easy for him to beat them in conversations. His architecture is comprehensible only in terms of its "everlasting" goal; he hates anything that is not stone, and he has only utter loathing for glass as a material for large structures, since it cannot conceal him and is breakable to boot.

His destructive lust is kept hidden at first. It seems all the more monstrous when it comes out. In late July of 1940, three days after the truce in France, he takes Speer and just a few others along to Paris, where he has never been. In three hours, he visits the Grand Opera, proving his thorough study of it ("You see how well I know the place!"), the Madeleine, the Champs Elysées, the Arc de Triomphe, the Eiffel Tower, the Invalides, where he pays his tribute to Napoleon, the Pantheon, the Louvre, Rue de Rivoli, and finally Sacré Coeur on Montmartre. After these three hours, he says: "It was the dream of my life to see Paris. I cannot tell you how happy I am that it has come true."

That same evening, back in his headquarters, in the small parlor of a farmhouse, he assigns Speer the task of recommencing the constructions in Berlin and he adds: "Wasn't Paris beautiful? But Berlin has to be much more beautiful! I often wondered before whether we shouldn't destroy Paris; but when we're finished in Berlin, Paris will only be a has-been. Why should we destroy it?" Speer is shocked that he can speak so calmly about destroying Paris, "as though it were the most obvious thing in the world." This shows the nearness of outdoing and destroying. Outdoing stands for victory, and if it works quickly, then it puts off destruction. The easy victory over France has saved Paris for the time being. Paris is to remain standing, in order to function as a has-been next to Berlin.

Soon thereafter, during that same year of 1940, Speer, at a dinner in the Reich Chancellery, watches Hitler "talk himself into an ecstasy of destruction." "Have you ever looked at a map of London? It is built in such a crowded fashion that one source of fire would be enough to wipe out the entire city as happened once, over 200 years ago. Göring wants to use countless firebombs with a whole new effect to create fire sources in as many parts of London as possible, fire sources everywhere. Thousands of them. They will then unite into a gigantic conflagration. Göring has the only right idea for it: high-explosive bombs won't work, but we can do it with fire bombs: totally destroy London! What can they do with their fire department once the whole thing gets going?"

Here, the lust for destruction is turned shamelessly against a city of eight million people, and it was probably the number of inhabitants that helped to intensify his lust. The union of thousands of fire sources into a gigantic blaze is presented like the creation of a crowd. Fire often serves as a symbol for the destructive crowd. Hitler is not content with the symbol, he transforms it into the reality for which it stands, and he employs fire as a crowd for destroying London.

This "ecstasy of destruction," at first all in Hitler's mind, happens to Germany in two different ways. What he has planned for London, though without success, becomes a reality in the German cities. It is as though Hitler and Göring had seduced and talked their enemies into utilizing this weapon, which they themselves invented. But the second and no less dreadful factor was that Hitler was so familiar with such thoughts of total destruction that they could not impress him deeply enough. The greatest horrors did not catch him unawares, he devised them himself and thought about them for a long time. The destruction of entire cities began in his head and was already a new military tradition by the time it seriously turned against Germany. Then, like everything else, the Germans had to "see it through." He refused to take note by personally witnessing the effects, and the destruction of neither Hamburg nor Berlin would have moved him to give up even one inch of conquered soil in Russia.

Thus came the situation that must seem monstrous today: the Reich was still spread over a good part of Europe while one major German city after another sank into ruins. The inviolability of his person in the narrower sense was assured. The larger person consisted in its expansion.

One cannot fully picture the destruction occurring in the mind of a paranoiac. His opposition, serving to extend and immortalize him, is aimed at this very infection by destruction. Yet it is within him, for it is part of him; and if it suddenly appears in the outer world, on whatever side, it cannot in any way surprise or astonish him. The violence of the processes inside him is what he forces as a vision upon the world. His mind can be as insignificant as Hitler's, he can, so to speak, have nothing to show that would have any value for a disinterested authority—but the intensity of his inner destructive processes makes him look like a visionary or prophet, a redeemer or Führer.

Divisions, Slaves, Gassings

During the war, Hitler's delight in the acute crowd around him swiftly wanes. He has grown accustomed to reaching his largest possible crowd, namely all Germans, by radio. Nor does he have any further opportunity to speak of a peaceful increase in the number of Germans. He is busy with war, which he regards as his real handicraft next to architecture. He now operates with divisions. They are already formed and under his command, he can do whatever he wants to with them. His chief goal now is to keep the generals in his hands. He has to convince the experts of war. For the moment, he can win them over with easy and surprising victories. The victories to which he called up the crowds earlier and the promise of which actually helped him to form the crowd—those victories now come true: the next stage.

Nothing is so crucial to him as being right despite the qualms of experts. Every prophecy that materializes becomes an inherent part of his self-confidence. Paranoia, which has two faces, doffs one, that of persecution, for the moment and consists totally of the face of greatness.

His head is never free of crowds, but both their makeup and their function have changed. He has won his Germans, now he gains *slaves*. They are useful and they will be far more numerous than Germans. But as soon as the war runs into difficulties, namely in Russia, and as soon as his own cities are threatened with bombs, another crowd becomes acute in him: the Jews, to be exterminated. He has gathered them, now he can annihilate them. He has already voiced his plans early and quite clearly, but when he seriously goes about with the extermination, he makes sure it remains a secret.

It was possible to be as close to the source of power as Speer was, and not be directly confronted with this annihilation. Here, Speer's testimony strikes me as especially important. He not only knew about the slavery stage, i.e. forced labor, he included it in his own jurisdiction. His plans were partly based on it. But he consciously found out about the extermination only much later, at a time when the war appeared lost. The actual revelations about the camps came to Speer at the end, when he was already fighting against Hitler; they had their utmost effect on him only in Nuremberg. This is credible because, for one thing, it prompts him to postulate a collective guilt in the leaders. He is decisive in his behavior under difficult circumstances (he has to assert himself against his fellow defendants, who regard him as a traitor). He is open in his statements, he glosses over nothing. He labors for years on his main enterprise, his memoirs, in prison, hoping to make any Hitler legend impossible. All these things presume the late shock at the revelations.

Thus, Hitler managed to conceal his most monstrous undertaking, the gassings, from the majority of Germans. But it was all the more operative in *his* mind. Any road back was blocked by that. There was no possibility for him to conclude a peace. There was only one way out: victory. And the more impossible it seemed, the more unique it became.

Delusion and Reality

Delusion and reality are hard to tell apart in Hitler, they incessantly overlap. But this alone scarcely distinguishes him from anyone else. The difference lies in the power of the delusion, which is not content with small satisfactions as is the case with most other people. In its closure, his delusion is primary and he is not ready to sacrifice the slightest bit of it. Anything that appears in reality is seen in terms of the delusion as a whole. Its substance is such that it can be fed by only one thing: successes. Failure cannot really touch him; it has only one function: to spur him on to new recipes for success. This unerringness of his delusion is what he considers his harshness. Everything he has seized remains there, and nothing crumbles. No building he ever plans to erect is so solid as his delusion. It is not a delusion permitting him to withdraw into himself and live next to the world: his delusion is such that he has to force it upon the world around him. The path that others used in only seemingly related cases—inventors or especially possessed creative people—the path of convincing individual people or putting out works to which they virtually entrust the achievement of conviction—that path is not his. It not only would be much too slow, but it does not fit in with the content of his delusion. Ever since the catastrophic outcome of World War I, he has been filled with the crowd of the fallen German soldiers, who cannot, so far as he is concerned, have fallen in vain, and thus, in a way peculiar to him alone, they have remained alive. He wants to change them back into that earlier crowd which existed when the war broke out. It is this crowd that makes up his strength; with the help of this crowd, i.e. by constantly referring to it, he is able to arouse new crowds and gather them around him. He is soon aware of the effectiveness of this power; and, with ceaseless practice and intensity, he develops into a master of crowds. To the extent that he deals with crowds, he realizes he can certainly make his delusion come true. He has discovered virtually the weak point of reality, the part where reality is most liquid, the part that intimidates most people, who fear the crowd.

His respect for the other, the static reality, does not get any greater however. The power nourished by crowds, power in a raw state, long remains the only one at his disposal; and even though it quickly increases, that is not the sort of power he really wants: his delusion demands the absolute political power in the state. Once he has achieved it, he can get at reality seriously. He is quite capable of distinguishing reality from his delusion. His sense of reality, which he greatly prides himself on, consists in exercising power. He employs it to gradually force the substance of his delusion on his environment, on his instruments. As long as things go well, it is impossible, and indeed undesirable for them to recognize the delusionary character of this structure, into which they are drawn and in which they take part. It is only with the failures that the unchangeable rigidity—that lunacy of his enterprise—becomes blatant. The gap widens between delusion and reality, and now the solidification of his belief in himself during the time of his good fortune turns out to be the misfortune of Germany, as it was for the rest of the world from the very start.

He still insists on his right to prophesy. He alone and nobody else has the right to foretell what will happen. The correctness of his predictions has been proven often enough. The reality of the future belongs to him, he has drawn it into his realm of power. He regards warnings as interfering with his future. They embitter him even when coming from his most time-tested assistants. He rejects them with all sharpness, as a kind of insubordination. His predictions have now taken on the character of orders which he issues to the future.

The ability to see through things, an ability inherent in both the paranoiac and the wielder of power, begins to reveal its delusiveness. That ability was useful to him when estimating his foes. He could divine their goals when they were still fully concealed. His "sixth sense" refers to that and to his correct predictions. Now that he is surrounded, he proves how poorly he sees through things. For a long time he regards the landing in Normandy as a ruse, the real landing has to come in the area of Calais. The steps he takes against the enemy are determined by this incorrect appreciation, from which nothing can make him deviate, to which he clutches unshakably until it is too late.

The abortive assassination attempt of July 20 causes the final, effective increase in his feeling of power. He survived almost by a miracle, it *is* a miracle. For once, Stalin becomes his model. He approves of Stalin's annihilation of the Russian general staff, and even though nothing factual is known about their treason, he assumes they must have been guilty because he hates his own generals. He orders the harshest measures for them and has them executed in the most degrading manner. Their execution gives him the most primitive sort of power: surviving one's enemies. He enjoys the films of these executions and has them screened in his intimate circle. But he saves a few victims for later, ordering their execution from time to time, according to the situation and his own needs.

On April 12, 1945, eighteen days before Hitler's death, Speer is urgently summoned to him. "He saw me and plunged towards me with a rare liveliness, as though possessed, pushing a news report into my hands: 'Here! Read this! Here! You never wanted to believe it! Here!' His words gushed out precipitously. 'This is the great miracle that I have always predicted. Who is right now? The war is not lost at all. Just read! Roosevelt is dead!' He just could not calm down."

Prolonging the war up till now appears justified. There seems to be a repetition of the events at the end of the Seven Years' War, when Frederick the Great of Prussia was saved from the worst danger by the death of his arch-enemy [Empress Elizabeth of Russia; translator's note]. Little contributed so strongly to the totally absurd prolongation of the war as the thought of this twist in an historic destiny. Frederick the Great was one of Hitler's early and *lasting* models: in the end, he was the only one.

In his bunker, that Speer compares to a prison, with nothing but ruins all around, with the Russians just outside of Berlin, of which little is left, Hitler is capable of hoping for a turning-point in the war from the death of a *personal* foe. Until the last, the real events are, for him, those between a few, very few powerful men; they are all that counts, the fate of the world depends on who survives whom. Nothing more clearly bears witness to the devastations wrought in his mind by the concept of power and his addiction to that concept. His last hope is hung on the death of Roosevelt, whom he scorned and despised as a "paralytic."

Yet in regard to the effect of historical models and to their danger, which is still not understood, it would be advisable to include Speer's description of that last scene in the bunker in all the schoolbooks in the world. For the moment, all we can do is to set up counter-models of complete truth in opposition to the undimmed effect of the disastrous models. The shame at this situation, the insight into its infamy, the essence of the false vision—they would all come together here in an indestructible impact.

1971

CONFUCIUS IN
HIS CONVERSATIONS

Confucius' distaste for oratory: the weight of chosen words. He fears their being weakened by glib and easy usage. The hesitation, the reflection, the time *before* the word is everything, but so is the time after it. Something in the rhythm of the isolated questions and answers raises their value. The quick word of the Sophists, the eager ball game of words—those are things he hates. The crux is not the impact of the swift response, but the sinking-in of the word that seeks its responsibility.

He also likes sticking to something that is present and explaining it. No long dialogues of his have come down, they would strike us as unnatural.

In contrast to him, his disciples become useful to the governing authorities less through their knowledge than through their eloquence. Hence, those of them who come up in the world through speech are not really pupils after his own heart.

Highly impressive in Confucius is his lack of success, especially when he wanders from town to town. One could hardly take him seriously if he had actually become and remained a government minister somewhere. He ignores power as it really is, he is interested solely in its possibilities. Power, for him, is never an end in itself, it is a task, a responsibility for the collective. He thus becomes a master of nay-saying and knows how to maintain himself fully. But he is no ascetic, he takes part in all aspects of life, never really withdrawing from it. It is only when mourning the dead that he acknowledges anything like asceticism, which serves to retain the dead more vividly.

His happiness, which never ends, is study. His antiquarian interests always concern what is human and they serve to order life. His penchant for order goes very far. Its ritual character is ultimately engrained in him. "He would not sit on a mat that did not lie properly." He has a flair for disparities and gives them their consciences.

Confucius allows no man to be an instrument. His dislike of specialization is connected to that, and it is a very important feature, important because it is still operating in modern China. It is not crucial to know this or that, it is crucial to be a human being with any individual knowledge.

But great emphasis is also placed on not acting out of calculation; that is, examined closely, not treating people as instruments. Whatever one may think about the societal origin of this attitude, which contains a scorn of commercial activity, the fact that it is clearly articulated, that it remained operative, if not decisive, through the study of Confucius' conversations—those facts are extremely important for what one might call the residue of Chinese culture as a whole.

The model man remains the man who does not act out of calculation.

Confucius is patient in striving for the ears of those who have power, the reigning princes. One cannot say that he flatters them; and if he does recognize their authority, it is only because he demands a great deal of them in its exercise.

He reveals no knowledge whatsoever of the nature of power, of its innermost essence. This knowledge is supplied later by his enemies, the legalists. It is very bizarre that all thinkers in human history who understand something about de facto power *approve* of it. The thinkers who are *against* power scarcely penetrate its essence. Their repugnance is so great that they do not care to study power, they fear being polluted, their attitude has something religious about it.

A science of power has been developed only by thinkers who approved of it and acted as its counselors. How can one gain power and more effectively hold on to it? What must one look out for in order to maintain it? What scruples must one discard if they prevent the exercise of power?

The most interesting of these connoisseurs of power who feel positive about it is Han Fei Tse, who lived 250 years after Confucius. A study of him is simply indispensable for the inveterate opponent of power.

Confucius' *Conversations* are the oldest complete intellectual and spiritual portrait of a man. It strikes one as a modern book; everything it contains and indeed everything it *lacks* is important.

One gets to know a very *complete* man in it, but not just *any* man. It is a man who is intent on being a model, and thereby having an effect on others. Every single quality—and very many are recorded—has a meaning. A loose arrangement, based on no recognizable principle, produces an altogether credibly acting, a thinking, breathing, speaking, silent being, who is one thing above all: a *model*.

In Confucius, one can learn with particular clarity how a model comes into existence and maintains itself. It is indispensable that one be inspired by another model, to which one holds fast under all circumstances, never doubting it, never giving it up, always wanting to reach it and yet never reaching it. Even if one does reach it, one can never hope to admit having done so. For the model that is reached loses its power. It can nourish only the man who sees himself at a distance from it. The attempt at spanning this distance, the attempt at getting at the model, as it were, can be renewed over and over again, but must never succeed. So long as such attempts do not succeed, so long as the tension of distance is maintained, the leap in the model's direction can always be undertaken anew. It is these seemingly futile attempts that count—seemingly futile, for they give more and more experiences, abilities, qualities.

Confucius sets up his model at a vast distance, it is the Duke of Chou, who lived five hundred years before him and to whom the majority of innovations in that new dynasty were attributed. To understand him, Confucius studies everything that happened then and since then, the historical documents, the songs, the rites. He examines these things, sifts and orders them; people later assumed that everything they knew about them was established by him. The duke appears to him in dreams; in later years, Confucius grew anxious if the duke did not appear for a while. He sees this absence of his model as a sign of disapproval, he has failed in too many things that the duke succeeded in.

But he was not his only model. One might say that he groups all Chinese history, to the extent that he feels he knows it, around models; at the start of each of the three historical dynasties, but even directly *before* the first of them, he puts one or two figures, who, as models, determine the period after them for a long time. He is not only aware of the huge importance of models, he also knows that they wear out, and makes sure they are renewed. His knowledge of their influence is something he reaps from himself and his pupils. His knowledge of counter-models comes from the rulers whom he tries to advise and who will not listen. As unpleasant as these counter-models are, he refuses to omit them. He introduces them into history, preferring to place them at the ends of dynasties. But he always makes sure they are conquered and dethroned by models in history.

This study of his models turns him into one himself, and it is bizarre that he has become much more of one and for a far longer time than they.

"A young man," says Confucius, "ought to be treated with utmost respect. How can you tell that he will not some day be as valuable as you are now? The man who has reached the age of forty or fifty without distinguishing himself in something—he deserves no respect."

Confucius acts accordingly in his long dealings with his own disciples. How carefully he observes them! How cautiously he assesses them! He makes sure never to harm them with premature praise. He lets himself go and is happy when they merit unlimited praise. He never censures without taking the harmful sting out of his censure. He lets his pupils criticize him and answers them. With all the principles he acts on, his assessment of character remains empirical. If two of them are together, he asks them for their innermost wishes and tells them his own. There is scarcely any reprimand to be felt in that, it is really a confrontation of different natures.

Yet he never conceals his deep love for Yen Hui, the pure and unsuccessful disciple; and when this favorite pupil of his dies at thirty-two, he does not hide his despair.

I know of no sages who took death as seriously as Confucius. He refuses to answer any questions about death. "If one does not yet know life, how should one know death?" No more suitable comment has ever been made on that topic. He knows very well that all such questions refer to a time *after* death. Any answer leaps past death, conjuring away both death and its incomprehensibility. If there is something *afterwards* as there was something *before,* then death loses some of its weight. Confucius refuses to play along with this most unworthy legerdemain. He does not say there is nothing afterwards, he cannot know. But one has the impression that he does not really care about finding out, even if he could. All value is thereby put on life itself; anything of radiance or earnestness that one has taken away from life by putting a good, perhaps the best part of its strength *behind* death is restored to life. Thus, life remains whole, it remains what it is, and even death remains intact, they are not interchangeable, not comparable. They never blend, they are distinct.

The purity and the human pride of this attitude are quite compatible with that emphatic intensification of the thought of the dead, as is found in *Li Ki,* the book of Chinese rites. This book contains the most credible things I have ever read about approaching the dead, about the sense of their presence on the days set aside for commemorating them. It is quite in Confucius' terms; it is, although recorded only later in this form, that which one always feels when reading his conversations. In a blend of tenderness and tenacity, which one scarcely finds elsewhere, he strives to increase the sense of veneration for certain dead people. Too little heed has been paid to this attempt at lessening the lust for survival, one of the most perplexing of tasks, and still unresolved today.

The man who mourns his father for three years, so utterly and so protractedly interrupting his normal activity, can in no way enjoy surviving, any possible satisfaction in survival is totally destroyed by the course of obligations for mourning. For in this period, one must also prove oneself worthy of one's father. One takes over his life in all details, one becomes one's father but by way of continued veneration. Not only does one not suppress him, one yearns for his return, and certain rites give one a feeling of his return. He lives on as a figure and model. One takes care not to go against his wishes, one has to prove oneself to him.

"After three days, one eats again; after three months, one washes again; after a year, one wears raw silk again under the garment of

175

mourning. Self-torment should not go to the point of self-destruction, so that death will not harm life. The period of mourning should not last beyond three years.

"The sacrifices should not be too frequent, otherwise they will become burdensome and their solemnity will be impaired. Nor should they be too infrequent, otherwise one will become indolent and forget the dead.

"On the day of the sacrifice, the son thought of his parents, he recalled their home, their smiles, their tone of voice, their attitudes; he thought of the things they enjoyed and the foods they liked to eat. After thus fasting and meditating for three days, he could see the people he was fasting for.

"On the day of the sacrifice, when entering the room of ancestors, he was looking forward to seeing them again in their ancestral seat; while walking around and in and out, he was serious as though sure to hear them moving or speaking; when going out the door, he would listen with bated breath as though hearing them sigh."

In all civilizations, that is the only earnest attempt I know of to wipe out the lust for survival. As such, one will have to think in a very unbiased fashion about this aspect of Confucianism in its origin, despite all subsequent degenerations.

For all the respect we thereby owe Confucius, it cannot be denied that a different goal was more crucial to him. He wanted to employ the memory of the dead in order to pin down tradition. He preferred this to laws, sanctions, and penalties. The tradition from father to son struck him as more effective, but only if the father was present to the son as a full person, not as a crumbling model. Three years of grief seemed necessary for turning the son completely into what the father had been.

It presumes great trust in what the father was. It wants to prevent a *worsening* from father to son. Nevertheless, we ought to consider whether it does not thereby impede a betterment.

1971

TOLSTOY
The Final Ancestor

Tolstoy's mania for self-accusal even in his early years is a contamination due to Rousseau. But his accusations collide with a compact self. He can rebuke himself for whatever he likes; he does not destroy himself. It is a self-accusal that gives him significance, it makes him the center of the world. Amazing how early he writes the story of his youth; that is the start of his activity as a writer.

He cannot hear about any new object without immediately laying down "rules" for it. The laws which he always has to find are his arrogance, but he is also seeking a persistency. He needs this because of death, which he has experienced early and frequently. At the age of two, he loses his mother, at nine his father; shortly thereafter, his grandmother, whom he looks at and kisses in her coffin.

But he is not precocious. He gathers his defiance for a long time. All his experiences submerge, unaltered, in his stories, novels, and dramas. They are strong experiences, and since they never crumble, they give him something monumental. Any man who maintains himself like that is a sort of monster. Others weaken by flowing away from themselves.

He sees truth too much as a law and grants his diaries something like omnipotence. With his early journals, which teem with embarrassing, but overestimated truths about him, he tries to educate his eighteen-year-old wife, lead her to his own, still precarious law. The shock he thereby inflicts upon her lasts for fifty years.

He is the kind of man who never gives up an observation, a thought, or an experience. Everything remains strangely conscious. He is spontaneous in his antipathies, his rejections; he is naive in holding on to conventional customs and notions. His forte is that he will not let himself be talked into anything, he needs fierce experiences of his own to arrive at new convictions. His accounts, à la Benjamin Franklin, which he begins so early, would seem ludicrous if everything in them were not reiterated with such frightening tenacity.

But there are exciting statements of his, which make up for a great deal in the diaries; for example, when, in a letter to his wife, he draws the Russo-Turkish War of 1877–78 fully into his life: "So long as it goes on, I will not be able to write. It is as though the city were burning. One doesn't know what to do. One cannot think of anything else."

The religious development of the *later* Tolstoy is marked by an inescapable compulsion. What he regards as a free decision of his mind is determined by an incredible identification: with Christ. However, his happiness—every peasant labor, that domination of the manual over him—has little in common with Christ.

Far more than Christ, he is a retrograde landowner, the lord who becomes a peasant again. To even the score for all crimes committed by masters, he utilizes the gospels. Christ is his crutch. The goal is the totally personal transformation back into a peasant. He is concerned not about the rights but about the existence of the peasant, which is not to be gained by violence. But he also wants to be *recognized* as a peasant.

His family, hindering him in this metamorphosis, becomes burdensome to him. His wife married the count and writer, she wants nothing to do with the peasant. She surrounds him with eight living children, who are nothing less than peasant children.

His property is divided up during his lifetime. He wants to be rid of it, and all the normal fighting of heirs takes place right in front of him among his wife and children. It is as though he intended to lure out the ugliest things in his family.

His wife decides to publish his works. She confers about the business with Dostoievsky's widow, whom she gets to know for that very purpose. One would think that two widows, very able widows, were sitting together.

In the last years of his life, Tolstoy is torn to bits by two enterprises, one could say: two businesses, the results of what he really was for decades.

His wife takes care of the publishing business, trying to make as big a profit as she can from selling his *Collected Works.* Chertkov, his secretary, takes care of his faith, the newly founded religion or sect. He too is an able man; he watches over any utterance of Tolstoy's and takes him to task. The pamphlets and brochures are propagated cheaply throughout the world. He usurps any statement by the founder that could benefit the faith, and he demands copies of the diary *in statu nascendi.* Tolstoy is devoted to his favorite disciple and allows him anything. He cares very much for this undertaking, less for his wife's, toward which he often feels only bitter hatred. But the two foundations have lives of their own and don't give a damn about him.

When he has a serious attack and seems on the point of death, his wife suddenly cries: "Where are the keys?" She means the keys to his manuscripts.

I have spent the whole night in a kind of enchantment with Tolstoy's life. In his old age, as the victim of his family and followers, as the object of all the things he most struggles against, his life has a meaning that none of his works attains. He tears the observer apart, any observer, for anyone looking at his life will find the embodiments of convictions that are the most important to him, right next to those that he despises profoundly. All are articulated, gasped out unsparingly, unforgettably, and keep recurring. He seems to unite the things that struggle violently against one another in the observer. What makes him most believable is his contradictions. He is the only figure of old age in our modern period whom one can take seriously. Since he utters *everything,* unable to deny himself any rebuke, any judgment, any law, he seems open on all sides, even those where he most sharply delimits himself.

It is acutely painful for me to watch a man who has seen through power in every form and pitilessly rejected it—war, law courts, governments, money—a man of this unheard-of and incorruptible clarity, make a sort of pact with death, which he has feared for so long. He approaches death by circuitous religious routes, deceiving himself about it until he is capable of flattering it. He thereby succeeds in losing most of his fear of death. He accepts death intellectually as though it were something morally good. He trains himself to watch calmly when his near and dear pass away. His daughter Masha, the only adult Tolstoyan in the family, dies at thirty-five. He witnesses her disease and her dying; he attends her funeral. He records contentment, he has come further with his death training, he has made progress, he approves of the dreadful thing; now, it is not even hard for him to do what he had to force himself to do a few years earlier when his favorite son Vanichka died at seven.

He himself *survives* once again and keeps growing older. He has no insight into the process of survival. He would be horrified to learn that the deaths of young members of his family strengthen his sense of life, actually prolonging his own life. In thinking about Christ, he does desire a martyr's fate for himself; but the worldly powers, which he hates, are careful not to touch him. All that happens is that the Church excommunicates him. His most loyal followers are exiled, he is left on his estate and may move freely anywhere else. He keeps writing what he wants to write, his things are printed somewhere or other, he cannot be silenced. He even weathers the most serious illnesses.

The things that the State cannot do to him are done to him by his family. It is his wife and not the government who openly hires guards for his estate. The life-and-death struggle he has to wage against her is not over his pamphlets and proclamations; it is over the most intimate daily accounts that he settles with himself: his diary. It is she, his wife, in league with his sons, who drives him to his death. She takes revenge for his war against her sex and against money; and it must be said that she is mostly concerned about money. The persecution mania, which he actually would have to develop, considering his uncompromising fight against powerful foes, develops in *her* instead. She makes him, the most open of all men, a conspirator at an advanced old age. He loves his teachings until the very end, and they are grotesquely embodied in his secretary Chertkov. He loves them so much that the relationship to Chertkov assumes a homosexual character in the eyes of his insane wife. The journals connected to the start of their marriage represent the real Tolstoy for her. By arduously copying his manuscripts, she makes them her own. Her paranoia tells her that nothing will remain of Tolstoy but the manuscripts and journals; she must have them.

However, the exemplary nature of his life, the incessant struggle with himself—into which she is drawn—are hated by her. With demonic strength, she manages to devastate the final years of his life. One cannot say she gets the better of him, for ultimately, after unspeakable torments, he flees. But even during the last days, when he thinks he is free of her, she is secretly close by; in the concluding moments, she whispers into his ear that she was there the whole time.

I was preoccupied with Tolstoy's life for ten days. Yesterday, he died in Astapovo and was buried in Yasnaya Polyana.

A woman enters his room; he thinks it is his favorite daughter, deceased, and he calls loudly: "Masha! Masha!" Thus he is fortunate enough to find one of his dead; and even if it wasn't his daughter, the deceptive instant of this good fortune was one of the last of his life.

Tolstoy had a difficult death; what a tenacious life. He did not make his peace with the Church. He was, however, surrounded by his disciples, and they protected him from the last emissaries of the Church.

His wife and his sons—all of whom except for the eldest, Sergei, were despicable men—lived in a luxury car at the railroad station of Astapovo, very close by. He felt his wife's eyes at the window and so the curtain was drawn. Six doctors, certainly not too many, were at hand; he fairly despised them, although preferring their care to his wife's.

I know of nothing more deeply moving than the life of this man. What is there about it that so compels me, that has been haunting me for ten days?

It is a *complete* life; until the very last moment, until death, it has *everything* belonging to a life. It is not shortened, deceived, or falsified by anything. All the contradictions that a human being is capable of are part of this life. Complete, known in every detail, it lies there before us, recorded in some form from youth until the final days.

The things that sometimes bother me in his work, a certain sobriety and reasonableness, benefit the self-depiction of his life. It has *one* tone, it is credible, perspicuous, and one is actually led to believe that a life can be perspicuous.

Perhaps there is no more important deception. For the idea that a man's life falls apart into countless details having nothing to do with one another—that may also be a notion that can be advocated; but it has gotten about too much and its consequences are not good. It deprives men of their courage to resist, because this courage requires a feeling of consistency. A man needs to have something in him that he is not ashamed of and that takes to task and records any necessary shame. This impenetrable part of his inner nature has something relatively constant to it and can be detected early if one seriously goes after it. The longer one can follow this constancy, and the longer the time of activity, the weightier a life is. A man who has possessed and known life for eighty years offers both a terrifying and necessary spectacle. He makes creation true in such a way as if he could justify it with insight, resistance, and patience.

This time, I have dealt only with Tolstoy's life and not his works.* Thus I could not be led astray by the things that I sometimes find boring in his works. His life is never boring, it is enormous; the end makes it an exemplary life. His religious and moral development would be worthless if it had not brought him into the dreadful situation of his later and latest years.

The fact that he did flee, that he did not die at home turned his life into a legend. But perhaps the time *prior to* his flight is more valuable. The resistance to anything that did not strike him as true changed the people closest to him, his wife and sons, into his enemies. Had he left his wife immediately, had he not been anxious about her life, had he turned his back on her (for which he had reasons enough) as soon as living with her became unbearable—then he could not be taken seriously. But he did remain, exposing himself as a very old man to her diabolical threats. His patience aroused the astonishment of the peasants around him, and some of them, with whom he spoke, *told* him as much. Their opinion was not something he scorned; of all people, they struck him as the best.

In the struggle he was forced to endure, he became—as he himself wrote—an *object;* that was the thing he could stand least.

He was not all alone. He had loyal disciples, including one whom he especially loved because he turned the rigor of the doctrine against Tolstoy himself. He also had a blindly devoted daughter. But that is precisely what makes the events around him so clear and concrete.

---

* I owe much to Troyat's biography, which draws richly on material available only in Russian.

Everything does not take place in him alone. Things occur as they do among human beings.

Tolstoy's life ultimately winds up as in *Auto-da-Fé:* the fight over the will, the burrowing through papers. A marriage that began with respect and understanding, with incessant and repeated copying of each page that he wrote, ends in the worst possible war of absolute misunderstanding. In their last years, both of them, Tolstoy and his wife, are as far apart as Kien and Therese. Their tortures are more intimate, of course, because, after decades of living together, they *know* more about each other. There are children in this marriage, there are followers of the prophet, and thus the stage of events is not so fearfully empty as in Kien's apartment. The depiction of the conflict in *Auto-da-Fé* is more detached and hence clearer perhaps; but since it operates with devices that Tolstoy rejected, it will appear more incredible to people of his "natural" attitude. Even in the midst of the worst affliction, he would certainly not have recognized himself as Kien, though he probably would have viewed his wife as Therese.

When very old, he peruses Korsakov's textbook of psychiatry for the symptoms of his wife's madness. He ought to know all of them quite accurately by now. But he has never truly confronted madness, he has always sidestepped it, he has scornfully left it to Dostoievsky.

Right before his escape, he is reading *The Brothers Karamazov,* specifically the part about Mitya's hatred of his father—in any event: hatred. He rejects it, he refuses to acknowledge it. Can it be that his moral rejection of hatred dims his view of Dostoievsky's thrilling portrayal?

In any event, he asks his daughter Sasha for the second volume of *Karamazov* for his flight.

1971

DR. HACHIYA'S
DIARY OF HIROSHIMA

The melted faces of Hiroshima, the thirst of the blind. White teeth sticking out of a vanished face. Streets lined with corpses. A cadaver on a bicycle. Ponds filled with dead people. A physician with forty wounds. "You're alive? You're alive?" How often does he have to hear those words? An important visitor: His Excellency. In his honor, he sits up in bed and thinks he's better.

At night, the only illumination: the fires of the city, blazing corpses. A smell like that of burning sardines.

When it happened, the first thing he suddenly noticed about himself: he was stark naked.

The stillness, the figures moving soundlessly, it is like a silent film.

The visits to the patient in the hospital: the first reports on the events, the annihilation of Hiroshima.

The city of the forty-seven ronins; was that why it was picked?

The diary of the physician Michihiko Hachiya covers fifty-six days in Hiroshima, from August 6, the day of the atomic bomb, until September 30, 1945.

It is written like a work of Japanese literature: precision, tenderness, and responsibility are its essential features.

A modern doctor, who is so Japanese that he believes steadfastly in the Emperor, even when the latter announces the capitulation.

In this diary, almost every page gives food for thought. The reader learns more here than in any later description, because he experiences the enigmatic nature of the events from the very beginning; everything is completely inexplicable. In the hardship of his own condition, among dead or injured people, the author tries to piece the facts

184

together; with increasing knowledge, his conjectures change, they turn into theories requiring experiments.

There is not a false stroke in this diary; nor any vanity not based on shame.

If there were any sense in wondering what form of writing is indispensable today, indispensable for a knowing and seeing man, then it is this form.

Since everything takes place in a hospital, the observation is constantly dependent on people: the people coming to the hospital and the people running it. People are named, within days they are dead. Others, from outer areas and towns, come to visit. People thought dead prove to be alive, and the joy at finding them is overwhelming. The hospital is the best in the city, a veritable paradise compared with the others, everyone tries to get in, and many succeed. The only nocturnal lights are the fires in the city: corpses being burnt are the givers of this light. Later, a group of three form around one single candle, they speak of the "pikadon," the event.

Each one tries to add to his own experiences with the accounts of others, it is as though one had to splice together scattered and random takes for a film, with bits and pieces coming along here and there. People go into the town, thread their way through the destruction or dig for treasures, they return to the new community of the dying and they hope.

Never has any Japanese been closer to me than in this journal. How much have I read about them before. Only now do I have the feeling that I really know them.

Is it true that one experiences people as deeply as oneself only in their greatest misfortunes? Is misfortune the thing that people have most in common?

The deep dislike of all idylls, the unbearableness of idyllic literature may be connected to that.

In the case of Hiroshima, we are dealing with the most concentrated disaster that ever broke in on human beings. At one point in his diary, Dr. Hachiya thinks of Pompeii. But not even Pompeii can offer a comparison. Hiroshima experienced a catastrophe that was carefully calculated by human beings and perpetrated by them. "Nature" is altogether out of it.

The sight of the catastrophe varied, depending on where it was experienced: within the city, where they only saw, but heard nothing, "Pika"; or outside, where they also heard it, "Pikadon." Very far into the diary, we find the depiction of a man who *saw* the cloud without immediate exposure to it. He was overwhelmed by its beauty: the colorful glow, the sharp edges, the straight lines spreading out into the sky.

What does *survival* mean in a catastrophe of such scope? This diary comes, as I have said, from a physician, a particularly conscientious, modern physician, accustomed to thinking scientifically; in the face of this phenomenon, one so novel and unique, he is unable to comprehend what it is all about. It is only on the seventh day that he learns—from a visitor from the outside—that an atomic bomb has struck Hiroshima. A friend of his, an army captain, brings him a basket of peaches. "It's a miracle that you've survived," he says to Dr. Hachiya. "After all, the explosion of an atom bomb is a terrible thing."

" 'An atom bomb!' I cried and sat up in bed. 'Why, I've heard about that bomb, supposedly it could blow up Formosa with no more that ten grams of hydrogen!' "

At a very early point, visitors come to congratulate Hachiya for being alive still. He is a respected and popular man, there are grateful patients, schoolmates, one-time fellow students, relatives. Their joy at his survival is boundless, they are amazed and happy, perhaps there is no purer happiness. They dote on him, but they are also surprised at a kind of miracle.

It is one of the situations in the diary that recurs most frequently. Just as his friends and kin are glad to find him alive, he too is glad at finding others alive. There are different variations of this experience: thus, he finds out that both he and his wife were assumed to be dead. An inmate in the hospital escaped from his blazing house without managing to save his wife; he thinks she is dead. He soon returns to the ruins and looks for her remains. In the spot where he last heard her screaming for help, he finds bones, which he carries back to the hospital and devoutly places in front of the altar. Perhaps ten days later, when he brings the bones to his wife's family in the country, he finds her there, safe and sound. She somehow managed to get out of the blazing house and was driven to safety by a passing military truck.

Here, it is more than survival, it is a return from the dead, the most powerful and most wonderful experience that human beings can possibly have.

Dr. Hachiya was director of this hospital, in which he now lies as a combination patient and doctor, and the most bizarre phenomenon is the irregularity of death. People who enter the hospital burnt or marked are expected to either die or recover. It is very hard to watch some of them getting worse and worse; but some appear to get over it and gradually feel better. They are already considered saved, and then they unexpectedly have a relapse, and are suddenly in real danger. Yet there are some, including nurses and doctors, who at first seem unscathed. They work with all their strength day and night; all at once, they show symptoms of the disease, it gets worse and worse and they die.

It is uncertain whether someone has escaped the danger; the delays in the effect of the bomb upset all normal medical prognoses. The physician realizes very soon that he is totally in the dark. He tries in every way, but so long as he doesn't know what the disease can be, he feels as if he were in a pre-medical age, and he has to content himself with comforting instead of healing.

While puzzling over other people's symptoms, Dr. Hachiya is himself a patient. Every symptom he discovers in others makes him uneasy about himself as well, and he secretly looks for it on his own body. Survival is *precarious* and far from being assured.

He never loses his respect for the dead and he is horrified to see it vanish in others. When he enters the wooden cabin in which a colleague, who has come from outside, is performing autopsies, he never fails to bow to the corpse.

The dead are cremated every evening in front of the windows of his hospital room. Right next to the place where that is happening, there is a tub for bathing. The first time he attends a cremation, he hears someone shouting from the bathtub: "How many have you burned today?" The lack of piety—here, a man who was alive just a while ago and is now being cremated, and there another, naked in a tub, right close by—fills him with indignation.

187

But after a few weeks, he and a friend are having their supper in his hospital room during such a cremation. He notices the smell— "like that of burning sardines"—and keeps on eating.

The sincerity and honesty of this journal are beyond suspicion. The writer is a man of great moral culture. Like anyone else, he is caught in the traditions of his background, he doubts none of them. His qualms and questions move within the sphere of medicine, where they are permitted and necessary. He believed in the war, he accepted the militaristic policies of his country, and although he observed certain things he did not like in the behavior of the officer caste, he considered it his patriotic duty to hold his tongue about them. But these very facts make his diary a lot more interesting. For we not only experience the destruction of Hiroshima by an atomic bomb, we also witness the effect on him of his gradual awareness of Japan's defeat.

In this totally destroyed city, people are not surviving enemies, they are surviving family, colleagues, fellow citizens. The war is still on, and the foes whom one wishes dead are elsewhere. People feel threatened by them, and the destruction of one's own people increases the threat. In the case of the bomb, death comes from above, one can only strike back at a distance, and one would have to *find out* about it.

The desire for that is very strong, that is why it seemingly comes true. After a few days, a man comes from another place and reports with utter certainty that the Japanese have hit back with the same weapon, devastating not one, no indeed, *several* big American cities in the same way.

The mood in the hospital instantly reverses, an exaltation takes hold of even the seriously injured. The people become a crowd again and believe they are saved from death by this diversion of death. So long as the exaltation lasts, many of them probably believe they do not have to die now.

On the tenth day after the bomb, the news of the capitulation has an even more serious impact. The Emperor has never yet spoken on the radio. To be sure, his speech is incomprehensible even now, it is in the archaic language of the court. But the superiors, who ought to know, do recognize the voice as his, and the content of the proclamation is translated. At the mention of the imperial name, all the people in the hospital bow. None of them has ever before heard the

Emperor's voice, that voice did not command the war. But now it is that voice which disavows the war. It makes them believe in the defeat, which they would otherwise have doubted.

The hospital inmates are affected more deeply by that news than by the destruction of their city, their illnesses, or the tormented death in full sight of many of them. Now, no diversion is conceivable anymore, injury and death must be borne with no reduction in their intensity. Everything is uncertain, but also hopeless. Many struggle against this hopelessness, which is passive; they would rather keep fighting. Two parties arise, one for and one against ending the fight. The crowd of the beaten, before fully disbanding, splits up into a double crowd. But the party in favor of continuing the war has much too hard a time: it is against the Emperor's orders.

During the next few days, it is curious to experience the splitting of power in Dr. Hachiya's consciousness, whereas during the war, power was so highly centralized. It splits into an evil power, the military, which led to the misfortune of the country; and a good power, the Emperor, which wants the good of the country. In this way, a power authority still exists for Hachiya, and the true structure of his own existence is not touched. His thoughts now gravitate incessantly to the Emperor. He, like the country, was the victim of the officers. He is deeply to be pitied; his life has become even more precious. He has been humiliated for something he did not even want: the war. This permits every loyal subject to look within himself for something that did not want the war. All at once, the observations about the officers, which one never dared to utter, become potent: their arrogance, their stupidity, their scorn for everyone who did not belong to their caste. Instead of the enemy, against whom one is no longer to fight, *they* become the foe.

The Emperor, however, was there the whole time, the continuity of life depends on his continuity: even during the catastrophe that befell the city, his portrait was saved.

Towards the end of the diary (on the thirty-ninth day, for that was when Dr. Hachiya first found out about it), we hear the story of how the Imperial Portrait was rescued. It is described down to the last detail. Right through the dying and the seriously injured, just a few hours after the explosion, the Emperor's effigy is carried to the river. The dying make way: "The Emperor's picture! The Emperor's picture!" Thousands are still burning *after* the portrait is put on a boat and carried away.

Dr. Hachiya is not yet sated with the first account of this salvation. It leaves him no peace, he looks for further witnesses, especially those who participated in the lofty action. He adds a further account to his journal. During these days, a great deal meriting praise has occurred in Hiroshima. Hachiya is fair and omits none of those things. He distributes his praises carefully and deliberately. But he speaks about the rescue of the Imperial Portrait with exuberant enthusiasm. One senses that of all the things that have happened, this, for him, is the most hopeful: it sounds as though it were the *survival* of the Emperor.

People keep coming, amazed that he is alive and congratulating him for it. Their joy is still palpable in his entries and infects the reader. For a long time, patients who have succumbed are cremated in front of the hospital's windows, the dying continues. It is like a new, unknown epidemic. Its exact reason, its course have not yet been researched. It is only with the autopsies that they gradually began to realize what they are dealing with. Hachiya's desire to investigate this new disease does not wane for an instant. The traditional structure of the country, culminating in the Emperor, survives intact in Hachiya; and equally intact is his modern medical mind. It was here that I first comprehended how naturally the two can go together, how little one interferes with the other.

The unimpeachable quality of this man, however, is his respect for the dead. It has already been said how hard it is for him to endure the fact that people get used to death; for him, it always remains something very serious. One does not have the feeling that, for him, the dead melt into a crowd, in which no individual counts anymore. He thinks of them as *persons*. One should not forget that he is a physician and thus professionally exposed to being blunted against death. But whatever has happened, one has the impression that he cares about each single person who has lived, each one just as he really was, just as he remembers him.

On the forty-ninth day after the calamity, a memorial day for the dead takes place. He rides his bicycle to town and seeks out every place that is hallowed by the dead, his own and also those whom he has learned about.

He closes his eyes to see a neighbor who has perished, and she appears to him. The instant he opens his eyes, the image vanishes, he closes them again and she reappears. He seeks his way through the remnants of the city, and one cannot say that he is wandering, for he knows exactly what he is looking for and he finds it: the places of the dead. He spares himself nothing. He pictures everything. He says he is praying for everybody. I wonder whether there were any people in Europe's cities who combed the devastation for the place of the dead and thus, with the clear image of the deceased in their minds, prayed for them—not for their immediate families, but for neighbors, friends, acquaintances, even for people they had never seen, and whose deaths they had only been told about. I hesitate to use the word "pray" in connection with Hachiya's actions on that day, but he himself uses it and calls himself on this and other occasions a Buddhist.

1971

GEORG BÜCHNER
Speech at the Awarding of the Georg Büchner Prize

Ladies and gentlemen, to express thanks for an honor that is given in Büchner's name strikes me as a foolhardy venture. For one thanks in words, and who would not have Büchner's in mind when his name is pronounced, and who could there be in any land on earth who had the right to place words of his own next to these words!

Thus, I would only care to say something very simple, namely that I know of no honor that I could view as being so great a distinction as this one, and I am happy to experience it. I thank the German Academy of Language and Literature, I thank the state of Hessen, I thank the city of Darmstadt, to both of which we owe *more and more* from year to year as the homeland of two of the clearest and freest human minds, Lichtenberg and Büchner.

I am no connoisseur of critical writing on Büchner, and it is highly questionable whether I even have the right to say anything about him to you, who are probably all connoisseurs of that literature. If there is anything I could offer by way of apology, it is the fact that he changed my life as no other writer has done.

The true substance of a writer, that which appears unmistakable in him, forms, I think, in a few brief nights, which differ from all others in intensity and effulgence. It is those rare nights in which he is yet quite beset with himself, so very much that he is capable of losing himself totally in his completeness. The dark universe that he consists of, that he feels space for without being able to grasp what it contains, is suddenly penetrated by a different, an articulated world, and the clash is so violent that all matter floating, scattered and at its own devices within him will light up at one and the same time.

It is the amount in which his inner stars notice each other across dreadful empty spaces. Now that they know they are there, everything is possible. Now the language of their signals can begin.

I lived through such a night in August 1931 when I first read *Woyzeck.* Throughout the entire previous year, I had lived in *Auto-da-Fé.* It was a retiring life, a kind of corvée, there was nothing outside of it, anything else happening in that year was repulsed. But now Kien had cremated himself with his books, and I felt my own books drawn into that fate in some incomprehensible way. It may have been guilt for permitting Kien to lay hands on books; it may have been justice in having to sacrifice my own books for his; but whatever it was, they denied themselves to me and I found myself burnt empty and blind in my self-created desert.

And so, one night, I opened up Büchner, and he opened himself up to me in *Woyzeck,* in the scene between Woyzeck and the doctor. I was thunderstruck, and it seems lamentable to put it so weakly. I read through all the scenes of the so-called fragment to be found in that volume, and since I could not admit that something like that existed, since I simply did not believe it, I reread them four or five times. I would not know of anything ever to affect me like that in my life, which was not poor in impressions. By dawn, I could not stand being alone with it anymore. Early in the morning, I went into Vienna, to the woman who was more than my wife, who also became my wife, and whom I would like to have among us today, now that she is no longer with us. She was far better read than I, *she* had read Büchner at twenty. Now I berated her for never, not even once, having mentioned *Woyzeck* to me, and there was hardly anything that we had not talked about. "Be glad you didn't know it," she said, "how could you have written anything yourself! But now that it's happened, you could also finally read *Lenz.*"

Which I did, in her house, that same morning; and *Lenz* made *Auto-da-Fé,* which I *was* proud of, shrink down terribly, and I realized how decently she had behaved towards me.

This is my own sole legitimation for speaking to you today about Büchner.

I think about the stations of Büchner's life, Darmstadt, Strasbourg, Giessen, Darmstadt, Strasbourg, Zurich, and it strikes me how close they are to one another. Even for those days, it was quite neighborly.

THE CONSCIENCE OF WORDS

The extent to which people felt that in Darmstadt, at least about Strasbourg, is shown in his mother's last letter to Büchner. Despite her relief at his arrival in Zurich, she writes: "I feel that since you've left Strasbourg, you are really abroad; in Strasbourg, I always believed you nearby." Only Zurich, which is truly not far, seems like a foreign place to her. It is certainly characteristic of the elan in Büchner's work that one never thinks of these proximities. Other writers may not have gotten any further away; that seems proper for them; in Büchner, one is astonished.

Nevertheless, we must recall *how much* Strasbourg was: the breeding-ground of a new German literature, Herder and Goethe in their youth. And a belated justice demands that we say how equally crucial *Lenz* was in those years. Memories that are no older than sixty years for Büchner, memories as close as anything that we might recollect from the time before World War I. But in between came the most far-reaching event in modern history, which has been replaced by even further-reaching events only in our generation: that event was the French Revolution. In Strasbourg, the effects of that Revolution were not stifled as in Germany at the same time. Büchner comes to France during the reign of the bourgeois king, when an intellectual life is starting to develop in many directions, soaked with politics, made fertile by opinions on public matters—a life so exciting and so modern that we are still drawing upon it now in certain respects.

In Strasbourg, Büchner has his first experience with a crowd: a few weeks after his arrival, the reception of Ramorino, the Polish freedom fighter, by the students and burghers. Three or four hundred students, with a black banner at the head of the procession, marched into the town, accompanied by an enormous crowd of people, all singing the "Marseillaise" and the "Carmagnole." And the air rang with shouts: "Vive la liberté! Vive Ramorino! A bas les ministres! A bas le juste milieu!"

In the Cathedral of Strasbourg, he meets a bearded, long-haired Saint-Simonist, who makes no small impact on him despite his gaudy costume. In Strasbourg, he witnesses a police assault on a demonstrating, protesting crowd. Büchner spent two years in this open world. What he brought there from home was invaluable. He came to Strasbourg not as a bleeding-heart youth, but with an exact eye for the physical, the individual, the concrete, which he owed to generations of medical forebears and the impressions in his father's house. It is a not insensitive, but straighter and more solid note in his youth: hardly a trace of poetic drafts, no self-mirroring, no arrogant airs of feebleness. He is the eldest son of a strong, prudent father, who ultimately lives to be seventy-five, and it does not strike me as pointless to recall the ages his three brothers reached: seventy-six, seventy-five, seventy-seven. Even his mother and sisters did not die young. In this large family, he is the only one to pass away early as the result of an unfortunate infection.

In Strasbourg, he learns to move about in French with complete ease, the one language is not displaced by the other. He makes friends, he gets to know Alsace quite well, and the Vosges. The new town, the new country are not such that one drowns in them. Two years in Paris would certainly have been quite different. The conspicuous thing about Büchner's life is that nothing is wasted. A nature that keeps its objects together, carefully distinguishing them, like individual people, like organs in a human being; playfulness does not become an end in itself, even dreams, even lightness have their sharp sides. A nature that is free despite the wealth of complexities, that views nothing as indissoluble and is thus, but only thus, very different from Lenz and quite reminiscent of Goethe.

No people or things are lost, and neither are any impulses that he has ever received: everything takes effect, he has no long deadlocks. It is amazing how swiftly and energetically he reacts to new circumstances. The return from Strasbourg and the narrow conditions of Darmstadt and Giessen torment him like a critical illness. But he makes his way out of the oppressive straits in the only way possible, by passing on the revolutionary impulses he has received, and without distinction as to person, unfalsified, in accordance with the essence— passing them on to people who are not after haughty separation. He founds the Society for Human Rights, the period of conspiracy begins, and with it his double life.

It can be shown in what form this double life continues after the failure of his action, how fruitful it is, how much he owes his oeuvre to it, how it leads to *Lenz* and even *Woyzeck*. The breadth of French conditions, which he experienced in Strasbourg, is brought home, to the confines of home; likewise, he takes along the most confining thing to threaten him, prison, on his escape from his homeland to

Strasbourg, and he keeps the fear of it alive in him even after he succeeds in reaching the paradise of Zurich.

Büchner's fear, which never left him again, has a special character, because it is that of a man who has fought actively against danger. His daring behavior in front of the investigating judge, his efforts to free his friend Minnigerode from the prison, the replacement by his brother Wilhelm when he is subpoenaed, his letter to Gutzkow, finally the successful flight—all these things demonstrate a powerful character, which completely recognizes his situation and refuses to give in to it.

However, one views the matter too simply if one ignores *Danton's Death,* which he scrawled out during the month of preparing for his escape. Danton too is able to recognize his situation; in his talk with Robespierre, he actually does his best to worsen it. He wants it to be irreparable, he wants it to be acute; but when he is faced with a decision to save himself or flee, he *paralyzes* himself with a sentence that frequently recurs: "They won't dare!" It is the line in the play that seems most obsessive; the very first time, it makes the reader uneasy, and finally, after several repetitions, he feels it the way one would like to feel a slogan of the Revolution, but in reverse. It reveals the actual subject matter of the play, namely: should one save oneself? Danton wants to *remain:* there is a desire for persistence in him that is stronger than any danger. "Actually I have to laugh at the whole business," he says. "There is a feeling of remaining in me, which says tomorrow will be like today, and the day after tomorrow and so on and on, everything will be like now. That's empty noise, they want to frighten me, they will not dare!"

The figure of this man, who does not want to save himself, has to be set up by the author, who does want to save himself. It is his own danger, the Conciergerie and the *Arresthaus* in Darmstadt are one and the same. He writes in a fever, he has no choice, he cannot grant himself any peace and quiet until he has Danton under the guillotine. He says so to Wilhelm, his younger brother, his closest confidant during these weeks, and he also tells him that he has to flee. But various things hold him back: the thought of the falling-out with his father, the concern for friends in prison, the belief that the authorities cannot get at him, and the lack of money.

"The belief that the authorities cannot get him!" In Danton's

196

mouth, that becomes, "They will not dare!" With this line of Danton's, Büchner tries to free himself from his own paralysis, it eggs him on to work against it. It strikes me as unquestionable that Büchner accepts Danton's fate, experiences it under a compulsion in order to escape his own.

Büchner's deeds adhere to him long after they are done, he looks back at them as if they were both undone and done. His flight, the central event in his existence, is outwardly successful, but the terror of the prison never fades from him again. He owes a debt to the friends he has left in Darmstadt, and he pays it by putting himself in their place. His letters from Strasbourg to his family are supposed to calm them and tell about his work and his prospects, but in reality they are filled with never ending disquiet. Refugees report to him about new arrests at home, and he passes all these items on to his family in detail. Although often better informed than they, he also expects their news about the same things. Nothing concerns him more, nothing interests him more. He, who is very aware of the value of freedom, whose work does everything to preserve it, as do his alertness and lucid appreciation of dangers—he feels as though he were also with his friends in prison. Their fear is his, one senses it when he writes about executions that have not even taken place. Ever since his second arrival in Strasbourg, one can speak about a new double life of his, which continues, albeit differently, his earlier life at home, in the time of conspiracy. The one life, external, factual, is the one he leads as an emigré, and he painstakingly tries to keep it free of any grounds for being extradited. The other life is the one he leads in his mind and feelings at home, with his unfortunate friends. The necessity of flight is still constantly imminent, the month of preparing for it in Darmstadt has never ended.

It is the fate of the emigré that he would like to believe he is safe. He cannot be, for those he has left behind—the others—are not safe.

Two months after his arrival in Strasbourg, Gutzkow, in a letter to him, mentions "your novella *Lenz*." Büchner, soon after his arrival, must have written to him about his plan for such a novella.

There would be much to say about the importance of his tale, about the things connecting Büchner to Lenz. Here, I would like to remark only one thing, which, measured by all that could be said, is certainly minor: the great extent to which the story is fed and colored by the flight. The Vosges were very familiar to Büchner, who had wandered through them with his friends; and he had also described them in a letter to his parents two years earlier. On the twentieth, when Lenz comes through the mountains, they are transformed into a landscape of angst. Lenz's condition, if it can at all be summed up in *one,* is a state of flight, which, however, falls apart into many, small, apparently senseless individual flights. No prison threatens him, but he is expelled, he is exiled from his homeland. His homeland, the only region in which he could breathe freely, was Goethe, and Goethe has banished him. Now he flees to places connected to Goethe, more or less remote; he comes, attaches himself, and tries to remain. But the exile, which is inside him and still in effect, forces him to destroy everything again. In small, befuddled motions, repeated over and over, he flees into water or out the window, to the next village, the church, a farmer's house, a dead child. He would have believed himself saved if he could have brought the child back to life.

In Lenz, Büchner found his own restlessness, the fear of flight which overcame him whenever he entered the prison to see his friends. He walked along a piece of his brittle road with Lenz, transformed into him and at the same time his companion, who saw him unswervingly from the outside as an Other. There was no end for it, no end for the expulsion, for the flight, there was only the same thing over and over again. "Thus he lived on." He wrote that last sentence and left him.

The Other, however, the man Büchner was known as in his milieu at the time, pursued a rigorous and tenacious scientific work on the nervous system of the barbels, thereby gaining the respect of natural scientists in Strasbourg and Zurich. He got his doctorate and went to Zurich for a test lecture.

In the Zurich period, which lasted no longer than four months, he succeeded in asserting and proving himself. He immediately became a docent, important men attended his lectures. A long letter to him testifies to his father's forgiveness. He likes Switzerland: "Friendly villages with lovely houses everywhere!" He praises the "healthy, strong people," and the "simple, good, purely republican government."

Right after that, in the same letter, the last extant letter to his family, written on November 20, 1836, the worst possible news flashes up like lightning: "Minnigerode is dead, as I am informed, that is to say, he was tortured to death for three years. Three years!" So close together: the salvation in the Zurich paradise and the mortal torment of the friend at home.

I think it was this news that led to the final manuscript of *Woyzeck*. Like no other work of his, it addresses the people at home. He may never have found out that the news was wrong. But in any event, it had its impact on him. Two years and four months have passed since Minnigerode's arrest; the fact that the time is prolonged into three years for him, who actually has always remained in Darmstadt, is not surprising. And yet this emphatic three recalls the imprisonment of another, that of the historical Woyzeck. Over three years passed between the murder of his mistress and his public execution. The case was known to Büchner, of course, from Court Councillor Clarus' report on the murderer Woyzeck.

Aside from the news of his friend's death in prison, aside from the acute memory of the oppressed and protesting friends at home, the conception of *Woyzeck* took in something else that would not necessarily occur to us: philosophy.

Part of Büchner's completeness is the fact that he confronted philosophy with grinding teeth. He has a faculty for it; Lüning, who met him as a student in Zurich, notices a "certain, utterly decided definiteness in making statements." Yet Büchner feels repelled by philosophical *language.* Very early, in a letter to his Alsatian friend August Stöber, he writes: "I am throwing myself with utter violence into philosophy. The artificial language is disgusting; I think that for human things one ought to find human expressions." And to Gutzkow, two years later, when he had already mastered this language: "I am becoming quite stupid in the study of philosophy, I am getting to know the poverty of the human mind from a new side." He delves into philosophy without becoming addicted, nor does he sacrifice a single grain of reality to it. He takes it seriously where it operates in the lowest, in Woyzeck, and he mocks it in those who feel superior to Woyzeck.

Woyzeck, a soldier, like the mountebank's monkey, "the lowest level of the human race," driven by voices and orders, a prisoner running around free, destined to be a prisoner, placed on prison fare, always the same, peas, degraded to an animal by the doctor, who dares to tell him: "Woyzeck, man is free; in man, individuality is transfigured into freedom," which only means that Woyzeck ought to be able to hold back his urine. Freedom to be resigned to any abuse of his human nature, freedom of enslavement for a few pennies, which he gets for feeding on peas. And then one is amazed to hear the doctor say: "Woyzeck, you are philosophizing again"—like the tribute paid by the booth-owner to the trained horse. But in the next sentence, the tribute is reduced to an "aberratio," and in the next, scientifically precise, to an "aberratio mentalis partialis," with a bonus.

The captain, however, the good, good man, who thinks he is good because things are good for him, who fears a fast shave like anything fast because of the tremendous time, because of eternity—the captain rebukes Woyzeck: "You think too much, that takes its toll, you always look so driven."

Büchner's study of individual philosophical doctrines affected *Woyzeck* in a different, a more hidden way. I am thinking of the frontal presentation of important characters, something that could be called their *self-denunciation*.

The assurance with which they exclude anything that is not they, the aggressive insistence on themselves, even in their choice of words, the heedless renunciation of the real world, in which, however, they strike about, powerfully and hatefully—all this has something of the offensive self-assertion of philosophers. These figures present themselves fully in their very first lines. The captain as well as the doctor and certainly the drum-major appear as proclaimers of their own persons. Mockingly or boastingly or enviously, they draw their borders, and they draw them against one and the same despised creature, whom they see under them and who is meant to serve them as an underling.

Woyzeck is the victim of all three. The doctor and the captain have learned their philosophy, and Woyzeck has real ideas to oppose them with. *His* philosophy is concrete, tied to fear and pain and contemplation. He is afraid when he thinks, and the voices driving him are more real than the captain's emotions at his coat, which hangs there, or the doctor's immortal pea experiments. In contrast to them, he is not presented frontally; from start to finish, he consists of live, often unexpected reactions. Since he is always exposed, he is always awake, and the words he finds in his alertness are words in a state of innocence. They are not ground up and misused, they are not coins, weapons, or stories, they are words, as though they had only just come into being. Even if he takes them over without understanding them, they go their own ways in him: the Freemasons hollow out the earth for him: "Hollow, do you hear? Everything hollow down there! The Freemasons!"

Into how many people is the world split up in *Woyzeck!* In *Danton's Death,* the characters still have much too much in common, they are all of a sweeping eloquence, and Danton is by no means the only man of wit among them. One can try to explain that with the fact that it is an eloquent time, and the spokesmen of the Revolution, among whom the drama takes place, have ultimately all attained prestige through the use of words. But then we remember Marion's story—it too is a summing-up, one could not conceive a more perfect one for her, and we must reluctantly resign ourselves to the idea that *Danton's Death* is a drama out of the school of rhetoric—to be sure, the most measureless of these schools: Shakespeare's.

It is distinguished from the plays of other disciples by its urgency and rapidity and by a special substance existing nowhere else in German literature and made up equally of fire and ice. It is a fire that forces one to run, and an ice in which everything appears transparent, and one runs to keep pace with the fire and tarries to peer into the ice.

Less than two years later, Büchner, with his *Woyzeck,* succeeded in performing the most perfect upset in literature: the discovery of the lowly. This discovery presupposes mercy; but only when the mercy is hidden, when it is dumb, when it does not articulate itself—only then is the lowly *intact.* The writer who gives himself airs with his feelings, who openly puffs up the lowly with his mercy, will sully and destroy it. Woyzeck is driven by voices and by other people's words, yet the driver has left him untouched. In this chastity regarding the lowly, there is no one comparable to Büchner even today.

In the last days of his life, Büchner is shaken with fever fantasies, today, little is known about their nature and content. These few items are in Caroline's Schulz's notes, in her own words. She writes:

"14th[February]. . . . Around eight o'clock, the delirium came back, and it was odd that he often spoke about his fantasies, judged them himself when we persuaded him they were not true. A recurrent fantasy was his imagining he had been extradited. . . .

"15th. . . . He spoke somewhat heavily when coming to his senses, but as soon as he was delirious, he spoke quite fluently. He told me a long coherent story: about his being brought out of the city yesterday, about first giving a speech in the marketplace, etc.

"16th. . . . The patient wanted to go out several times because he imagined he could be imprisoned or believed he already was imprisoned and wanted to escape."

I think if we had these fantasies in their true wording, we would be very close to Woyzeck: even in this report, which is reduced and mellowed by grief and love and which lacks the terror of a driven man, we can feel something of Woyzeck himself. Büchner still had Woyzeck in him when he died on the nineteenth.

It is not pointless to meditate over Büchner's possible later life, because it keeps one from looking for any sense in his death. It was as senseless as any death, but his death makes this senselessness particularly blatant. He was not fulfilled despite the weight and maturity of the works he left behind. It is part of his nature that he would never have been completed, not even later. He stands there as the pure exemplar of man who has to remain incomplete. His many abilities, alternately pinch-hitting for one another, testify to a nature that, in its inexhaustibility, demands an endless life.

1972

THE FIRST BOOK
Auto-da-Fé

The title is misleading, for the book that was to become my first was conceived as one of eight books that were drafted at the same time, in the course of one year, from autumn 1929 to autumn 1930. The manuscript of the first of these novels, on which I then concentrated and which evolved during the following year, bore the name *Kant Catches Fire*. Under this title, it remained in my home as a manuscript for four years, and it was only when it was about to be published, in 1935, that I supplied the title it has since had in German: *Die Blendung* (blinding, dazzlement).

The chief character of this book, today known as Kien, was designated as B. in the early drafts, the initial being short for "Bookman." For that was how I saw him, as a bookman, and so intensely that his connection to books was far more important than he himself. His consisting of books was his sole quality at the time; for the moment, he had no others, I gave him the name Brand (conflagration). This name contained his end: he was to end in a fire. While I did not know in detail how the novel would develop, one thing was certain at the start: he would set fire to himself and his books, burning up with his library in that self-created fire. That was why his name was Brand, and thus the two early designations for him, Bookman and Brand, were all that was certain about him at the very beginning.

However, one more thing was certain, and it must be called decisive for the book: the counter-figure of Therese, the small-minded housekeeper. The model for her was as real as the bookman was unreal. In April 1927, outside of Vienna on a hill overlooking Hacking, I had rented a room in Hagenberggasse. I had already lived in a few student digs in town and now I wanted to live outside for a change. The Lainz deer park with its old trees attracted me, and the advertisement for a room right near the wall of the deer park leaped to my eyes. I went to have a look at the room, the landlady opened and took me up to the second story, which contained nothing but this room. She herself lived downstairs with her family on the main floor. I was thrilled with the view; beyond a playground, you could see the trees of the archbishop's large garden and on the other side of the valley, on top of the facing slope, there was the walled town of the mentally ill, Steinhof. I made up my mind at first sight, I had to be in this room, I discussed the details with the landlady in front of the open window. Her skirt reached to the floor, she held her head at an angle sometimes throwing it to the other side; the first speech I heard from her is taken up verbatim in *Auto-da-Fé:* about the young people of today and potatoes that already cost twice as much. It was a fairly long speech, and it irritated me so much that I fixed it in my mind immediately. It is true that I often heard it again word for word during the next few years. But I could not possibly have forgotten it after the first time.

At this first viewing, I stipulated that my girlfriend could visit me. The landlady insisted it had to be the same young lady, my "fiancée," every time. My indignant reply that it was only one put her at ease. I also had a lot of books, I said. "Excuse me," she said, "that must be so with a student." There were more problems with my final request: I wanted to hang up the pictures that I always had. She said: "The lovely wallpaper. Does it have to be thumbtacks?" I said yes hard-heartedly. For six years, I had been living with large reproductions of the frescoes in the Sistine Chapel, and I was thus the thrall of Michelangelo's prophets and sibyls, whom I would not have sacrificed even for this room. She saw my resoluteness and gave in reluctantly.

I spent six years in that room, and I owe it not just the character of Therese. The daily view of Steinhof, where six thousand lunatics lived, was the thorn in my flesh. I am quite sure that I would never have written *Auto-da-Fé* without that room.

But things had not gotten that far yet, I was still a student of chemistry, going to the laboratory every day and writing only in the evenings. Nor would I want to give the false impression that the character of Therese, who came into being only three and one half years later, had more in common with the landlady than her way of

204

speaking and outer resemblance. She was a retired post office employee, her husband too had worked for the post office, and two grown children lived with them. Only Therese's first speech is real, everything else is quite freely invented.

A few months after I moved into this new room, something happened that exerted a deep influence on my later life and also on the creation of *Auto-da-Fé*. It was one of those not too frequent public events which move an entire city so deeply that it is no longer the same afterwards.

On the morning of July 15, 1927, I was not in the Chemical Institute on Währingerstrasse as usual, I was at home. I was reading the morning newspapers in the coffeehouse in Ober Sankt Veit. I can still feel the indignation that overwhelmed me when I took hold of the *Reichspost;* it had a gigantic headline: "A Just Verdict." There had been shooting in Burgenland, workers had been killed. The court had acquitted the murderers. The judgment was designated, no, trumpeted as a "just verdict" in the organ of the government party. It was that mockery of any sense of justice rather than the acquittal itself that triggered an enormous excitement in the workers of Vienna. From all parts of the city, the workers marched in closed processions to the Palace of Justice, which with its sheer name embodied injustice for them. It was a completely spontaneous reaction, I personally felt just how spontaneous. Taking my bicycle, I zoomed into the city and joined the procession.

The workers, usually well disciplined, trusting their Social Democratic leaders, and content that Vienna was ruled by them in an exemplary fashion, were acting *without* their leaders on that day. When they set fire to the Palace of Justice, Mayor Seitz, standing on a fire engine, tried to block their way with his right hand raised high. His gesture was futile: the Palace of Justice was *burning*. The police were ordered to shoot, ninety people were killed.

That was forty-six years ago, and the excitement of that day still lies in my bones. It was the closest thing to a revolution that I had physically experienced. A hundred pages would not suffice to describe what I saw. Since then, I have known very precisely that I need not read a single word about what happened during the storming of the Bastille. I became a part of the crowd, I dissolved into it fully, I did not feel the least resistance to what it did. I am surprised that I was nevertheless able to grasp all the concrete details occurring before my eyes. I would like to mention one of them.

In a side street, not far from the burning Palace of Justice, but still off to the side, a man, very sharply distinguished from the crowd, stood with high flung arms, wailing and moaning over and over again: "The files are burning! All the files!" "Better than people!" I told him, but that didn't interest him, all he could think of was the files. It occurred to me that he might have some connection to the files, an archivist, he was inconsolable. He struck me as funny, even in this situation. But he also annoyed me. "They've been shooting down people!" I said angrily, "and you carry on about files!" He looked at me as if I weren't there and repeated with a moan: "The files are burning! All the files!" He was stationed to the side, but it was not undangerous for him, his lament was not to be missed, I too had heard it.

A few years later, when I sketched the *Human Comedy of Madmen,* I gave B., the bookworm, the name Brand. The fact that his name and fate derived from that Fifteenth of July was something I was not conscious of, it would have been embarrassing for me if I had realized the connection, and perhaps I would even have thrown out the entire plan. Nevertheless, the name Brand began hemming me in as I wrote the novel. So much else happened, and the end, which a reader should not think of in advance, seemed too blatantly foreshadowed in this name. I redubbed him Kant, and he bore that name undisturbed for a long time. In August 1931, four years after July 15, Kant set fire to his library and perished in the conflagration.

But that was a late, unforeseen consequence of July 15. Had anyone, at that time, announced such a literary result, I would have ripped him to shreds. For right after that, in the days of utter dejection, when one could think of nothing else, and the events one had witnessed were still taking place in front of the mind's eye, haunting one night after night even in sleep, there was only one legitimate connection with literature, and that was Karl Kraus. My idolization of him was at its highest level then. This time, it was gratitude for a very definite public deed, I don't know to whom else I was ever so grateful for anything. Under the impact of the massacre, he put up posters everywhere in Vienna, demanding the "resignation" of Police

Commissioner Johann Schober, who was responsible for the order to shoot and the ninety deaths. He did it alone, he was the only public figure to do so; and while the other celebrities, of whom there was never any lack in Vienna, did not wish to lay themselves open to criticism or perhaps even ridicule, he alone found the courage for his indignation. His posters were the only thing to keep one upright in those days. I walked from one to another, stopped at each, and I felt as if all the justice of this earth had gone into the letters of his name.

The year following this event was completely dominated by it. Until summer 1928, my thoughts revolved around nothing else. More than ever, I was resolved to find out what a crowd really is, for a crowd had overwhelmed me from the inside and the outside. I seemingly continued my chemistry studies and started the work for my dissertation, but the task I charged myself with was so uninteresting that it barely scratched the skin of my mind. I devoted every free moment to studying the things that were really important to me. In various, apparently very farflung ways, I tried to approach what I had experienced as a crowd. I looked for it in history, indeed, in the history of *all* cultures. I was more and more fascinated by the history and early philosophy of China. I had already begun with the Greeks much earlier, in my Frankfurt period. Now I delved into the ancient historians, especially Thucydides, and the philosophy of the pre-Socratics. It was natural for me to study the revolutions, the English, French, and Russian; but also the significance of crowd in religions started dawning on me, and my desire to know all religions, which has never left me since then, commenced in that time. I read Darwin, hoping to find something in him about crowds among animals, and I perused books on insect states. I must have slept very little, for I read all through the night. I took a number of notes and tried to write a few essays. They were all provisional and preliminary work for the book on crowds. But now, considering it from the standpoint of the novel, I see how many traces those passionate and diverse studies left in *Auto-da-Fé,* which was finished just a few years later.

In summer 1928, I came to Berlin for the first time, and that was the next decisive event. Wieland Herzfelde, founder of the Malik publishing house, was looking for a young man to help him with his work on a book, and he had found out about me from a friend. He invited me to come to Berlin during the semester break, to live in his place and also work there. He received me heartily and did not make me feel how inexperienced and unknown I was. I suddenly found myself in a nexus of Berlin's intellectual life. He took me along everywhere, I met his friends and countless other people; sometimes, say at Schlichter or at Schwanecke, a dozen of them at once. Let me name only the three who were most on my mind: One was George Grosz, whose drawings I had admired since my schooldays in Frankfurt; Isaac Babel, both of whose books I had recently read, and they had made the deepest impact on me of all books in modern Russian literature; Brecht, of whom I knew only a few poems, but there was so much talk about him that people were curious, and besides, he was one of the very few younger writers whom Karl Kraus tolerated. Grosz gave me an *Ecce Homo* folder, which had been prohibited; Babel took me along everywhere, especially to Aschinger, where he felt most at home. I was overwhelmed by the openness of both men, who spoke to me about anything whatsoever. Brecht, recognizing my naïveté, instantly and understandably irritated by my "lofty attitude," tried to shock me with cynical remarks about himself. I never saw him without his telling me something bewildering about himself. I sensed that Babel, to whom I could scarcely offer anything, liked me for the very innocence that drove Brecht to cynical remarks. Grosz, who had read little, preferred asking me about books, and he was not the least bit shy about having titles recommended to him.

There would be a great deal to say about that Berlin period, and I am not really saying anything now. The only thing I would like to mention today is the contrast to Vienna. In Vienna, I knew no writers, I lived alone; since everything was made taboo by Karl Kraus, I had no desire to meet any writers. At the time, I did not yet know about Musil and Broch. Many, indeed most things that were highly regarded in Vienna were fairly worthless, and it is only today that we know what important things were being done then, almost behind closed doors, pushed aside and ignored by the public, for instance the works of Berg and Webern.

Now I suddenly found myself in Berlin, where everything was open, where the new and interesting things were also famous. I moved about only among these people, who all knew each other. They led a fast and vehement life. They frequented the same cafés, spoke about one another without the least qualms, loved and hated each other in all openness, their peculiarities presented themselves in the very first sentences, it was as though they were striking out at people with themselves. Never before had I seen articulated people so different and so peculiar and all in a heap. It was child's play recognizing on the spot a man who had something to him, harmlessly in contrast to Vienna, there was no lack of such people. I was in the most expansive excitement, and at the same time I was terrified. I took in so much that it had to confuse me. Yet I was resolved not to let myself be confused, and this refusal to yield to inevitable confusion had painful consequences.

The most difficult thing for a young Puritan—which I still was because of the special circumstances of my early years—was the wilder sexuality. I saw much that I had always despised. It was incessantly presented to us, it was part of the character of life in Berlin back then. Anything was possible, anything *happened;* compared with that, Freud's Vienna, in which so much was *talked* about, seemed harmlessly chattery. I had never before felt so close to the entire world at each of its places at once, and this world, which I could not master in three months, seemed like a world of lunatics.

It fascinated me so much that I was unhappy upon having to return to Vienna in October. Everything lay in me, unseparated and unmastered, a gigantic tangle. I terminated my studies in winter and passed my examinations in spring. I felt slightly as if I didn't know what I was doing, for underneath everything was the new chaos, that would not go to sleep. I had promised my friends to come back to Berlin in summer of 1929. The second visit, lasting another three months or so, was somewhat less feverish. I lived for myself and forced myself to follow a quieter life style. I saw many people again, but not all. I went to other parts of Berlin, I went to pubs alone, meeting a different kind of people there, particularly workers, but also burghers and petit bourgeois, who were not intellectuals or artists. I took my time and I made my jottings.

Now, when I returned to Vienna in the fall, the amorphous tangle began to clear up. It was all over with chemistry forever, I only wanted to write. I had ensured myself a livelihood with a few books by Upton Sinclair, which I was to translate for the Malik publishing house. I was a free man, and I continued the manifold studies that were close to my heart, that I had begun prior to Berlin, those preliminary works for the book on crowds. But the thing preoccupying me most after my return from Berlin, the thing that wouldn't let go of me was—the extreme and frenzied people I had met. In Vienna, I once again lived alone in the room I have already spoken of. I saw almost no one, and in front of me, on the facing hill, I always had the city of lunatics, Steinhof.

One day, the thought came to me that the world should not be depicted as in earlier novels, from one writer's standpoint as it were; the world had *crumbled,* and only if one had the courage to show it in its crumbled state could one possibly offer an authentic conception of it. However, this did not mean that one had to tackle a chaotic book, in which nothing was comprehensible anymore; on the contrary, a writer had to invent extreme individuals with the most rigorous consistency, like the individuals the world consisted of, and he had to place these extreme individuals next to one another in their separateness. I made that plan of a human comedy of lunatics and sketched eight novels, each focusing on a figure on the verge of madness, and each of these figures was different from all others down to his language, down to his most secret thoughts. His experiences were such that no one else could have had the same ones. Nothing could be exchangeable and nothing could mix with anything else. I told myself I was building eight spotlights to illuminate the world from the outside. For a year, I kept working on these eight characters alternately, depending on which attracted me most in a given moment. There was a religious fanatic; there was a technological visionary, who only lived in cosmic plans; there was a collector; a man obsessed with truth; a spendthrift; an enemy of death; and finally, a pure bookman too.

Parts of these extravagant drafts, only small parts unfortunately, are still in my possession, and when I was reading through them recently, the élan of that time awoke in me again, and I understand why I remember that year as the richest year of my life. For in early fall 1930, there was a change. The bookman suddenly became so important to me that I pushed aside all other drafts and concentrated fully on him. The year in which I had indulged myself in everything was replaced by a year of downright ascetic discipline. Every morning, never omitting a day, I worked on Brand, as he was now called. I had no plan, but I avoided the heat of the previous year. To keep from being swept away too far, I kept reading Stendhal's *The Red and the Black.* I wanted to proceed step by step and I told myself it had to be a severe book, ruthless towards both myself and the reader. A deep dislike of the prevailing Viennese literature kept me immune to anything pleasant or agreeable. The most popular thing was of an operatic sentimentality, and there were also the lamentable feature-writers and chatterers. I cannot say that any of these people meant anything to me, their prose filled me with disgust.

When I ask myself today where I got the rigor of my work, I come to very heterogeneous influences. I have already named Stendhal, it was certainly he who made me stick to clarity. I had just finished the eighth chapter of *Auto-da-Fé,* now titled "Death," when Kafka's *Metamorphosis* came into my hands. Nothing more fortunate could have happened to me at this point. There, in utmost perfection, I found the antipode to literary non-commitment, which I hated so much; there was the rigor that I yearned for. There, something was achieved that I wanted to find for myself. I bowed to this purest of all models, knowing full well that it was unattainable, but it did give me strength.

I believe that a familiarity with chemistry, with its processes and formulas, also went into this rigor. Thus, retrospectively, I can by no means regret the four and one-half years I spent in the laboratory, an occupation I regarded as unintellectual and confining. That time was not lost, it proved to be a peculiar discipline for writing.

Nor was the year of drafts lost. Since I was working on all these drafts at once, I had accustomed myself to moving simultaneously and leaping about in various worlds that had nothing in common, that were separated from one another down to their last details, down to their languages. This benefited the consistent separation of the characters in *Auto-da-Fé.* What was earlier the separation between novels now became the separations within a single book. So, although the material of those drafts remained largely unused, the method of *Auto-de Fé* was formed through them. Even the things that remained unwritten in the eight novels, the secret juices of the *Human Comedy of Madmen* flowed into *Auto-da-Fé.*

Despite my satisfaction at my daily progress in writing, at its never letting me go and my never wanting to stop, I felt tormented by the concrete reality of the sentences as I committed them to paper. The cruelty of the man who forces himself to deal with a truth mostly tortures himself; the writer does a thousand times more to himself than to the reader. There were moments in which this sensitivity almost persuaded me to terminate the novel—against my better judgment. My refusal to give in to these temptations is something I owe in part to the reproductions of the Isenheim Altar, which had replaced the Sistine frescoes in my room. I was embarrassed in front of Grünewald, who had undertaken something enormously difficult and stuck to it for four years. Today that strikes me as bombastic. But any worship of truly great things, if it becomes too intimate, has something arrogant about it. At the time, these details in Grünewald, which I always had around me, were an indispensable goad.

In October 1931, after a year, the novel was finished. Brand, as we now know, had changed his name in the course of the work, he was now Kant. However, I had qualms about the identity with the philosopher's name, and I knew I would not keep it. Likewise, the title of the manuscript was a provisional *Kant Catches Fire.*

The novel retained every detail of the form it now had. Except for the title and the sinologist's name, nothing was altered. It consisted of three parts, and I had each one bound separately in black linen, and then I sent the three heavy tomes in an enormous package to Thomas Mann. Upon opening it, he must have thought they formed a trilogy. In the accompanying letter, I struck a haughty and dignified tone. It is hard to believe, but I was of the opinion that my sending the book was an honor to him. I was sure he merely had to open any of the volumes and would then be unable to put it down again. In a few days, the three volumes came back unread; he apologized, saying he didn't have the strength. I was absolutely convinced I had written an exceptional book, and even today, it is still an enigma from where I drew this certainty. My reaction to the wretched brush-off was that I decided to let the manuscript lie and not undertake anything with it.

I stuck to my resolve for a long time. Then I softened now and again. By giving readings from the manuscript, I emerged more and more from the isolation of my life in Vienna. I read Musil and Broch, was deeply impressed by their works, and also met them. Likewise I got to know other people who meant a great deal to me: Alban Berg, Georg Merkel, and Fritz Wotruba. My book existed for them and a few others before it existed for the public. I wanted to assert myself only with them, the real stars in Vienna, and some of them became my good friends. I in no wise regarded it as a humiliation that for four years I could not find a publisher who would venture to put out the novel. Now and then, quite seldom, I gave in to a friend's urging and submitted the manuscript to a publishing house. I would get letters explaining how risky a publication would be, but these letters were almost always respectful. Only Peter Suhrkamp made me feel very distinctly his deep distaste for the novel. Every rejection increased my certainty that the book would live later on. Then, in 1935, when it was really about to come out, Broch urged me, with a stubbornness unusual for him, to give up the name Kant. I had always planned to, but now it really happened. The man was now called Kien (pinewood), something of his combustibility got back into his name. Along with Kant, the title *Kant Catches Fire* likewise disappeared, and I decided upon the new and definitive title: *Die Blendung*.

Perhaps I should also mention that Thomas Mann now read the book immediately. He wrote that of all the books of that year, this novel, together with *Henri Quatre* by his brother, occupied him the most. His letter, containing a few intelligent and many flattering things, moved me in a conflicting way; it was only upon reading it that I realized the absurdity of the wound that his refusal had caused me four years earlier.

1973

THE NEW KARL KRAUS

Speech Given at the
Berlin Academy of the Arts

The census has revealed that Vienna has 2,030,834 inhabitants. Namely, 2,030,833 souls and me." There is no utterance by Karl Kraus that more perfectly sums up his attitude and his essence than the single lean sentence of this gloss. The subject is a population figure, the population of Vienna, designated as a certain number of souls, whereby the word signifies the opposite of what it originally meant and still means today. The plural puts it near Gogol's dead souls, they are souls that are no longer souls. Their pluralism deprives them of life. All together are juxtaposed to an individual known as "I," and this "I" balances them, the weight and value of this I are greater than those of all the other inhabitants put together.

Such a claim has never been made so nakedly, one might call it a fluke that it exists in this tersest of all wordings. It stands behind the 30,000 pages of the *Fackel* [Kraus's journal—translator's note], which never lacks for life despite its armored language. This claim signifies that the One can challenge these millions, it contains his murderous intention as he confronts the total population of a metropolis, each and every single one, and it is important that this city be named by its name: Vienna.

The *Fackel* issue containing this inconspicuous gloss is dated January 26, 1911. Seen retrospectively, that was a relatively harmless time, and it may be considered unsuitable to ascribe a murderous intention to the writer of this simple line. At first sight, he expresses nothing more than a penchant for *separateness*. It is unbearable to be counted as a number in a census. The larger the figure, the more incomparable a man feels when learning it—a man who breathes, lives, reads, judges, hates—the more incomparable he feels towards those who are merely counted along as numbers in that figure. Nothing more seems to be expressed in this opposition, and one has to be infected by Karl Kraus after years of familiarity with his oeuvre to see anything else in his utterance. Distrust was the supreme virtue for him when he began writing the *Fackel,* his aim was to see through things ruthlessly; and during the thirty-six-year run of his journal, he succeeded like no one else in practicing that virtue. He infected many people and he may have helped some achieve their own way of looking through things, a way they held on to as long as he to his.

Hence, he cannot be excluded from being seen through himself, he has to put up with being an object of the same practice, which he exercised with incomparable mastery throughout his life. So I insist on sniffing a homicidal intention in that meager gloss, aimed at the entire statistically comprehended population of Vienna, and I would like to support my allegation with several of the many sentences that he wrote down in 1911 or earlier.

In its first issue, the *Fackel*'s motto was not a sonorous *What we are running,* but *What we are running over.* One could attribute that to a punsterism with no overly great importance. Yet leafing through later issues, we stumble over sentences like the following:

"If he kicks the bucket before my very eyes, he mocks me for the meagerness of my trophies." One page further: "What care I about the events? The plunging rock may be shaped as it will: the way the Austrian brain sewage splashes about is still the only spectacle for whose sake I pay an income tax to this state." That was printed in the summer of 1907.

In the attacks on Alfred Kerr during 1911, four successive issues of the *Fackel* contain the following titles: "Little Pan Is Dead," "Little Pan Is Still Rattling," "Little Pan Already Stinks," "Little Pan Still Stinks." And there are sentences like: "Whereas other polemicists make themselves popular by losing their breath, the survival of my objects always keeps reinspiring me. They may consider that I persecute the great down to their very shades and will not release them even there." Or: "It is my doom that the people I wish to kill up and die on the sly." Or: "Now he's gone and leaves me nothing to do but put him on a bier."

I am by no means falsifying his ways when I put Karl Kraus's murderous desires at the fore of this reflection. No moral treatise is intended here. I want to try to grasp him as he was. But to forestall any misunderstanding, to prevent any false notions in his belittlers, of whom there was never any lack, I want to say immediately that I consider him the greatest German satirist, the only one in the literature of this language whom one has the right to name next to Aristophanes, Juvenal, Quevedo, Swift, and Gogol. Those names are few. One could also add Ben Jonson and Nestroy. But still, the list remains very small, and it obviously does not comprise the writers of a literary genre in a narrower sense. What they have in common is a very definite kind of substance, which I would simply call "murderous." They attack whole groups of people, but also individuals, with a hatred that would otherwise—i.e., if they were not capable of writing—lead to murder. Their victims are not always known by name, but the ghosts of those among them who still mean something to us today, like Socrates or Euripides, could bear witness to the rage of the assault upon them.

The case of Karl Kraus is particularly bizarre because his entire enormous oeuvre is within our reach. Wherever we open to, it is filled with lust and voracity for attack. Insignificant as many of the objects and causes may seem to us, everything about them can still be found out. They are not so remote from us in time as to exist only on the pages of the *Fackel*. Many of the victims, having escaped, were still alive recently, others are still alive today. I knew quite a number of them, and I always kept comparing them with the figures they became in Kraus's writings. An inexhaustible fascination emanated from these clashes, infinitely many things could be learned about the process of satire.

What annoys today's reader of the *Fackel,* what makes it unbearable for him over long stretches, is the evenness of assault. Everything happens with the same strength, everything is drawn as equally important into one and the same language. One senses that the attack is an end in itself, a superior strength is demonstrated where absolutely no strength would be necessary; the victim vanishes under the incessant blows, he is long since gone, and the fight continues.

Besides, victories look suspicious now. There have been so many victories in our century, such costly, such senseless, such fruitless ones—most people, not just those who can think about it, are fed up with victories, fed up as perhaps no one else in the past. Even the gesture of victory disgusts us; something in the automatism of human actions, which was oriented towards victories throughout known history, is about to change radically.

Thus, the intellectual victors, who incessantly have to attack, fight, and win, who cannot help demonstrating their superiority, make us feel uneasy, we find them irksome, we turn away from them. For this reason, there are some who will have nothing to do with Karl Kraus, and I would say that they are the best among his detractors. However, they overlook something that is probably decisive: No one, literally no one, did as much to propagate that attitude as Karl Kraus.

For he was the only person to fight against World War I from start to finish and in every single detail; World War I, in which the victors on all sides were put on pedestals. His fight was not theoretical, there was no lack of intellectual protests against the war; nor did he advocate the standpoint of any one party. As important as such parties were, as immense as the results of their attitude, so long as it was consistent—he nevertheless was really the only one to wage the struggle alone. And if, among the more than two million souls of that Viennese census, soon many felt as he did—he nevertheless confronted every single phenomenon of the war. There was not *one* voice that he did not hear, he was possessed with every specific timbre of the war and rendered it compellingly. Whatever he satirically foreshortened in this case was foreshortened effectively; whatever he exaggerated was exaggerated so precisely that it only first existed in this exaggeration and remained unforgettable. The world war entered *The Last Days of Mankind* completely, unsparingly, uncomfortingly, without embellishment, without reduction, and above all and most important, without habituation. Whatever was repeated in that play remained horrifying through every single repetition. One is amazed that there was ever a hatred of such proportions, a hatred befitting even the world war, sinking its teeth into it with a visionary fury and not letting go for four years.

Compared with that, the hatred of the combatants themselves was weak, the fighters who had sunk their teeth into an enemy that was set up for them and daily painted in the falsest colors. They leaned on each other, their attitude was a general one, they were also faced with a double threat of death: from the foe, who was as ill-used as they, and from their own superiors. Karl Kraus carries his Aetna of hatred in himself alone, he had been practicing it for fourteen years of the *Fackel;* in large, in small, in petty actions he had mastered everything that now came to his aid. He had stocked up an arsenal of the most versatile weapons without guessing what he would use them for, his military exercises are all presented in the *Fackel,* it is not necessary to treat each of them as sacrosanct; some, like the roasting of Maximilian Harden or the grand essay *Nestroy and Posterity,* are admirable, others are off target or boring. But all in fall, they benefited the thing that will always be regarded as his true achievement, because of which he is counted among the great, the deadly satirists of mankind.

Today, I have not undertaken to convince you how great this accomplishment was. There would certainly be a great deal to say about it, but I find it hard to believe that there could be even one person among you who was not overwhelmed by this work—*if* he confronted it. Hardly anyone could venture to write an introduction for *The Last Days of Mankind.* It would be both arrogant and superfluous. The introduction is carried inside by everyone born in this century and doomed to live in it. The monstrous placenta of the First World War, the very movement that led to the Second, together with its conclusion, is still before our eyes, and the threat it ended with is something we are well aware of. It has entered the conception of the future, in which, for the first time, we are all involved together. Blindness towards this is no longer possible. I do not want to tire you with a repetition of what I have said about the "split future." The man who has the hope (and I would not know of anyone who could possibly not have it) that we could still succeed in escaping from the black half of this future, which threatens annihilation, into the other half, that of the good life, which has no less possibility plus all desirability on its side—that man realizes that the most crucial thing is knowing what we are like, knowing what people, who are in no respect different from us, are capable of. This knowledge cannot be complete enough, it cannot be extreme enough.

There are two ways of reading *The Last Days of Mankind:* either as the painful introduction to the truly last days now imminent; or also as an overall picture of the things we have to discard if we wish to avoid these truly last days. The best thing would be to find the

218

strength for experiencing this work differently at different times, namely in both ways.

Yet however one has experienced it—it has always been a riddle how this work could come about. One can so easily say that a man carries an Aetna of hatred inside him, especially when he has said it about himself. But what enabled him to nourish this hatred for four whole years, that uncommonly complex hatred, which, unlike the earlier satires of the *Fackel,* does not aim at any individual foe or any alleged monster. How can a man consist for four whole years of hundreds and hundreds of voices, which acutely contain their vileness and their own condemnation at once? How can a man endure such uncounted horror? I attended a hundred lectures by Karl Kraus; for nine years I let every spoken and written word of his take effect on me: for five years without resistance, for four with growing criticism. But I never knew who he was, he remained the most incomprehensible of all men for me, when I was entranced by him as well as in the period of incipient skepticism. I could grasp his impact on others and on myself, but who he was and how he existed remained an unanswerable enigma for me.

A short while ago, the key to Karl Kraus was found. Since the publication of his letters to Sidonie von Nádhérny,* there has been a *new* Karl Kraus, and this is the one I would like to speak to you about today. But I first have to say how grateful I am to the redactors of these letters, the men who did the real, very difficult work, Walter Methlagl and Friedrick Pfäfflin. The notes supplied by Friedrich Pfäfflin, which fill nearly the entire second volume of the publication excel in tact and conscientiousness: any understanding is impossible without these notes, and one has to live with the letters for a good while to gauge the high value of this achievement.

On September 8, 1913, Karl Kraus was introduced to Sidonie by her cousin, Count Max Thun, in the Café Imperial. There is hardly anything by Kraus about the first meeting; we are all the more thankful for a passage in Sidonie's diary a few days later, quoted by

---

* Karl Kraus, *Letters to Sidonie Nádhérny von Borutin.* Edited by Heinrich Fischer and Michael Lazarus. Redaction by Walter Methlagl and Friedrich Pfäfflin. Munich: Kosel Verlag, 1974.

Pfäfflin. There are just a few key words, but several illuminate the power of that first meeting. They spoke about the writers who were much talked about in that time. With some amazement, one reads about Sidonie's influence on Rilke's poems. Perhaps it was an effusive compliment of Kraus's. Next to it comes the sentence: "Nothing for you, I am going to write now."

That very first night, they went to the Prater together. "Fiacre, Praterallee, floating stars" that's what she wrote. He spoke about her voice, lamenting, clear, and yet scarcely audible, fading. About her gaze, which was fixed in the distance. If one could only be where those eyes saw! Earlier, during supper in a hotel bar, she had spoken about the desert in which she now lived. Only three months had passed since the death of her favorite brother Johannes. He had taken his own life during a trip to Munich. She couldn't get over it, her parents had died earlier, this brother, Johannes, one year her senior, had been the most important person to her. He was twenty-nine when he took his life. All she had left now was her twin brother Karl, with whom she lived in Janowitz. When one gets to know her later, one feels that her grief is a sort of paralysis: all emotion dried up, everything meaningless that might move one after such a dreadfully sudden death. Thus she now saw her life in the image of a desert. He, endowed with a peculiar sensitivity to death, inconsolable at seventeen over the death of his mother, later over the death of twenty-two-year-old Annie Kalmar, whom he idolized as much as she her brother Johannes, overwhelmed by her sorrow, which had spread as a desert around her, and overpowered by her beauty, filled with compassion and admiration for her—Kraus, in the most lightninglike way, which was typical of his decisive reactions, made up his mind to lead her out of the desert. The strength with which he saw and understood her, the way in which he addressed the dead man in her, with tenderness and respect for him, as though he had personally known him and realized how greatly he deserved this grief—the unquestionable nature of this action, the vehemence and thoughtfulness of an admiration that omitted nothing, that embraced her fully—all these things subdued her, and she felt, with *his* certainty, that she had met the man whom she most needed.

During the swift nocturnal drive through the Prater, he said things about her that had something somnambular in them: he said she

220

needed freedom, travel, movement. "He recognizes my essence," she writes. In those first hours, he granted her the things that later were to cause him the greatest torments. She, however, during this drive, spoke the sentence that she did not record herself; we find it only eight years later in one of his letters; she said: "Come with me!" And she meant that he should accompany her to her freedom. In all these years, it was the only challenge, the only active thing that came from her.

In late November, he visited her for the first time in Janowitz. A castle, in a wonderful park, with ancient trees, among which a five-hundred-year-old poplar particularly entranced him. Here, Sidonie lived as mistress of the animals, with horses and hounds, swans and nightingales. To have some notion of Sidonie's effect when welcoming a guest at Janowitz, one only has to read Rilke's letter about his visit to Janowitz seven years before.* The fact that Kraus's experience was different, that he was more amazed and more excited, with Janowitz as the paradisal contrast to an accursed world, which he lashed and ransacked night after night, does not lessen the value of Rilke's portrayal. For it too bears witness that these are not just any castle, any park, any inhabitants of such a place. Rilke too felt the unity of the mistress and the park and he was moved by that in a more profound way than he was willing to admit to some of his more influential castle patronesses. His twenty-year correspondence with Sidonie was meant as much for Janowitz as for her; he loved thinking of it as an ultimate haven, though he no longer cared to use it when he knew Karl Kraus was there. The new year, 1914, brought Kraus back to Janowitz. He was emphatically touched by the mistress of the place and the place itself and all its inhabitants. They shifted to his center; he referred everything to them from now on; Janowitz became the solid pole of faith in his existence. Here, everything was perfect and good, nothing was spoiled. Here, one did not have to look through anything, all was as it appeared, but heightened, transfigured. In Karl Kraus's world, nothing is different. There is the despicable and the lofty; and between them, nothing. The dullness and mediocrity constituting the world of most people are unknown to

---

* Rainer Maria Rilke, *Briefe an Sidonie Nádhérny von Borutin*. Edited by Bernhard Blume. Frankfurt/Main: Insel Verlag, 1974.

him; the stuff of life, which he acquires violently, contains nothing indifferent. "Do you know how I *see?*" he writes in a letter, meaning the gaze to which it is given to grasp *forever.* This gaze misses nothing, but it is also *decision,* it contains adoration or damnation, and since most of it is damnation, his destiny is to yearn for worship.

Yet damnation is movement, an incessant plunge into hell, a plunge that he brings about—and so he has even greater need of rest, the inviolability and immobility of what finds favor in his eyes.

Sidonie is not alone at Janowitz, she lives with her twin brother Karl, who figures in the letters as Charley. She dotes on him, he is the only one left of her immediate family. But she is also under a kind of guardianship; it is the brother's task to watch over her as a young woman. It has always been taken for granted that she will marry within her social class, and she too sees a future of that sort as natural; her diary often speaks about it. This conventional part of her nature is embodied by her brother; and much as Sidonie needs freedom, she does not contest her brother's right; she yields to his supervision. The true nature of her relationship to Karl Kraus has to remain a secret.

It is a secret that is hard to keep. He sneaks into her room at night when visiting the castle and while the servants and her brother are asleep. There are nocturnal strolls in the park, there is one special meadow that he loves; it becomes a code word in his letters and turns up in his poems. During this winter, Sidi is overcome by her love and mentions Karl Kraus frequently in her letters to Rilke. She takes it for granted that she will find sympathy in one poet for the other, as though an alliance of minds could fortify her against the prejudices of her class. Perhaps she was toying with the thought of an official connection with Kraus. Rilke, enjoying her confidence, because he has always kept at a distance despite all his tributes to her, senses the danger and becomes Karl Kraus's most effective enemy. In his much-discussed letter of February 1914, he warns of being too close to Kraus. In a thoroughly cautious way—it is one of his longest letters—he insinuates, without using the word Jew, the natural alienness of Karl Kraus. It is an embarrassing letter, most embarrassing probably because of the caution hidden behind carefully weighed hints. The reader also senses that the demonstrative concern for Sidi camouflages another concern, for Janowitz, which Rilke would like to maintain as a refuge and keep free of that other, stronger influence.

Nevertheless, it is only fair to recall that Kraus, albeit in his more open way, had also begun his acts of war against the rival on the evening of his very first encounter with Sidi. When Rilke's name came up, Kraus said: "Nothing for you. I am going to write now." These words, already mentioned, are in Sidi's diary; one may doubt the accuracy of the recording, but the gist is certainly true. There are signs that Rilke's warning took effect, something changes in the tone of her letters to Karl Kraus. He registers it with no inkling of Rilke's attack. From now on, Sidi certainly did not consider marrying Kraus. It becomes all the more important for both to maintain the secrecy of their love. Kraus's alertness is stupendous. His distrust, which bypasses her, goes against anyone coming into contact with her; remarks about Sidi in his presence, and even those brought to him by others, are avenged with the same annihilatory hatred that he expends on public matters.

Most of the time, the two are separated, and so the first thing to stress is his excitement in waiting for her letters. "I spent all day waiting yesterday. On the alert for any telegram dropping into the box. . . . More than twenty times, I dashed into the hall when I thought I heard the lid clap down." He receives her letters acoustically, he hears them fall into the mailbox.

This extreme dependency on letters is one of the few aspects in the correspondence reminiscent of Kafka's relationship to Felice. His expectation is often disappointed, like Kafka's: then he demands letters from her again and uses the most powerful, the most tyrannical devices on her to get what he wants. These demands contrast strangely with the tone of worship that usually marks his letters.

Keeping this love a secret from everybody, especially from Sidi's twin brother Charley, often leads to humiliating conditions for him, which, however, he accepts for her sake. Even for visits to Vienna, she has to find reasons that sound plausible to her brother. Her conditions often make their love impossible and increase his passion. She dictates the circumstances, for only she is familiar with the exact dynamics at Janowitz, and thus *she* remains in control. Intellectually, however, he is always indisputably in control; thus, he is all the more depressed by the enslavement to external circumstances.

From the very start, he invites her to his lectures, thereby luring her to Vienna. There she has a certain seat in the second row, and he always refers to it, even when she cannot possibly come. He tells her far in advance whenever he plans anything, and he calls her the chief person at the lectures, as though she were more important than he, who is lecturing. She enjoys his triumphs, they are performed for her. If she is hindered or far away on a trip, he reports to her about them. Thus, we learn a great deal about the significance of the lectures for him. His serious way of preparing for them, the care and attention going into each program, the intoxication at their effect—for all that and a great deal more, there is invaluable testimony in the letters, they are worth reading for that alone. It sometimes happens (and no one who ever heard him would believe it) that he feels something like timidity at the thought that she may not come. At times, he insists on at least *seeing* her beforehand. "I have to stand before people on Saturday evening, Sunday afternoon, and Monday evening. It is naturally quite impossible if I do not see you first."

Kraus never makes fun of himself in public. Nowhere in his oeuvre is there a single sentence against himself. He attacks, he awaits attacks, and he protects himself. He notices the tiniest chink in his armor and stops it up. Nothing can happen to him, and nothing does happen to him. This alone makes it fascinating to see him where he is weak and also acts weak: in these letters.

She did not invite him to Janowitz as often as he would have liked, and he suspected that she sometimes would rather be alone there, even when her brother was traveling. But things soon became more threatening to him when her old wanderlust awoke. A friend of hers, Count Guicciardini of Florence, whom she knew a year longer than Kraus, wanted to meet her in Venice at Whitsuntide. She agreed unhesitatingly, even though she had promised Kraus to spend these days with him near Vienna. "Why are you doing this?" he writes to her, offended. "Perhaps I will one day be the one who travels off incognito and whom no call will hold." And yet he resigned himself; after all, he was the one who, at their first encounter, had recognized and praised her urge for freedom. During this absence in Venice, he hit upon the idea of buying a car, and he hoped to thereby tie her wanderlust to him. With a chauffeur, he picked her up in Graz, spending a few days with her on the drive back. The car now became important for their relationship; shortly thereafter, he came to Janowitz for a longer visit. On June 28, he returned to Vienna late at night, and learned from an extra edition of a newspaper on Nussdorfer Strasse that the heir to the Austrian throne, Franz Ferdinand, had been assassinated.

Even that early, he was accused of a preference for aristocrats. That was connected, of course, with his visits to Janowitz; the real reason could not be known to anyone. I cannot find that aristocrats are treated any better than other people in his real work, *The Last Days of Mankind.* He expressed sympathy for only one aristocrat, and that was a murdered man, Franz Ferdinand. The mockery of the corpse, the shameful obsequies for the murdered couple aroused his fury, and this indignation in turn affected his attitude towards the living man, he spoke respectfully about the qualities of the pretender to the throne. Everywhere else, he is more ruthless towards aristocrats than others: since they were more powerful, they had a greater share of the blame for the disaster than men who were simply powerless bit players in the war. That July, Kraus took a trip of several weeks through the Dolomites with Sidi and her brother Charley. At Lake Misurina, they found out that war had been declared. Charley returned home instantly to take care of things at Janowitz. Kraus and Sidi remained alone in the Dolomites for a week. It strikes me as very important that Kraus and Sidi spent this alarming time together, cut off from the rest of the world. She despised the war no less than he. She was distressed about Rilke, who she thought was in Paris, and she wrote him on the spot. Her letter had lines that could have been by Kraus; she not only despised the war, she despised it in *his* words. They went home, he to Vienna; a few days later, he was in Janowitz again. The attitude he shared with Sidi—their joint rejection of the war hysteria—was expressed in letters from Vienna: "Things are bleak here.
. . . Yesterday, the Viennese restaurants crossed all French and English terms out of their menus. The general state is getting more and more idiotic. . . . At Janowitz, you cannot imagine the nastiness now becoming visible as enthusiasm. My best to the neutral swans!
. . . If one could only sleep through this year! Or be *worthy* of dear peace in Janowitz!"

He failed to notice that they were seeing too much of him at Janowitz. Perhaps he was careless as well. Charley had his own troubles, which were linked to the outbreak of the war but of a more practical nature. He wanted to have his sister's ear; the fact that she was being taken up more and more by Kraus went on Charley's nerves. He sensed the growing intimacy between them. One day, when Kraus unexpectedly arrived at Janowitz to take Sidi for a long drive, there appeared to be some kind of embarrassing scene. Sidi's letters tried to mediate between the two men, it was useless, her brother did not wish to see Karl Kraus at Janowitz anymore.

In this first month of the war, Kraus was paralyzed by the events, he felt them so deeply that he was dumbstruck. He hated to write, he even wrote fewer letters. He clung to the image of Janowitz, the "island," as he called it. The things he had attacked earlier were in no ratio to the calamity that had now broken in on all people; no man has ever gone through such a change of proportions. Most intellectuals helped themselves by swimming along in the general current and doing their bit for sparking the war crowd. Even writers whom he venerated, like Gerhart Hauptmann, gave in without resistance to the hysteria of the war. Kraus experienced this blindness as a physical torment. The first lesson to be learned was silence; the silence he turned against the false voices was the real island. But he also realized the danger that this silence might be misunderstood. In November, he finally explained it publicly. He gave the speech that began with the words: "In this great time. . . ." It contained sentences like the following: "Do not expect any word of my own from me. I could not say anything new; for in the room one writes in, the din is enormous, and whether it comes from animals, from children, or simply mortars, one should not decide now. The man who encourages the deed violates both word and deed and is twice despicable. The calling for that has not died out. Those who have nothing to say because action has the word, they keep speaking. If anyone has anything to say, let him step forward and hold his peace!"

This address was correctly understood, even when published in December as a meager issue of the *Fackel*. Silence, so enormously eloquent, was taken as an announcement. December brought another reading, not from his own works, and then yet another in February 1915, with a new explanation for the silence. That was all. Nothing else came for a long time. The silence went on and on. The first real *Fackel* appeared in October 1915 over a year after the outbreak of the war.

It is possible only now to comprehend what happened. During that first winter of war, Sidi deprived him of his voice. She gave it back to him in the summer of 1915. Shedding light on this is quite important. The loss of Janowitz, after her brother's refusal to receive him, had struck Kraus very deeply. Sidi wrote him that her attempt at mediating had failed. Charley remained adamant. She herself was in Italy again, this time in Rome and Florence, where she met Guicciardini. She had announced her trip in a letter to Kraus: "In Italy, I am being awaited with yearning." Again he resigned himself, but his nervousness increased; he sensed how much Guicciardini meant to her. Gradually, not without consideration of his sensitivity, she initiated him into her plans: she wanted to marry Guicciardini.

She was fed up with being under her brother's tutelage and was looking for some way out. She saw her freedom in the only place in which a woman of her background could expect it: in marriage. It had to be with someone of her own class, for she needed her brother's permission. That alone left Kraus out of the picture, but she did not wish to marry him, for she would hardly have found freedom in a marriage with Kraus. Count Guicciardini, the same age as Kraus, seemed like the right man. He had been wooing her for some time; he was pleasant and he was ready to allow her the freedom without which she did not care to marry. Her relationship to Kraus would not change; instead of in Janowitz, they would meet in Italy.

Kraus was distrustful of her plan, he could not stand the thought of officially sharing her with another man; he was even more upset by the idea of her leaving Janowitz: it was only there that she was mistress of the animals. Even if he were not allowed to visit, he nevertheless *saw* her there. "I am very importunate," he writes her, still holding back, "I want to save my world." He sends her the poem "Love without Vanity," originally titled "Everything or Nothing." She remarks: "Sent to me as a protest because I couldn't see him as much as he wished, because of other considerations and obligations." Thus begins the long series of poems dedicated to her. She tries to encourage him to work; he replies shortly after that November lecture: "Don't talk to me about work. I am sufficiently liberated by the few pages. For a long time into the future, there won't be anything else to do, or to say to the gory world. Everything I am belongs to you. Don't you want it?"

He is mortally afraid for her when she doesn't write: "Isn't it known that a madman lives in Vienna, doubly miserable because he is always aware of his condition? . . . I know I am asking too much. . . . Please don't put me at ease. Life cannot suffice for my immoderation, and hence neither can love if it has to put up with life. . . . It would have been heavenly. Some day I could be the 'positive' one, the most positive, most lovingly assert to a creature that does honor to the Creator—when something shouts: 'Too late!' "

I am quoting only a few sentences from long letters, demonstrating his despair. At New Year's, he spends a few days with her in Venice. She then goes on to Rome, and he writes her there: "Your two last days in Venice—what a weary epilogue! With painful eyes among the sights—as though it were a commandment of nature!"

Like any traveler unwilling to neglect anything, she fills the days with the fleeting view of obligatory places and objects. Whatever they may be, he regards them as false heightenings in connection with her, for she is the highest. He cannot bear having her stand worshipful in front of anything. It would irritate him less if she went about calm and proud and not too long among other things and would permit the most famous pictures and sculptures to bow to her. He writes her that she is *the* sight, the one, the true; how could the others, who are so much less, be so important to her.

During February, he writes her a series of very long letters. Fearing they could wind up in the wrong hands, he speaks of himself in the third person as B. In these letters, he tries to get hold of himself, he most subtly describes the way he feels. One is amazed to experience him as a novelist. Such a combination of passion and psychological analysis exists nowhere else in him. He is not attacking, he is portraying; the precision of his self-insight recalls the great French writers.

Only it is not a novel but an account, day by day and occasionally several times a day, of his true state. She must have answered in a way that was not unworthy of his way, and one regrets the loss of her letters. Not infrequently, naked despair breaks through in his lines. He suffers, as he writes, from hallucinations, and each one comes true with every word that he receives from her. When she contests what tortures him, she says things that confirm the delusion. He is most excited in long telegrams, trying to force a meeting with her.

All at once, he finds himself unexpectedly in Rome. "I came here last night from Florence in order to say goodbye to you. . . . I don't know what I'm writing. I've been standing in the street since yesterday and I'm half dead." He asks her for five minutes that same evening, for he is traveling on immediately. A chauffeur brings her the letter. He waits nearby in the car.

It was the high point of the crisis and the start of recovery. She saw him right away. He remained in Rome; the next day he wrote effusively: "You strode over my heart, you wanted to smash my brain. . . . Yesterday you saved me, and that was more grace than the pain of the last few weeks." She had convinced him, he wanted to test his own strength now and, for the first time, he gave in to her marriage plan. She asked him to write a poem for her wedding, he wrote it and handed it to her the next day, it was called "For Sidi's Wedding Day." Later, it was renamed "Metamorphosis" and heads the book *Words in Verses.* She had also asked Rilke for a poem for the same occasion, and he had written it on the spot.

Karl Kraus remained in Rome for a while, very close to her, but profoundly terrified by her obligations and her exhaustion. He was still very unstable, she complained that he was different every day, he felt he was partly to blame for her exhaustion, to which he contributed. But this time, when they separated, it was only for a brief period. A few days later, she came to him in Vienna and they traveled—miracle of miracles!—to Janowitz. There must have been a reconciliation between her brother and him. The wedding in Rome was a month away; the preparations, which were much discussed, brought the two men together. Here in Janowitz, Karl Kraus found himself again. Here, Sidonie was no longer so driven and she became as she had been in the past. In these two days, both of them found their security for one another again. He referred later to the "spirit of April 1"; and the next letter, which he wrote her when she was in Rome, was signed "Karl von Janowitz."

The change was total. One finds a sentence there, and one scarcely believes one's eyes: "Writing seldom doesn't wear on the nerves." He does *"not* have the feeling of being deprived," and he is delighted at mere cards. He discusses her wedding present with Charley: a mirror. Once he even mentions work: "Everything has become much easier." But very soon he says: "Work interrupted by putting order in old things. Library, writings. Would like to have everything in such a way that it would be possible to give up the apartment suddenly." He seems—and this was inconceivable for him just recently—to have grown to like the idea of moving to Italy.

Then he went to Rome to be close to her during the wedding which was scheduled for May 6. The wedding guests were all gathered in Rome. But the war, whose effect on their relationship he had so greatly feared, now became his ally. Italy's entry in the war against Austria was imminent, and the Austrian guests, for whom this meant internment, fled Rome in a panic. The nuptials did not take place. As though rewarded for his self-control and his ultimate resignation to the hated project, Karl Kraus was released from his fears at one swoop.

Sidi went to Switzerland to recover from the excitement. He, in Vienna, felt he would have to *earn* seeing her again; but just two weeks later he met her in Zurich. A new car, purchased in Switzerland, was ready; they took off, with Sidi at the wheel, accompanied by the old Irish nurse, who had lived with Sidi since her childhood. For five weeks, they drove all over Switzerland, to the most beautiful places, discovering one that entranced him with its name and was to achieve great significance for him: Thierfehd on the Tödi.

This time, upon returning to Vienna, he plunged furiously into his work. "Outside," he writes, "the air is that of Sodom, the dreadful shout 'Extra, extra!' is there, with children being born and men dying under it—but it cannot do anything more to me." It was no new work as yet: he was putting together the volume *Destruction of the World by Black Magic,* which consisted of *Fackel* articles from before the war. He reworked every single sentence, as was his habit. "My present joy at work makes up for the numb waiting of years, which, however, was certainly necessary. . . . I am now working in the most hostile world, I am strong from work and for it, and I *therefore* need, far more than in the empty period, the last human heart listening to me. . . . Whatever I think is thought for you, whatever I write is written for you, and you know that these five hundred pages, thoroughly worked over, belong to you. . ."

Since his faculty for torture had turned away from her, he turned to the objects making up his true calling. "Yesterday was . . . a tormenting day. The war knocked at my door too, not just at yours. I received the news that one of the few people who had behaved decently to me and my work is in a horrible situation, waiting to be called to the front as a *release*. The incident is so dreadful that I do not want to portray it for you in writing." That man was Ludwig von Ficker, editor of *Der Brenner,* and Kraus moved heaven and hell to ease his predicament.

The same letter tells of another adventure, which could be ridiculous if it weren't highly important for him as a source of strength. The clairvoyant and graphologist Raphael Schermann, who was creating a sensation in Vienna, had written an analysis of Kraus's hand, writing without knowing him personally and with no clue as to his identity. Kraus found this analysis to be so phenomenal that he copied it down for Sidi. Since it showed him as he wanted to be seen (he dispatched it to Sidi to influence her), I would like to quote the most important parts:

> "A rare mind; a writer who writes dreadfully grippingly. . . .
> "When he commits himself to a cause, he pursues it until death. His language and his tongue are like a 42-centimeter mortar. . . .
> "When he faces an enemy, he will not budge until the enemy is on the ground. He is afraid of nothing, *and if a thousand people are present,* he advocates his cause so vociferously and grippingly that everyone collapses virtually hypnotized. [A comment by Karl Kraus: vision of a lecture hall.] . . . He must have fought enormous fights in his life. He is always ready for an attack, holds his weapon in hand ready to fire so that no attack can catch him unprepared.
> "The impact is so strong that I cannot get away from it. A dreadfully sharp observer, even sharper in criticizing. No mere mortal can approach him. . . .
> "His work has brought him many insults and persecutions, but he has always carried the day. . . .
> "No vanity whatsoever, not even personally. . . .
> "His nerves are overstrained. He allows himself no relaxation. . . .
> "He understands more about the war than some people running it, *but he can say nothing.*"

The tone of this analysis, half of which is quoted here, is certainly crude and charlatanlike. It is written in a language that Karl Kraus would have mocked to death had he read it in a newspaper. But the crucial thing here is how it affected him at that specific time. Incidentally, he underscored one phrase in it: ". . . and if a thousand people are present." For in the struggle to which he would very soon resolve himself, he all alone, he would have to reckon with more than a thousand opponents. The analysis of his handwriting promised him victory even in such a fight. The direction of the struggle, however, is predicted in the final sentence: "He understands more about the war than some people running it, but he can say nothing." Here, the last part, "but he can say nothing," is underscored by him. These rousing words end the letter, and the reader feels—to remain in the jargon of both the analysis and the period—that an *explosion* is imminent.

However, in the next letter, two days after that, "after one of the most dreadful of days . . . letters from prisoners and from a poor, sick soldier," he copies twenty-six lines for her from Paul's Epistles to the Corinthians. These are lines that can be linked to his plan. Let me quote three of them:

"The spiritual man, however, can judge anything; but him no one can judge.

"If I must boast about myself, I will boast about my sufferings.

"Who is afflicted with suffering that I do not suffer with him? Who is offended, and I do not feel the most burning pain?"

And now, one week later, comes the letter for which I have made you come this long way. It is the most important in the entire correspondence, and I would like you to hear most of it:

"I have seen too much misery in the past few days and yet I have drawn work from it—a work that is finished only when the victims march right past my window at six in the morning. I want to tell you what kind of work it is, the first section of which was now completed in three days and nights. . . ."

He quotes a diary page, written a few days earlier and meant for her as well:

"Now, while in front of my desk, as though towards it, the daily, inescapable, horrible shout rings out, afflicting the human ear for all time: 'Extra! Extra!,' I have been spending an hour in Thierfehd. And nothing, nothing has changed! No idea, whether thought, spoken, or screamed, could be strong enough, no prayer ardent enough to penetrate this matter. In order to *show* such powerlessness, should I not therefore present all the things I *cannot* do now—at least do something: put myself on the line? What is left?

"The road must be taken. . . . The things to be shouted out should throttle me so that they won't otherwise choke me. On the street, I am no longer sure of my nerves. Yet it would be better if it happens by plan and only in such a way as to happen for the one person for whom I live and do not wish to live anymore if *she* believes that further silence will endanger one's *own* human dignity, that it can no longer be endured—this still testimony of deeds, nay, of words, which have snuffed out the memory of mankind for all cosmic times. This is one person without whom nothing can happen, because everything happens for her.

"Now from this exhaustion, a spark has sprung out, and a plan has come into being for a work that, to be sure, if ever it could come forth, would be tantamount to putting oneself on the line. Nevertheless, and for that very reason, it has to be written to its end. The first act, the prelude to the whole thing, is finished and could exist by itself. But to whom will it penetrate? Switzerland . . . is failing here, perhaps she will help later; if not, then America.

"But, whatever may or may not happen, I am now freer. . . ."

The prelude to *The Last Days of Mankind* was thus completed, in three days and nights. He is aware of how dangerous this work is and he views it as putting himself on the line. He lives in the capital city of the belligerent country and attacks *by name* all who are taking part in this war. He spares no one, least of all those with power and responsibility, for whom it would be child's play to silence him. He could land in jail, he might even be murdered. The fact that it did not happen says nothing for the moment of his decision. He sees the danger and walks towards it: he has every right to say that he is putting himself on the line. The things he wants to shout out will throttle him, which means that he could be strung up as a traitor. In this war, as he writes much later, there are 10,000 gallows. If he does not shout it out, he will have to choke on it. But he does not want to shout it unsystematically, it has to be a work, and he feels capable of it only if it happens for the person for whom he is living: Sidi.

For it was she who viewed his silence as perilous for his own human dignity, which had demanded of him that he *speak*. She had talked to him about his work in the chaos of winter, he had rebuffed her. His public declaration of silence in November, suitable to the events, had been an empty shell which he had been clutching stubbornly, as was his way, until finally, it broke to smithereens under her influence and for her sake.

Many things came together in this decision to produce a work that he would not have risked earlier, he would not have had the strength. There was the private war of the past winter, in which he was torn apart, in which he was almost broken, an atmosphere of menace and despair, excluding anything that was not Sidi. There was the trip through Switzerland, the sealing of their peace in an environment of peace (Thierfehd had become the symbol for that), and the sudden shift back to Vienna, to the yelping voices of war. Since his return, every letter of his spoke about those voices, he was possessed by them, as with the recruits, the victims, marching past his window every morning at six. There was the personal news from the war, letters by strangers and by friends, to whom his heart was wide open. There was (it played its part and hence cannot be omitted) the graphologist's analysis, which encouraged him to wage a murderous struggle against an enormous superior force; it promised him everything needed for such a battle. Ultimately, there was the impact of St. Paul's words, reminding him he had to sacrifice himself.

But the most important element in everything was Sidi: by living in terms of her, he drew his unity from her, something without which such a work could not have been launched. The endurance of love, which he awaited from her, became likewise the endurance of the genesis of that work. She left him when the war ended and the work was done.

However, we are anticipating his enterprise too greatly. In this same letter, as he began to work, he announced his arrival at Janowitz on August 1, he would be "laden with work." There, he spent the whole of August, writing his drama and preparing a big war issue of the *Fackel*. From then on, he never stopped working again.

You will hear nothing more from me about the further circumstances of his great passion. The letters of the next three years, until the end of the war, would require a different sort of treatment. And they may not be all that important. The most important things are in the work itself, in *The Last Days of Mankind* and in the big war-issues of the *Fackel,* the first appearing in October 1915. My goal was to bring you to the point at which this work could no longer be held up. It is, to use an image of Stendhal's, the moment of crystallization. *This* crystallization contains both passion and labor, but he manages to keep the work itself, *The Last Days of Mankind,* perfectly free of the woman without whom it would never have been.

It is a particular tension which he needs for it from now on. He needs Janowitz—an island, to be sure, but an island in enemy territory: any soil from which war is waged is enemy territory for him. He also needs to cross over to Switzerland, the genuine paradise of peace, he needs it more and more often. He could have decided to settle there, like others who hated the war, for instance Romain Rolland. But he so greatly wanted to publish the *Fackel* in Vienna, fight against the censors wherever he could confront them, doggedly wrest phrase after phrase away from them. And even more, he wanted to feel the war in the place where all its threads ran together, in the Austrian capital. So he visited Sidi in Switzerland and then returned to Vienna. Every new confrontation with the war sharpened the barb of his hatred. Nor could he rebuke himself for so often escaping the war, since in those very regions of peace, in Janowitz and especially Switzerland, he worked on *The Last Days of Mankind* with growing strength and passion.

The letters to Sidi cover twenty-three years of his life. I have tried to familiarize you with two of them, the most important years. I see it as a supreme veracity in Karl Kraus that he desired the publication of the letters to Sidi. We owe it to him to pay them serious heed, thereby fulfilling his very last wish.

1974

THE WRITER'S PROFESSION
Speech given in Munich
in January 1976

Certain words have lain in helpless weariness for some time, they were avoided and concealed, their use aroused mockery, they were constantly drained until they shrank up and became ugly warnings. One of these words is the German word *Dichter,* a writer or poet. If a man nevertheless did take up the activity of writing, which existed as always, he called himself "someone who writes."

One might have thought it was a matter of giving up a false claim, winning new standards, becoming more rigorous towards oneself, and especially avoiding anything that leads to unworthy successes. In reality, the opposite happened: the very people who struck out ruthlessly at the word *Dichter* consciously developed and intensified the methods of creating a stir. The petty notion that all literature is dead was proclaimed in high-flown words, printed on costly paper, and discussed seriously and solemnly as though the topic were a complex and difficult intellectual structure. Certainly, this particular case soon drowned in its own ludicrousness. But other people, not sterile enough to exhaust their energy in a proclamation, wrote bitter and very talented books, called themselves "someone who writes," and very soon made names for themselves. They did what the *Dichter* of yore used to do: instead of lapsing into silence, they kept writing the same book over and over again. As incapable of improvement and as worthy of death as mankind appeared to them, it still had one function left: to applaud them. Anyone who did not feel like doing so, who got tired of the same old ejaculations, was doubly damned: first as a human being, which was a pretty worthless thing to be; and then as someone who refused to recognize the writing man's endless addiction to death as the only thing that still had any value.

You will understand that, considering such phenomena, I feel distrustful of both the man who merely writes and the man who self-complaisantly still labels himself a *Dichter*. I see no difference between them, They are as alike as two peas in a pod, any prestige they have attained strikes them as a vested prerogative.

For in reality, no man today can be a writer, a *Dichter,* if he does not seriously doubt his right to be one. The man who does not see the state of the world we are living in has scarcely anything to say about it. The endangerment of the world, once a principal theme of religion, has shifted into this world. Its destruction, rehearsed more than once, is seen with a cool eye by those who are not writers; there are people who calculate the chances of destruction, make a profession out of that, and thereby get fatter and fatter. Ever since we entrusted our prophecies to machines, predictions lost all value. The more we split away from ourselves, the more we entrust to lifeless authorities, the less we can control what happens. Our growing power over everything, whether animate or inanimate, and especially over our own kind, has produced a counter-power, which we only seemingly control. A hundred, a thousand things could be said about it, but they are all familiar, that is the odd thing about it, every detail has become a daily news item, a heinous banality. You would not expect me to repeat all that; I have planned something else for today, something more modest.

Perhaps it is worth the trouble to think about whether there is anything in this situation of the earth with which writers, or the people one regarded as such until now, could make themselves useful. Despite all strokes of fate that the word *Dichter* had to suffer for them, something of its claim has remained. Literature may be what it may be, but there is one thing it is not, anymore than the human beings still clutching it: literature is not dead. If a man represents it today, what should his life be like, what should he have to offer?

By chance, I recently stumbled upon a jotting by an anonymous author, whose name I cannot give you simply because no one knows it. This jotting bears the date August 23, 1939; that was a week before the outbreak of World War II. And it goes:

"But everything is over. If I were really a writer, I would have to be able to prevent the war."

What nonsense, people say today, since we know what has happened since then; what presumption! What could a single person have prevented, and why a writer of all people? Can we conceive of any claim that is further from reality? And what distinguishes this sentence from the bombast of those whose sentences deliberately brought the war?

I was irritated by that line, I copied it down with mounting irritation. Here, I thought, here I have found the thing that most repels me about the word *Dichter,* a claim that contrasts so grossly with what a writer could do at best, an example of the blustering that has discredited the word *writer* and filled us with mistrust as soon as a member of the guild beats his breast and comes out with his colossal intentions.

But then, during the next few days, I felt to my astonishment that the sentence wouldn't let go, it kept haunting me, I plucked it out, chopped it up, pushed it away, and pulled it out again as though it were solely up to me to find some meaning in it. The way it began was already odd: "But everything is over," an utterance of a complete and hopeless defeat in a time when victories ought to begin. Whilst everything was focused on victories, he is already expressing the bleakness of the end, and in such a way as if it were inevitable. When one takes a closer look at the sentence, however—"If I were really a writer I would have to be able to prevent the war!"—it turns out to contain the very opposite of blustering, namely an admission of complete failure. Even more, it expresses the admission of a *responsibility,* and at those points—this is the amazing thing—where we could speak least of all about responsibility in the normal sense of the word.

Here is a man who obviously means what he says, for he is saying it quietly, is turning against himself. He is not establishing a claim, he is giving it up. In his despair at what *has* to happen now, he accuses *himself,* not the true bearers of the responsibility, whom he certainly knows precisely, for if he did not know them, he would think differently about what is to come. Thus the source of the original irritation remains one thing: his idea of what a writer ought to be and the fact that he considered himself one until the moment, when, with the outbreak of the war, everything collapsed for him.

It is precisely this irrational claim to responsibility that gives me pause to think and captivates me. One would also have to add that words, deliberate and used over and over again, misused words, led to this situation, in which the war became inevitable. If words can do so

238

much—why cannot words hinder it? It is not at all surprising that a man who deals with words more than other people do will also expect more of words and their effect.

Hence, a writer—and perhaps we have found this somewhat too quickly—would be a man who sets great store by words and likes to go about among them, perhaps even more so than among people, he is at the mercy of both words and people, but has more confidence in words, also pulls them down from their seats in order to reinstate them with even greater aplomb, questions and feels them, caresses, scratches up, planes, paints, indeed he is actually capable, after all his intimate impudence, of creeping away from them with reverence. Even if he appears as a spoiler of words, as he often does, he is a spoiler out of love.

All his activities conceal something that he himself does not always know about, something that is usually weak, but at times of a force that tears him to bits, namely the will to stand up for anything that can be grasped in words, and to atone personally for any such failure.

What value can this assumption of a fictive responsibility have for other people? Does its unreal character not deprive it of any effect? I believe that what a man takes upon himself is viewed more seriously by all other people, even the most limited, than what is forced upon him. Nor is there any state closer to events, any more profound relationship to them than feeling responsible for them.

If the word *Dichter* or writer was tattered for many people, it was because they associated make-believe and lack of seriousness with either word, something that withdrew so as to avoid trouble. Men entered one of the most somber periods in history, unable to recognize it until it was already breaking in upon them; and the combination of lofty airs and aesthetics, in all nuances, was not something to inspire respect. The false confidence of writers, their misunderstanding of reality, which they approached with scorn and nothing else, their denial of any connection to reality, their inner remoteness from everything that really took place (for it could not be gleaned from the language they used): understandably, eyes that saw harder and more accurately turned away in horror from so much blindness.

One may object by pointing out sentences like the one I have begun with. So long as such sentences exist—and naturally there are more than one—taking responsibility for words and deeply feeling the recognition of total failure, we will have the right to hold on to a term that was always used for the authors of the essential works of mankind, works but for which we could not even have an awareness of what constitutes mankind. We use these works in a different way from, but no less than, our daily bread; we are nourished and carried by them. Even if nothing else were left, even if we did not know how much they carry us, while at the same time, we are futilely seeking something in our age that could hold a candle to them—were we to be confronted with them, only one attitude would be possible: If we are very severely against the age and especially against ourselves, we can reach the conclusion that there is no such thing as a *Dichter* today, yet we have to passionately wish that there *were* such a person.

That sounds very summary, and it has little value if we do not try to make clear for ourselves what a *Dichter* must have to satisfy this demand.

The first and most important thing, I would say, is that he be the keeper of metamorphosis—keeper in a twofold sense. For one thing, he will make mankind's literary heritage, so rich in metamorphoses, his own. Today, when the writings of nearly all early cultures have been deciphered, we know how rich that heritage really is in metamorphoses. As late as the previous century, everyone dealing with that most intrinsic and most enigmatic aspect of man, the gift of metamorphosis, had to stick to two fundamental books of Antiquity: a late work, Ovid's *Metamorphoses,* an almost systematic collection of all the known, mythical, "higher" metamorphoses; and an early work, the *Odyssey,* which focused on the adventurous metamorphoses of one man, Odysseus. These metamorphoses culminate in his coming home as a beggar, the least man imaginable; and the perfection of the successful disguise has never been attained, much less surpassed, by any later poet. It would be ridiculous to expound on the impact of these two books on the modern European cultures, even before the Renaissance and certainly after that. Ovid's *Metamorphoses* flash up in Ariosto as in Shakespeare and in countless others; and it would be very wrong to believe that their effect on the modern age is exhausted. Odysseus, however, is still crossing our path even today: the first character in world literature to enter its most central existence; it would be hard to name more than five or six figures with such charisma.

He is probably the first character who was always here for us, but not the oldest, for an older one has been found. Just barely a hundred years ago, the Mesopotamian *Gilgamesh* was discovered and its importance recognized. This epic begins with a metamorphosis: the natural man Enkidu, living among the animals of the wilderness, turns into an urban, civilized man, a theme that truly concerns us today, when we have learned very precise and concrete things about children who have lived among wolves. Enkidu dies after becoming Gilgamesh's friend, and thus there is an enormous confrontation with death, the only such confrontation that does not leave a modern man with the bitter aftertaste of self-deception. At this point, I would like to offer myself as a witness to an almost incredible process: no work of literature, literally none, has so decisively determined my life as this epic, which is four thousand years old and, until one hundred years ago, was unknown. I encountered it at the age of seventeen, it has not let go of me since then, I have returned to it as to a Bible; and, aside from its specific effect, it has filled me with expectation for things still unknown to us. It is impossible for me to regard as completed the corpus of traditional things that serve to nourish us. And even if it should turn out that no written works of such importance are to follow, there still remains the enormous reservoir of oral traditions among the primitive peoples.

For here there is no end of metamorphoses, such as we are talking about. One could spend a lifetime collecting and re-enacting them, and it would not be a bad life. Tribes, sometimes consisting of just a few hundred people, have left us a wealth that we certainly do not merit, for it is our fault that they have died out or are dying before our eyes, eyes that scarcely look. They have preserved their mythical experiences until the very end, and the strange thing is that there is hardly anything that benefits us more, hardly anything that fills us with as much hope as these early incomparable creations by people who, hunted, cheated, and robbed by us, have perished in misery and bitterness. Scorned by us for their modest material culture, blindly and ruthlessly exterminated, they have left us an inexhaustible spiritual legacy. One cannot thank scholarship enough for rescuing it; its true preservation, its resurrection to our life are up to the poet, the *Dichter*.

I have called the *Dichter* the keeper of metamorphoses: but he is a keeper in a further sense as well. In a world of achievement and

241

specialization, a world that sees nothing but peaks, towards which one strives in a kind of linear focus that exerts all strength on the cold solitude of the peaks while scorning and blurring the adjacent things, the many, the real things, which do not offer themselves for any help towards the peaks—in a world that prohibits metamorphosis more and more because it hinders the overall goal of production, which heedlessly multiplies the means of its self-destruction while simultaneously attempting to stifle whatever earlier human qualities are still extant—in such a world, which one might label the most blinded of all worlds, it seems of cardinal significance that there are people who, nonetheless, still keep practicing the gift of metamorphosis.

This, I think, would be the true task of the *Dichter*. That gift, once universal, but now doomed to atrophy, has to be preserved by any means possible; and the *Dichter,* thanks to that gift, ought to keep the accesses *between* people open. He should be able to become *anybody and everybody,* even the smallest, the most naive, the most powerless person. His desire for experiencing others from the inside should never be determined by the goals of which our normal, virtually official life consists; that desire has to be totally free of any aim at success or prestige, it has to be passion in itself, the passion of metamorphosis. It would require an ever open ear, but that would not be enough, for a majority of people today are scarcely able to speak, they express themselves in the phraseology of newspapers and public media and say the same things more and more without *being* the same. Only metamorphosis, in the extreme sense in which the word is used here, would make it possible to feel what a man is behind his words; the true existence of whatever there is of life could not be grasped in any other way. It is a mysterious process, its nature has scarcely been examined, and yet it is the only real approach to another human being. People have tried different ways of naming this process, they have spoken of empathy; for reasons I cannot now discuss, I prefer the more demanding word "metamorphosis." But whatever name one uses, hardly anyone can dare to doubt that we are dealing with something real and very precious. In his never ending practice, in his compelling experience of all sorts of human beings, all, but particularly those who are paid the least attention, in the restless manner of this practice, not atrophied or paralyzed by any system—that is where I see the real profession of the *Dichter*. It is conceivable, it is even probable, that only a portion of his experience goes into his work. How to judge that is again part of the world of achievements and peaks, and that cannot interest us today, we are now trying to grasp what a *Dichter* would be like if there were such a man, we are not after the things he leaves behind.

If I now totally ignore what passes for success, if I even distrust it, then I do so because of a danger that everyone knows to exist in himself. The striving for success and success itself have a *narrowing* effect. The goal-oriented man on his way regards most things not serving the goal as ballast. He throws them out in order to be lighter, it cannot concern him that they are perhaps his best things; important for him is the point he attains, he swings himself higher from point to point and reckons in yards. The position is everything, it is determined externally, it is not he who creates it, he does not take part in its genesis. He sees it and aspires to it; and as useful and necessary as such efforts may be in many endeavors of life, they would be destructive for the *Dichter,* as we would like to see him.

For he above all has more and more space to create in himself. Space for knowledge, which he acquires for no recognizable purpose, and space for people, whom he experiences and absorbs through metamorphosis. In regard to knowledge, he can acquire it only through the honest and clean processes determining the inner structure of every branch of knowledge. But in the choice of these areas, which may lie far apart, he is led not by any conscious rule, but by an inexplicable hunger. Since he opens himself up to the most disparate people at once, understanding them in an ancient, pre-scholarly way, namely through metamorphosis, since he is thereby in a constant internal motion, which he cannot weaken or terminate (for he does not *gather* people, he does not put them side by side in an orderly fashion, he merely encounters them and absorbs them alive), since he receives violent pushes from people, it is quite possible that the sudden turn to a new branch of knowledge is also determined by such encounters.

I am aware of the astonishing nature of this demand, it cannot but arouse protest. It sounds as though he were aiming at a chaos of contradictory and conflicting things in himself. For the moment, I would have little to say against such an objection, it is very weighty. He *is* closest to the world when he carries a chaos inside himself, yet he feels—that was our point of departure—responsibility for this chaos,

243

he does not approve of it, he does not feel at ease about it, he does not regard himself as grand for having room for so many contradictory and unconnected things, he hates the chaos, he never gives up hope of overcoming it for others and thereby for himself as well.

To utter anything of any value about this world, he cannot push it away and avoid it. Despite all purposes and plans, it is more of a chaos than ever before, because it is moving faster and faster towards self-destruction. And it is as a chaos and not *ad usum Delphini,* namely for the reader, smoothened and polished, that he has to carry it in himself. But he must not fall prey to the chaos; using his experience of it, he must fight it and oppose it with the impetuosity of his hope.

What then can this hope be and why is it valuable only if nourished by the metamorphoses, the earlier ones, which he appropriates through the inspirations of his readings, the contemporary ones, which he appropriates through his openness for the people around him now?

For one thing, there is the force of the characters who have come to tenant him, who do not abandon the space they now occupy in him. They react out of him, as though he consisted of them. They are his majority, articulated and conscious, they are—since they *live* in him—his resistance to death. One quality of myths that are handed down orally is that they have been repeated again and again. Their vitality is like their definiteness, they are not destined to change. It is possible only in each individual case to find what makes up their vitality, and perhaps they have not been studied enough in terms of why they have to be repeated to others. It would be quite possible to describe what happens when one meets them for the first time. Today, you cannot expect such a thorough description; any other would be worthless. I only wish to mention one thing: the feeling of certainty and incontestability, *that* was what it was, that was the only thing it could be. Whatever it is that one experiences in myths, as incredible as it would have to appear in some other context, here it remains free of doubt, here it has a single unalterable shape.

This reservoir of unquestionability, from which so much has reached us, has been misused for the most peculiar borrowings. We know only too well the political abuse that has been perpetrated with it; warped, thinned, and distorted, even such inferior borrowings can intrinsically hold out for a few years until they burst. Borrowings of quite a different sort are those of science. Let me mention merely one striking example: whatever one may think of the truth of psychoanalysis, it has drawn a good portion of its strength from the word "Oedipus," and the serious criticism of that discipline is trying to attack it in that very word.

All the abuse perpetrated with myths can explain why people have turned away from them, a process typical of our age. They are felt to be lies because only the borrowings are known, they are discarded along with those borrowings. What they offer in metamorphoses seems merely unbelievable. Of their miracles, people recognize only those that come true as inventions, and we fail to realize that we owe each such invention to its archetypal image in myths.

The thing, however, that along with the specific individual contents makes up the true essence of myths is the metamorphoses practiced in them. It is through them that man has created himself. It is through them that he has made the world his own, through them he takes part in the world. We can see that he owes his power to metamorphosis, but he also owes something better to metamorphosis, he owes it his compassion.

I do not hesitate to employ a word that may seem improper to the practitioners of the mind: it is banished (that too is specialization) to the realm of the religions, there it may be named and administered. Otherwise, it is kept remote from the objective decisions of our daily life, which are determined more and more by technology.

I have said that a man can be a *Dichter* only if he feels responsibility, even though he may do less than others to realize it in individual actions. It is a responsibility for life, which is destroying itself, and one should not be ashamed to say that this responsibility is nourished by compassion. It is worthless if it is proclaimed as an indefinite and universal feeling. It demands the concrete metamorphosis into every individual thing or person that lives and exists. The *Dichter* learns and practices metamorphosis in myths, in the literature that has come down to us. He is nothing if he does not incessantly apply them in his environment, in his milieu. Myriad life, which enters him, which remains sensorily divided into all its individual phenomenal forms, does not coalesce within him into a mere concept, it gives him the strength to oppose death and thereby becomes something universal.

It cannot be the *Dichter*'s task to deliver mankind over to death. Not closing himself off to anyone, he will be stunned to learn of the growing power of death in many people. Even if all people consider it a futile undertaking, he will shake away at it and never, under any circumstances, capitulate. It will be his pride to resist and fight—with devices different from theirs—the envoys of nothingness, who are growing more and more numerous in literature. He will live by a law that is his own, but not tailored to him. This law is the following:

One shall repulse nobody into nothingness who would like to be there. One shall seek nothingness only to find a way out of it and one shall mark the road for everyone. Whether in grief or in despair, one shall endure in order to learn how to save others from it, but not out of scorn for the happiness that the creatures deserve, even though they deface one another and tear one another to pieces.